The Sea Their Graves

NEW PERSPECTIVES ON MARITIME HISTORY
AND NAUTICAL ARCHAEOLOGY

UNIVERSITY PRESS OF FLORIDA

Florida A&M University, Tallahassee
Florida Atlantic University, Boca Raton
Florida Gulf Coast University, Ft. Myers
Florida International University, Miami
Florida State University, Tallahassee
New College of Florida, Sarasota
University of Central Florida, Orlando
University of Florida, Gainesville
University of North Florida, Jacksonville
University of South Florida, Tampa
University of West Florida, Pensacola

UNIVERSITY PRESS OF FLORIDA
Gainesville · Tallahassee · Tampa · Boca Raton
Pensacola · Orlando · Miami · Jacksonville · Ft. Myers · Sarasota

THE SEA THEIR GRAVES

AN ARCHAEOLOGY OF DEATH AND REMEMBRANCE IN MARITIME CULTURE

David J. Stewart

James C. Bradford and Gene Allen Smith, series editors

Copyright 2011 by David J. Stewart
All rights reserved
Published in the United States of America. Printed on acid-free paper.

First cloth printing, 2011
First paperback printing, 2019

24 23 22 21 20 19   6 5 4 3 2 1

Library of Congress Cataloging-in-Publication Data
Stewart, David J. (David James) 1968–
The sea their graves : an archaeology of death and remembrance in maritime culture /
David J. Stewart.
p. cm.—(New perspectives on maritime history and nautical archaeology)
Includes bibliographical references and index.
ISBN 978-0-8130-3734-9 (cloth : acid-free paper)
ISBN 978-0-8130-6420-8 (pbk.)
1. Sailors—Great Britain—Social life and customs. 2. Sailors—United States—Social life and customs. 3. Sailors—Death—History. 4. Sepulchral monuments—History. 5. Death—Social aspects—History. 6. Burial—History. 7. Great Britain. Royal Navy—History. 8. United States. Navy—History. 9. Seafaring life—History. 10. Maritime anthropology.
I. Title.
V737.S74 2011
394.'4—dc23   2011018968

The University Press of Florida is the scholarly publishing agency for the State University System of Florida, comprising Florida A&M University, Florida Atlantic University, Florida Gulf Coast University, Florida International University, Florida State University, New College of Florida, University of Central Florida, University of Florida, University of North Florida, University of South Florida, and University of West Florida.

University Press of Florida
2046 NE Waldo Road
Suite 2100
Gainesville, FL 32609
http://upress.ufl.edu

For Heidi, as before,
And now for Atticus and Katharina too

Sometimes on Neptune's bosom our ship is tossed with waves,
And every minute we expect the sea must be our graves.

From "Sailors for My Money" by Martin Parker, seventeenth century

Contents

List of Illustrations ix
Preface and Acknowledgments xiii

1. Introduction 1
2. "Death Stands Ready at the Door":
   The Dangers of Maritime Life 34
3. Values for a Dangerous World 70
4. "The Natural Sepulchre of a Sailor":
   Burial at Sea as Ritual Performance 105
5. "Was Never Since Heard Of": Remembering the Missing 133
6. "Rocks and Storms I'll Fear No More":
   The Anchor and the Cross 167
7. Conclusions: A Living Tradition 202

Notes 221
Bibliography 239
Index 253

Illustrations

Figures

1.1. Mossop/Gilberry family gravestone, recording the loss of Wilfred Gilberry and the *Andacollo* 3
1.2. Community monument commemorating the sinking of the steamer *Atlantic* 25
1.3. Crew monument from the Seamen's Bethel, New Bedford, MA, commemorating two sailors who never returned 26
1.4. Ledger slab for Master John Varrall, who was killed by falling into the hold of his fishing smack in 1846 27
1.5. Read family gravestone, Portland St. George, Dorset, U.K. 28
1.6. Bow-shaped pulpit in the Seamen's Bethel, New Bedford, MA 29
1.7. Broken headstone of Master Mariner William Walliss, Hull Holy Trinity, East Yorkshire, U.K. 31
2.1. Monument for HMS *Eurydice*, 1878 35
2.2. Denison family monument, Stonington, CT 41
2.3. Memorial for the *Queen* transport 43
2.4. Detail of the *Queen* memorial 44
2.5. Mural plaque for British mariner Alfred Nicholls 47
2.6. Cenotaph for Benjamin Ewen 48
2.7. Gravestone of John Peirce 51
2.8. Broken column monument commemorating three brothers who died in three separate incidents 54
2.9. Monument for Cadet Bowyer Hamilton Guy Freer 55
2.10. Gravestone of mariner William Palmer 58
2.11. Detail of Palmer's stone, showing harbor scene and Palmer's vessel 59
2.12. Cenotaph for Captain Samuel Tucker, Portland, ME 59

2.13. Detail of James Stephenson's gravestone 61
3.1. Statue at the Fishermen's Memorial in Gloucester, Massachusetts 71
3.2. Monument for Royal Navy Captain Colin Andrew Campbell 74
3.3. Detail from Campbell's monument, depicting the burning of HMS *Bombay* 75
3.4. Gravestone of William Henry Allen, an American naval officer killed during the War of 1812 77
3.5. Monument for midshipman Thomas Barratt Powers, RN, who was killed in the War of 1812 78
3.6. Monument to three sailors, including a native Pacific Islander 79
3.7. Thomas Bennett's civilian-style gravestone set amid standard military stones 81
3.8. Crew monument for eleven sailors from HMS *Ariadne* who drowned while attempting to save a shipmate who had fallen overboard 83
3.9. Reconstruction of Octavian's campsite memorial for the Battle of Actium 85
3.10. HMS *Ganges* monument 95
4.1. Gravestone of Henry Howard, who was buried at sea in 1851 130
5.1. Obelisk for lost sailor Walter Ewer 135
5.2. An early memorial for an absent sailor: the gravestone of Captain John Hyer 137
5.3. The earliest empty grave recorded during the survey 141
5.4. Three seafaring sons of the Cobb family are commemorated with this cenotaph 143
5.5. Marblehead Charitable Seamen's Society monument 146
5.6. Marble plaque for Lt. Charles Webbe, which hints at his widow's grief over his loss 162
5.7. Gravestone for George Williams, which states that "his grave was in the deep" 164
6.1. Detail of monument for Gilman Low, showing anchor and biblical verse 177
6.2. Anchor and chain wrapped around cross 178
6.3. Angel holding anchor on crew monument for HMS *Severn* 179
6.4. Anchor incorporated into "IHS" Christian symbol 179
6.5. Another version of the "IHS" anchor, this time on a Celtic cross 180

6.6. Stained-glass window commemorating Captain John Downey, RN, who drowned when the packet *Briseis* foundered in 1838   189
6.7. Detail of the lower left panel of the Downey memorial   190
6.8. Detail of the lower center panel of Downey's memorial   191
6.9. Detail of gravestone of Robert Smith   193
6.10. Anchor and phrase "in sure and certain hope" on the gravestone of seaman John Scriven   199
7.1. Bermuda's Lost at Sea memorial   204
7.2. A modern religious maritime memorial   210

Table

1.1. Ten-year trend in fatality rates for selected high-risk occupations in the United States   6

Preface and Acknowledgments

The literature of the sea is replete with stories of shipwrecks. Since humans first took to the sea, ships and lives have been lost. Shipwreck tales contain all of the elements that make for exciting reading—tragedy, romance, bravery, hubris, and sacrifice, to name a few. Thousands of books have been written about maritime disasters. And yet those stories seldom address the question: what happened next? Survivors' stories are sometimes discussed to an extent, but little has been written about what happens to the dead. This book is about what happened next. Those who perished in maritime tragedies were more than statistics. They were real people with real lives and feelings. Those left behind suffered tremendously when their loved ones failed to return from the sea. Mariners, like other groups who work dangerous occupations, developed a close-knit group culture. Deaths at sea disrupted the fabric of this culture and necessitated actions designed to mend social structure. The forms that these actions took, from the ritual of burying a body at sea to the creation of memorials to honor the missing, can tell us a great deal about how maritime people saw their world.

This is not a study about monuments that honor famous people. Plenty of those exist already. For comparative purposes, the memorialization of naval heroes such as Horatio Nelson and John Paul Jones will be discussed, and even Winston Churchill makes a brief appearance, but by and large, this is a study of people who seldom find their way into history books but who nevertheless deserve to be remembered. I would rather tell you about Mrs. Charles Webbe of Cornwall, who lost her husband to the North Atlantic in 1839, and how she tried to cope with it through the memorial that she created, or about the respect that the crew of HMS *Ariadne* felt for eleven of their shipmates who sacrificed their lives while trying to save one man. Life is not made up of the fabulous and extraordinary, but of the commonplace and everyday. The everyday world of sailors included the very real possibility that death could strike at any moment. These are the stories that they told on their memorials, and in order to understand maritime culture, we need to listen to them.

This study crosses a number of disciplinary boundaries. My own training is in nautical archaeology and folklore. To understand maritime death rituals, I have had to delve into fields such as sociology, psychology, semiotics, death studies, and religious history. No doubt I have made some mistakes along the way. To scholars in those fields, I beg your indulgence. In my defense I offer a quote from Henry Glassie's *Material Culture*, which inspired this work.

> The scholarly discipline teaches discipline. It creates technicians, rigorous in procedure and exposition. Then scholars mature. Finding the world is not divided as the academy is divided, they bumble into territory beyond their expertise and become amateurs committed to a transdisciplinary intellectual practice.... Without betraying discipline itself, the care in their craft, intellectuals break out of disciplinary confinement, abandoning the comforts of youth in order to speak of things that matter. Our work must begin, but it cannot end in our divisive disciplines of nurture.

This quote sums up my core philosophy of nautical archaeology: in order to arrive at the best understanding of maritime life, we must examine all forms of evidence, be they texts or artifacts. This will entail a certain amount of bumbling along the way. In this book I have tried to speak of the things that mattered to maritime peoples from the Age of Sail, and I hope that I have done right by them.

My work would not be possible without the continued support of my wife and family. Numerous others have helped shape this book as well. I would like to thank Sylvia Grider, Kevin Crisman, James Bradford, Tom Green, Fred Hocker, George F. Bass, Fred van Doorninck Jr., and Jenny Moody. My colleagues at East Carolina University have been particularly supportive over the last four years as this book took shape, and I would like to thank in particular Larry Babits, Brad Rodgers, Nathan Richards, Mike Palmer, Carl Swanson, Wade Dudley, and Gerry Prokopowicz. Every scholar suffers from moments of doubt. During those times, words of encouragement from George F. Bass, Richard Gould, Brian Fagan, and Bruce Dickson were greatly appreciated.

Preliminary results of this study have been published in *Mortality* (volume 10, 2005, pp. 276–85), the *International Journal of Nautical Archaeology* (volume 36, 2007, pp. 112–24), and *The Historical Archaeology of Military Sites: Method and Topic* (Texas A&M University Press, 2010).

1

Introduction

On a spring day in 1865, the ship *Andacollo* weighed anchor and departed Callao, Peru, bound home for Liverpool. The vessel was under the command of Captain Wilfred Gilberry, who had spent a large part of his life at sea. Though still relatively young (Gilberry celebrated his fortieth birthday during *Andacollo*'s passage to South America), Gilberry had captained both sailing vessels and steamships on transatlantic voyages for more than a decade prior to taking command of *Andacollo*. An experienced sailor, Gilberry was well aware of the dangers of ocean travel. A decade previously, Gilberry, then in command of the *Governor*, had come across the Spanish ship *Nuestra Senhora de Begona* sinking in the middle of the North Atlantic. Gilberry's crew successfully rescued all of the Spanish sailors before their vessel slipped beneath the waves.[1]

Andacollo itself was as new as her captain was experienced. Built in Liverpool in 1864, the brand-new clipper ship spent time at Glasgow, Scotland, outfitting for her voyage to the Pacific. Newspaper advertisements extolled the virtues of the "splendid new Liverpool-built Iron Clipper" and promised to provide "first rate conveyance" for freight and passengers destined for Lima, Peru.[2] *Andacollo* departed Glasgow on February 2, 1865, and arrived at Lima's port of Callao, called by one visitor "the largest, safest, and most beautiful of any in the South Seas," on April 23, after a relatively quick passage of two and a half months.[3] Entering the harbor, *Andacollo*'s crew would have seen "a busy looking place—flags of all nations, and vessels of all kinds" at anchor in the roadstead.[4] At Callao, *Andacollo* spent a month offloading goods and taking on new cargo in preparation for the return voyage to England. In contrast to its splendid harbor, the town of Callao itself was described by travelers as a "dreary, uninviting place" with a sky that, while appearing perpetually gray, never seemed to produce a drop of rain.[5] Despite these shortcomings, *Andacollo*'s crew probably enjoyed their time ashore, mingling with local people and fellow sailors from around the world. It was to be their last.

On May 30, *Andacollo* left Callao behind, bound for Valparaiso, Chile, en route home to Liverpool. As it made its way down the coast of South America, *Andacollo* sailed out of history. The ship never arrived at Valparaiso, nor did it return to its home port in the British Isles. Back home in Liverpool, fears mounted throughout the summer of 1865 as no word came. By October, all hope had been lost.

> MISSING VESSEL—A fine new Liverpool ship, the Andacollo, was posted yesterday at the Underwriters' Rooms as missing, nothing having been heard of her since she sailed from Callao for Valparaiso on the 30th of May last. All hope of her safety is now abandoned. She was a very fine iron clipper ship, of 864 tons register, built in the autumn of last year, by Messrs. T. Vernon and Son, for Messrs. Imrie and Tomlinson, and was under the command of Captain Gilberry.[6]

No trace of the vessel was ever found. The ship simply vanished at sea, as have so many others over the centuries. It is possible that it foundered in a storm, or wrecked on the rocky coast of South America. The crew might have survived for a time or plunged instantly to a watery grave. Most likely, no one will ever know. But they were not forgotten.

This book is about the ways that English and American seafarers remembered those who died, and, by extension, what this tells us about maritime peoples as a group. Although Gilberry and *Andacollo* disappeared, the tale of their loss remains; it is documented on a gravestone in St. James' Cemetery in Liverpool, England. The stone is no longer *in situ*, and is so badly weathered that one must kneel in front and examine it carefully in order to learn the story that it tells (figure 1.1). The full inscription reads:

IN SACRED REMEMBRANCE
OF
WILFRED MOSSOP,
Master Mariner of this Port.
Born at Whitehaven December 7th, 1786
Departed this life December 12th, 1848
"Therefore be ye also ready."

HANNAH, his Daughter,
Died at Whitehaven December 31st 1854
Aged 23 Years
WILFRED GILBERRY,
his Nephew: Born 17th April 1825:
left Callao 30th May 1865, in command of
the ship "Andacollo" bound for Valparaiso
and has never since been heard of.
ISABELLA GILBERRY,
Wife of the above,
departed this life December 11th 1883
Aged 56 Years[7]

Gilberry's remembrance comprises a mere five lines, tucked into the middle of an unremarkable stone from one city cemetery. Originally, it would have been surrounded by nearly identical stones, making Gilberry's remembrance difficult to see, save by the most determined observers. Why,

Figure 1.1. Mossop/Gilberry family gravestone, recording the loss of Wilfred Gilberry and the *Andacollo*. St. James' Cemetery, Liverpool, U.K. Photo by author.

then, was he included at all, especially since his body had been lost on the far side of the world? Although they knew that his corpse would never rest in the grave, Gilberry's family nevertheless felt it necessary to put his story on the family gravestone. Thousands of similar memorials exist in churchyards and cemeteries throughout the world. These memorials represent an almost totally unexplored avenue into the study of maritime life. Collectively, they tell us about the beliefs of an occupational group whose sense of self and collective worldview was shaped by the deadly environment in which they lived and worked.

A Singularly Deadly Profession

It would be hard to find an occupation that has been more romanticized than seafaring during the Age of Sail (for the purposes of this study, roughly the fifteenth through the early twentieth centuries). From the comfort of dry land, novelists and scholars alike weave tales about lusty jack tars living a life of adventure. Those who spent time on heaving decks, and their loved ones ashore, knew better. While the life of a sailor did have its adventurous moments, the reality was usually quite different than popular depictions would have one believe. Seafaring is hard, dirty, dangerous work. Today, commercial fishing consistently ranks as the world's deadliest occupation. In the United States, data from the Bureau of Labor Statistics shows that commercial fishers have an average occupational fatality rate of about 121 per 100,000 workers per year over the ten-year period from 1998 to 2007, a figure that ranks highest among all occupations (table 1.1).[8] During this same period, the average fatality rate for the U.S. workforce as a whole was just over four deaths per 100,000 workers. This means that fishers are thirty times more likely to die on the job compared to all other U.S. workers. Even occupations we think of as dangerous, such as police work and firefighting, do not have nearly the fatality rate of commercial fishing. Fishing is about four times as deadly as coal mining or truck driving. Fishers are almost eight times more likely to be killed on the job than police officers, and more than seven times as likely as firefighters. The only occupations that come close in terms of danger are logging, flight crew work, and high steel construction work. Logging actually has a higher fatality rate than fishing in some years, but when averaged over time, fishing is slightly more deadly. Pilots and high steel workers certainly face dangerous situations, but even so, fishing is still about 1.5 and 2.1 times as deadly, respectively. While not as deadly as fishing, U.S. sailors also have a high on-the-job fatality rate. From 1998 to 2007, the average rate was more than 45 deaths per 100,000 workers, putting seamen behind loggers, flight crew workers, and high steel construction workers. The fatality rate for U.S. sailors, however, was still about eleven times higher than that of the workforce as a whole.

Data from the United Kingdom show the same deadly trend for commercial fishing. In 2008, the Marine Accident Investigation Branch published a study that examined the extent and causes of deaths aboard U.K. registered fishing craft.[9] This study was prompted by data that showed that the fishing industry fatality rate was 115 times higher than that of the workforce as a whole.[10] The study found that from 1992 to 2006, U.K. fishers had a fatal accident rate of 126 per 100,000, a number slightly deadlier than that of U.S. commercial fishing.

In the United Kingdom, however, merchant seafarers do enjoy a safer workplace than their U.S. counterparts. In a series of articles, Stephen Roberts has analyzed merchant shipping deaths over much of the past century.[11] His analyses show that merchant seafaring safety improved throughout the twentieth century, with a drastic decline in fatality rates over the last few decades. Early in the century, merchant shipping fatality rates averaged more than 200 deaths per 100,000 workers. Recent rates are much improved. For the decade 1996 through 2005, the fatality rate was only 10.7 per 100,000 workers. Even so, during the last half century, U.K. merchant shipping has still been anywhere from twelve to twenty-four times as deadly as the national occupational average. While recent improvements offer hope to those who make their living on the sea, Roberts points out that a large part of the decline in fatality rates over the past twenty-five years is due to U.K. vessels being re-registered under flags of convenience.[12] In other words, the danger has been outsourced. More dangerous vessels may now be registered in countries with less stringent safety regulations, and therefore the sailors who man them probably face a similar degree of risk as their predecessors. To sum it up, in the United States and the United Kingdom, commercial fishing is consistently the deadliest occupation one can pursue. Fatality rates range from thirty to more than one hundred times higher than that of the rest of the workforce. Merchant seafaring is not as deadly as fishing, but still ranks among the deadliest occupations and has significantly higher fatality rates than the workforce as a whole. It is important to keep in mind that these data

Table 1.1. Ten-year trend in fatality rates for selected high-risk occupations in the United States

Fatalities per 100,000 Workers

Year	All Workforce	Commercial Fishers	Loggers	Flight Crew	High Steel	Maritime (excluding fishing)	Coal Miners	Commercial Truck Drivers	Firefighters	Police
1998	4.5	137.3	141.6	80.5	82.5	37.1	23.8	29.2	19.0	11.6
1999	4.5	162.5	129.5	65.7	60.6	49.1	30.6	28.8	20.4	11.0
2000	4.3	108.3	122.1	100.8	59.5	46.4	35.2	27.6	15.4	12.1
2001	4.3	151.2	127.8	64.0	57.7	39.0	36.7	25.3	16.5	13.5
2002	4.0	71.1	117.8	69.8	58.2	46.6	25.2	25.0	16.6	11.6
2003	4.0	115.0	132.9	98.3	52.1	41.8	34.6	26.8	17.4	20.9
2004	4.1	90.9	92.4	92.4	47.0	65.9	29.9	28.0	10.8	18.2
2005	4.0	118.4	94.1	68.6	55.6	47.6	26.8	29.2	11.5	18.5
2006	4.0	147.2	84.6	90.4	61.0	41.3	49.5	27.5	16.6	16.8
2007	3.7	111.8	86.4	70.7	45.5	41.2	28.4	26.2	17.4	21.8
Average	4.1	121.4	112.9	80.1	58.0	45.6	32.1	27.4	16.2	15.6

are from modern industrialized nations, with well-developed lifesaving systems and workplace safety regulations. In the Age of Sail, mariners faced a much more dangerous workplace environment.

Fatality statistics for the Age of Sail are more difficult to calculate, but one thing is clear: seafaring was a great deal more dangerous than it is today. By the mid-nineteenth century, public scrutiny was brought to bear on dangerous workplaces, and governments were coming under pressure to do something about them. Public opinion in favor of greater safety regulations prompted Queen Victoria to appoint the Royal Commission on Loss of Life at Sea to study the industry and suggest ways of improving safety. The commission's final report, issued in 1887, reveals how much deadlier seafaring in the nineteenth century was.[13] From 1871 to 1886, the commission recorded a total of 25,395 sailor deaths on British registered vessels. The fatality rate, however, was up for debate. Statistics from the Board of Trade showed an average of between 210,000 and 217,000 seafarers employed per year. Using these figures, the fatal-accident rate would have been about 731 per 100,000 seafarers. The shipping industry, however, disputed the Board of Trade's figures, claiming that actually around 300,000 British sailors were employed in any given year.[14] The reason why shipping industry leaders sought to inflate the number of employed seafarers is obvious; if there were more sailors, then the fatal-accident rate was consequently lower. Even using their higher estimate of seamen, however, the fatal-accident rate for 1871 to 1886 would still be about 529 per 100,000 seamen. Both of these estimates should be considered too low, however, because they do not include two crucial factors. The commission only included deaths due to shipwrecks, founderings, drownings, or other accidents aboard ships at sea. Fatalities that occurred in port were not factored in, and would have raised the annual rate. Even more importantly, deaths due to disease were not included. Disease should have been considered, however, because it represented one of the main occupational hazards for seamen. Fatalities due to disease are estimated to have been between 1,300 and 1,400 annually.[15] Factoring in disease, the annual fatality rate for 1871 to 1886 would be about 1,330 to 1,376 per 100,000 sailors, if using the government's employment figure of 217,000, or close to 1,000 deaths per 100,000 if using the shipping industry's figure of around 300,000 employed seamen.

A low estimate, then, for the U.K. merchant shipping fatality rate in the second half of the nineteenth century was somewhere around 1,000 deaths per 100,000 seamen annually, with higher estimates somewhere above 1,300 per 100,000. Given the disparity between sets of data, these numbers should be viewed as a general reflection of the deadliness of U.K. seafaring rather than as absolute facts. Still, using the most conservative estimate, late-nineteenth-century British merchant seamen died at a rate about five times higher than that of their early-twentieth-century counterparts, more than twenty times higher than that of modern U.S. sailors, and about one hundred times higher than that of U.K. merchant seafarers today. This rate is about ten times higher than those of modern U.K. and U.S. commercial fishing, the deadliest occupation in either of these countries. It is safe to say that nineteenth-century seafarers faced a substantially greater risk of dying on the job than do modern sailors.

In earlier centuries, seafaring must have been at least as deadly, if not more so. It is impossible to calculate accurate fatality rates due to the paucity of reliable statistics before the mid-nineteenth century. Some information, however, can be gleaned. Outbreaks of disease could kill scores of mariners at a time. On the Cadiz expedition of 1625, for example, an outbreak of typhus proved fatal for more than one-quarter of the men in the English fleet (some 5,000 casualties).[16] During Anson's ill-fated circumnavigation from 1740 to 1744, a staggering 1,051 out of 1,955 men never returned.[17] In 1810, while engaged in the Napoleonic Wars, the British Royal Navy suffered a total loss of 5,183 sailors.[18] This figure represents an incredibly high mortality rate of 3,647 deaths per 100,000 workers, based on Lloyd's figure of 142,098 men serving in the navy that year.[19] To be sure, this figure is for a navy during a time of war, but most deaths occurred due to shipwrecks, accidents, and disease rather than enemy action.[20] In other words, even in a wartime military context, most sailors died for the same types of reasons as their civilian brethren. Statistics from the famous fishing port of Gloucester, Massachusetts, reveal that a total of 2,351 lives and 428 vessels were lost between 1830 and 1882, an average of 44 fatalities per year.[21] This was a significant number of fatalities for a city whose population numbered only about 7,500 in 1830.[22] These examples represent only a few incidents, but nevertheless provide some idea of the huge number of lives lost over the centuries.

Not all agree about the deadliness of seafaring. Some authors have commented on what seemed to them to be low fatality rates among nineteenth-century sailors. Elmo Paul Hohman examined the account books for fifteen voyages made by eight mid-nineteenth-century American whaling vessels. He determined that sixteen deaths occurred among the 489 crewmen—a mortality rate of 3.3 percent. A further study by Hohman of twenty-three voyages by ten whaling vessels revealed a death rate of 2.6 percent (30 out of 1,141 total whalemen).[23] Based on these studies, Hohman posited a relatively low mortality rate among American whalemen, a conclusion seemingly supported by Margaret Scott Creighton's study of more than one hundred diaries of American merchant seamen and whalers from 1830 to 1870. Creighton calculated that the average American merchant vessel or whaler suffered a mortality rate of approximately 5 percent over the course of three years at sea.[24] There are two problems with these approaches. First, they are based on a relatively small number of vessels and voyages. More significantly, the number of fatalities seems low because the authors quote percentages (3.3, 2.6, and 5 percent, respectively) that seem small. In reality, these percentages actually indicate very high fatality rates. Converting them to the standard system used today—number of fatalities per 100,000 workers—reveals just how high they really are. The numbers quoted by Hohman yield 818 and 657 deaths per 100,000 workers, respectively, if one assumes an average four-year cruise. If the cruise duration was shorter, which may in fact have been the case, then the fatality rates would be even higher. It is not possible to calculate a rate from Creighton's data, because she does not supply the number of fatalities or total number of crew members. However, a 5 percent mortality rate means a death rate of 1 in 20. Even spread over a three-year cruise, this equals a high fatality rate.

Further investigation into Age of Sail archives might yield additional data for calculating fatality rates, but the point is clear. Modern commercial fishing ranks as the deadliest profession one can pursue, while merchant seafaring is more dangerous than most other occupations. In the Age of Sail, seafaring was anywhere from ten to possibly more than a hundred times as deadly as it is today. Before the advent of modern workplace safety codes, other occupations were also more dangerous than their modern counterparts. Miners, for example, often suffered fatality rates on par with seafarers. U.S. coal mining had a fatality rate of 367 per 100,000 workers during the first decade of the twentieth century.[25] Hard rock metal mining in the western United States was equally deadly, if not more so, with estimated fatality rates ranging from 225 to 600 per 100,000 miners during the late nineteenth and early twentieth centuries.[26] E. H. Hunt's examination of British labor history shows that seafaring ranked consistently among the deadliest occupations, although tin mining sometimes surpassed it.[27] John Rule claims that Cornish tin and copper mining was probably the most dangerous occupation in nineteenth-century Britain.[28] For the period of 1849 to 1853, Rule cites a fatality rate of 3,351 per 100,000 workers aged 45 to 55, and 6,317 per 100,000 workers aged 55 to 65.[29] According to these data, Rule estimates that Cornish mining was about 50 percent more deadly than seafaring. The statistics, however, are not so easily comparable. The mining-fatality data includes miners who died due to the effects of disease, whereas the statistics for seafaring fatalities typically did not. Cornish metal miners contracted debilitating lung diseases from years of breathing dust in a low-oxygen environment, a fact that accounts for why fatality rates increased with age. In addition, the maritime statistics typically did not include fatalities from fishing vessels, which were considerably more deadly than merchant seafaring. Given the nature of nineteenth-century statistical recordkeeping, it is difficult to compare one occupation with another accurately, but it seems likely that the fatality rates for seafaring ranked right alongside other dangerous occupations such as mining. Equally important, seafaring existed as a deadly occupation for much longer than many other hazardous forms of work. The heyday of Cornish metal mining lasted from about 1740 to 1860, whereas seafaring has a much longer history. Although reliable statistics for earlier centuries are impossible to calculate, there is no reason to believe that fatality rates were any lower than in the nineteenth century. They were, in all likelihood, probably higher. At times, other high-risk occupations such as logging and mining may have met or exceeded the fatality rate of seafaring, but a sailor's occupation has consistently ranked among the world's deadliest. Seafaring is as deadly a profession as any that humans have ever pursued.

In addition to the sheer number of fatalities, there is another factor that makes death at sea even worse. Not only were sailors in greater statistical danger than landsmen, but the tragic nature of death at sea made fatalities there even more notable. At sea, humans in frail wooden craft were at the mercy of powerful natural forces. Storms were frequent occurrences, and all mariners could expect to face many over the course of a career. Storms can whip the ocean into a frenzy, generating towering waves that toss ships about like toy boats in a bathtub or drive them to ruin upon the land. Two motifs, rocks and storms, exemplify the dangers of the natural world and feature prominently on maritime memorials.

Natural phenomena aside, the ship itself is a dangerous place to work, and thousands of mariners met their end in accidents involving falling from the rigging, drowning, or being crushed by shifting cargo. The threat of armed conflict was always present, and the weapons of the time, though crude by modern standards, inflicted gruesome wounds on the human body. If these threats were not enough, a sailor could also find himself at the mercy of diseases contracted in some exotic port of call or caused by malnutrition or the crowded nature of shipboard life.

Realizing the many appalling ways that a man could die at sea represents the second key to understanding the hold that death had on the maritime mind. When he embarked upon a life at sea, a man knew that he stood a decent chance of being shipwrecked, plunging to his death from the rigging, being mutilated by cannon or sword, expiring from a gruesome disease in some tropical backwater, falling overboard and drowning, being washed overboard in a storm, drowning by the upsetting of a boat, perishing from malnutrition, being presented with the choice of burning to death aboard a flaming vessel or jumping over the side to drown, or sinking into the depths aboard a foundering ship. He not only faced a statistically greater chance of dying than his counterparts on land, but the nature of death at sea made it even more awful. The shadow of death loomed always over mariners and had a great hold on their collective subconscious. Consequently, it influenced their group values and beliefs to a substantial degree.

Sailors: Culture, Component, Subculture, Folk Group?

A foundational premise of this book is that sailors possess a distinct occupational culture. While seemingly straightforward, the idea of *maritime culture* has been a subject of some contention within maritime archaeology. In the mid-1990s, J. R. Hunter sounded a cautionary note regarding the use of the term. Hunter's main objection came from the fact that it is impossible to find any culture that is strictly maritime in character. Every maritime group, noted Hunter, is part of a larger culture, and the boundaries between what is and what is not maritime in a society can be extremely difficult to determine. Instead of the term *maritime culture*, Hunter prefers *maritime component*, by which he means the elements of a society that are related to seafaring. Hunter's argument is valid; no culture seems to be entirely maritime in nature. But it is also a bit of a straw man, because it is not clear that other scholars ever intended the term *maritime culture* to exclude seafaring as part of a larger cultural system. Hunter specifically cites the work of Keith Muckelroy and Christer Westerdahl. Neither, however, considers maritime culture a self-contained entity that precludes membership in a wider society. Muckelroy was the first scholar to discuss maritime culture extensively; as Hunter notes, Muckelroy seems to have been the one who coined the term. It is clear, however, that Muckelroy never considered maritime culture to be something separate from a larger cultural system. Instead, Muckelroy considered maritime culture to be one of many subcultures within a society. Examples of other such subcultures include religious groups, members of the military, urban dwellers, and rural farmers. Muckelroy noted that within each subculture "there are special aspects to their economic, political, social, etc., organisation which are different from those in other sub-cultures, although interrelated with them."[30] This statement makes it clear that Muckelroy viewed maritime culture as only one of the possible components within a society, not as a way of life somehow separate from any other form of culture. Westerdahl's conception of maritime culture is entwined with his concept of the *maritime cultural landscape*. Westerdahl variously defines the maritime cultural landscape as "the unity of remnants of maritime culture on land as well as underwater" and "the whole network of sailing routes, old as well as new, with ports and harbours along the coast, and its related constructions and remains of human activity, underwater as well as terrestrial."[31] There is nothing here to preclude seafaring from being part of a larger cultural matrix, and Westerdahl makes it clear here and in his discussion of maritime enclaves that he considers seafaring life to be part of a wider system.[32]

I also take exception to Hunter's claim that because they exist within a larger cultural matrix, "maritime components are no more than extensions or reflections of the broader culture to which they belong and are integral rather than isolated economic or social elements."[33] Integral they may be, but that does not mean that there are not true distinctions to be found among the subcultures that make up a culture. In modern industrialized nations, for example, subcultures based on age, occupation, race, ethnicity, gender, and religion can be found, to name only a few. These subcultural groups retain features that reflect their parent culture, but also possess traits of their own that make them distinct cultural units. Mariners, a subculture based on occupation, can be viewed as a distinct unit of study, and in fact the idea that seafarers formed a distinct group within their parent culture is an idea that dates back more than two millennia. In Homer's *Odyssey*, the ghost of Teiresias tells Odysseus:

> Go forth, taking a shapely oar, until thou comest to men that know naught of the sea and eat not of food mingled with salt, aye, and they know naught of ships with purple cheeks, or of shapely oars that are as wings unto ships. And I will tell thee a sign right manifest, which will not escape thee. When another wayfarer, on meeting thee, shall say that thou hast a winnowing-fan on thy stout shoulder, then do thou fix in the earth thy shapely oar and make goodly offerings to lord Poseidon.[34]

Homer understood that in his time there were people who knew nothing of the sea and who would think that a ship's oar was a farming implement. The passage implies that Odysseus and the people inland share a panhellenic culture, as shown by their ability to communicate, but that there was nevertheless a distinction between those who made their living from the sea and those who dwelled far away from it. I am not arguing here that the *Odyssey* is historically accurate, but rather that it reflects an idea that existed in ancient Greek society. Whether the *Odyssey* is history or legend, or whether Homer reflects ideas from the Bronze Age or the Greek Dark Age, makes no difference. The point is clear: for more than 2,500 years, at least, the concept of a difference between maritime and terrestrial culture has existed. In the Age of Sail, mariners likewise lived within a parent culture, but nonetheless shared traits that made them distinct as an occupational group. Whether we choose to call this *culture*, *component*, or *subculture* does not really matter. Instead, the question is how, as scholars, can we isolate and study the characteristics of maritime occupational life, which can be, as Hunter has astutely pointed out, admittedly difficult to separate from its parent culture?

The approach that I will use in this book examines sailors as a *folk group*, a concept borrowed from the field of folkloristics. The term refers to groups of people who come together to perform an action or series of actions, and as a consequence of their shared experience, develop a set of group values and beliefs that they express through various means.[35] The term excludes groups that are formed purely for some functional reason but whose members do not interact to develop a set of shared ideas and customs. The passengers on a transatlantic airliner, for example, spend many hours together, share meals, and chat, yet they do not develop a set of group ideas and traditions during their flight. The flight crew, on the other hand, are members of a folk group. Flight-crew lore expresses the way the group views things that are important to it, and includes cautionary tales for preventing accidents, ways to deal with unruly passengers, and thoughts on negotiations with management.[36]

Exploring the concept more closely, folklorist Barre Toelken has provided what I consider to be the best definition of a folk group: "any group of people who share informal vernacular contacts that become the basis for expressive, culture-based communications."[37] Understanding this statement requires a brief discussion of several key concepts in folkloristics. Central to the idea of folklore is that folklore is *informal*. That is, it is not learned as part of an official, institutional process. One goes to institutions such as universities to learn a formal curriculum. While there, however, students participate in their groups' traditions, which can include such things as exchanging stories about professors, dressing a particular way, and going to wild parties. Such lore is learned not from the curriculum but from interaction with other group members. By the same token, mariners in the Age of Sail learned how to be sailors from other sailors, not from textbooks. Today, even in occupations that include formal training, much information regarding job skills is still passed on informally from worker to worker. Firefighters, for example, attend schools on the correct techniques for fighting blazes, but also learn much by observing and working with their peers.[38]

Informal learning is a hallmark of all occupations, but not all can be considered folk groups. An occupational group becomes a folk group when its members develop the second part of Toelken's definition: "expressive culture-based communications." This means that the group develops ways of being and acting that articulate the group's understanding of what it is and what it should be. In a nutshell, the group develops a set of values and beliefs and a particular worldview. These ideas are expressed through the group's traditions, which can cross a range of genres such as personal-experience narratives, jokes, proverbs, rituals, songs, and material culture. The group maintains and perpetuates itself through the performance of its traditions. Newcomers to the group learn the ways of the group by observing and interacting with other group members. They typically become full-fledged members over a period of time, which includes progressing through a series of stages marked by rituals following the member's completion of each step.

Toelken goes on to say that the term folk group

> Is therefore not a static label to be applied simply where people are observed to be loggers, quilters, Ozarkers, or Russian Old Believers; rather, the term should indicate a dynamic system of human interchange where the members of any group interrelate on a high context level of attitude, reference, connotation, sense of meaning, and customary behavior, precisely as members, and to be members, of that group. And the group persists not because it has a certain number of bodies, but because its members continue to use their shared vernacular system of reference.[39]

Unpacking this statement reveals several other key aspects of a folk group. Group beliefs are not static; on the contrary, traditions change over time. Dynamism is a key concept in folklore studies, and means that, at any given time and place, folklore will reflect the culture that produces it. This, indeed, is what gives folklore its value to scholars: by interpreting its form and meaning, we can understand something about the culture that produced it, and see how cultural ideas change temporally and spatially.

Another key tenet is that simply being a member of a particular occupation, ethnicity, or religion does not make one a member of that folk group. There is a difference between cutting down trees and being a member of the logger folk group. To be included in the latter, one must participate in the "way of being"—the traditions that express the group's beliefs and worldview.[40]

Folk groups are *high context* groups, a term that Toelken borrows from anthropologist Edward T. Hall. Hall derived his concept of high and low context from the study of communications, and explains it in this way:

> A high-context (HC) communication or message is one in which most of the information is either in the physical context or internalized in the person, while very little is in the coded, explicit, transmitted part of the message. A low-context (LC) communication is just the opposite; i.e., the mass of the information is vested in the explicit

code. Twins who have grown up together can and do communicate more economically (HC) than two lawyers in a courtroom during a trial (LC), a mathematician programming a computer, two politicians drafting legislation, two administrators writing a regulation, or a child trying to explain to his mother why he got into a fight.[41]

Thus, a high context group is one in which members share a great deal of information that is not privy to nonmembers, and also conduct themselves according to a set of customs that are known to the members of the group but often seem strange and mysterious to outsiders.

In his classic article "The Esoteric-Exoteric Factor in Folklore," William Hugh Jansen provides a detailed exploration of the relationship between groups and outsiders. *Esoteric* refers to the way that the group sees itself, while *exoteric* means the way that outsiders view the group. Jansen explores the functions and development of internal group lore. Esoteric lore "frequently stems from the group sense of belonging and serves to defend and strengthen that sense."[42] Jansen notes three factors that typically give rise to esoteric lore within a group. First, it typically develops in groups that are isolated in some way from other parts of society. Isolation promotes the development of strong group bonds. It also tends to foster exoteric lore about the group, because isolated groups come to be seen as different or strange to the rest of society. Isolation was obviously a prime factor in the development of esoteric group lore among sailors; other groups similarly isolated, such as cowboys and loggers, feature similar sets of lore. The second factor that leads to esoteric groups occurs when group members possess some specialized knowledge or skill. This often includes a specialized vocabulary that group members master, but which is not understood by outsiders, even those who speak the same language. For occupational groups, specialized knowledge often takes the form of job-related skills. Again, these factors obviously applied to sailors, who possessed the knowledge of how to handle a ship and used many terms that landsmen did not understand. Jansen's third factor for the development of esoteric groups occurs when a group is seen as being particularly different or interesting in some way. This factor results in the development of exoteric lore about the group, but is another way in which differences between the group and the rest of society are highlighted. This factor largely accounts for the reason why we romanticize occupations like seafaring, police work, firefighting, and cowboying: they are seen as having some qualities that make us wish we could participate. Young boys and girls want to run away to sea or off to the range; even adults tend to romanticize such occupations because they symbolize escape from the mundane realities of life.

Not all folk groups develop the same level of intimacy. Among occupational groups, the highest context groups seem to develop in professions where group members must form close bonds because the work is particularly dangerous or stressful. This is one reason why the folk-group concept is particularly suitable for studying sailors. Other occupations whose members form close bonds include loggers, miners, pilots, military units engaged in combat, cowboys, and high-steel workers. All of these groups have in common a shared dangerous workplace environment that shapes their group values and worldviews. As we will see, the values and worldview that arise out of these occupations share much in common.

Returning to Toelken's discussion, he also makes the point that a folk group is not dependent on size. Rather, it is about a certain number of people performing a common set of traditions. Membership can therefore be as few as two or run into the millions. Examples of the former, known as *dyads* to folklorists, would be married couples or close military buddies, while African-Americans and Catholics would be two examples of folk groups whose membership numbers in the millions.[43] Generally speaking, the higher the number of members, and the greater their diversity, the greater the chance for subgroups within the larger group. The larger the group, the lesser the chance that members will know other members. In the case of especially large groups such as religions, it would indeed be impossible for any one person to know everyone else. Members could still recognize other members, however, by their performance of the group's traditions. A sailor would have recognized a fellow sailor by such things as dress and vocabulary, in the same way that an American Catholic can understand the rituals being performed by Filipino Catholics if he or she happened to visit their church in the Philippines.

The folk-group concept possesses several features that make it useful for studying maritime culture. First, the group has an existence beyond any one member. Members may come and go, but the group exists as long as there are members actively participating, that is, carrying on the group's traditions and passing on its values and beliefs. This is particularly well suited to seafarers because many sailors did not work at sea for their entire career. A man might sign on for one voyage, and then leave seafaring forever. If he left the group and ceased performing its traditions, then he would no longer be considered a member of the group. On the other hand, a man could leave seafaring, but continue to participate in maritime traditions, in which case he would still be considered a member of the maritime folk group. A good example of the latter is Richard Henry Dana Jr., whose book *Two Years before the Mast* stands as a classic of maritime literature. During his time at sea, Dana embraced maritime culture and continued to perpetuate group traditions after returning to life ashore. Massachusetts statesman Henry Adams, who knew Dana in the late 1840s, described his appearance and character.

> [H]e affected to be still before the mast, a direct, rather bluff, vigorous seaman, and only as one got to know him better one found the man of rather excessive refinement trying with success to work like a day-laborer, deliberately hardening his skin to the burden, as though he were still carrying hides at Monterey. . . . he forced himself to take life as it came, and he suffocated his longings with grim self-discipline, by mere force of will.[44]

Dana's traits, as Adams describes them—bluffness, a hardness of self against the elements, taking life as it came—are characteristics that marked men in the maritime folk group. The fact that Dana still acted like a seaman more than a decade after returning from the sea shows how deeply such characteristics can become imbued in members of a high context folk group, and how one can still be a group member even though he no longer actively works in the occupation. It follows that a person can also be a group member for a period of time, leave the group, and later return. The key is not time spent in or out of the occupation, but rather whether or not one actively participates in the group's customary behavior.

Another feature that makes the folk-group approach useful for studying maritime life is that being a member of one group does not preclude membership in other groups. Most people, in fact, are members of numerous folk groups at any given time in their lives. A person can belong to groups based on age, occupation, gender, ethnicity, nationality, and religion, to name only a few of the more common ones. They might also join groups with shared leisure interests. Viewing mariners in this way eliminates Hunter's objection that maritime culture does not really exist because it is always part of a larger culture.[45] An occupational folk group such as seafaring is only one of many groups that a person belongs to, and forms a subculture within a larger culture.

It follows from the previous concept that the notion of an occupational folk group implies a great deal of diversity among its members. Some folk groups are based on particular genders or ethnicities, but membership in occupational folk groups cuts across these lines. This is particularly apropos for sailors because they came from many different ethnic, national, and religious backgrounds, and yet when working together as sailors, they performed traditional behaviors that grew out of their shared workplace experience. Because of the group's diversity, however, the maritime folk group contained numerous subgroups. Such subgroups share many traditions and beliefs with the parent group—otherwise they would not be a part of it—but they also possess their own traditions that reflect each subgroup's particular concerns. The folk-group approach is flexible enough to allow for such subgroups and for any one of them to become units of investigation.

Toelken points out that membership in an occupational folk group is not limited only to those who perform the actual on-the-job tasks. Instead, the group is composed of the "total community" of people involved in the particular occupation.[46] As long as a person participates in the group's traditions, he or she is a member of the group. When studying maritime culture, this concept is useful because it allows for examination of all of the diverse subgroups that make up the larger group. For example, women at sea were the exception rather than the rule, but women nevertheless formed a key component of maritime culture. In roles as diverse as sailors, mothers, wives, tavern keepers, and prostitutes, women participated in maritime work and thus can be included in the maritime folk group. As we will see, the participation of women was an important part of maritime memorialization, because it was often the women left behind who put up memorials. Such memorials reflect not only the beliefs of the group as a whole, but also the specific concerns of the female gender subgroup within the group.

Because of the diversity that exists in an occupational folk group, group values and beliefs exist, but they are not monolithic. A group has to hold some beliefs and parts of a worldview in common or it would cease to exist, but individuals and subgroups within the group certainly have their own beliefs. For example, one group value that we will see in the memorials is the idea of taking care of shipmates, sometimes even to the extent of sacrificing one's own life to do so, but this did not stop white sailors from discriminating against black sailors. A white mariner might risk his life to save a black shipmate from drowning and still discriminate against him. In the first instance, he would be following the belief of the larger group, while in the second instance, he would be following the feelings of his ethnic subgroup toward a person of a different ethnic subgroup.

Sailors and inhabitants of maritime communities ashore represent a classic example of an occupational folk group. The skills possessed by mariners, and the dangerous environment in which they work, helped create a body of shared tradition unique to maritime peoples. While numerous collections of nautical lore from the Age of Sail have been published, most folkloristic studies of maritime communities have dealt with modern groups. Folklorists have yet to apply the folk-group approach to the study of past maritime peoples. Part of the reason for this is the problem of trying to record shared traditions from people who are long since dead. One solution to this problem is to combine theoretical concepts from folk-group research with methodologies from archaeology. Memorialization practices represent one form of shared tradition that can be examined through archaeological research. Maritime peoples used memorials and mortuary rituals to express their conception of the world. To date, this category of material remains largely untouched by maritime scholars. This is a pity, because mortuary rituals are one of the best ways to learn about the things that a group cherishes—its group beliefs, values, and worldview.

Memorials: The Material Culture of Memory and Beliefs

Archaeologists tend to equate the beginning of gravestone scholarship with the work of James Deetz and Edwin Dethlefsen, but before their studies, other scholars had already recognized the value of memorials as vehicles of cultural ideas. Most early studies of memorials were performed from an art historical perspective; that is, memorials were examined for their artistic value. This approach focused on elaborate elite memorials and largely ignored the simple gravestones of non-elites. Nevertheless, early scholarship yielded several valuable insights. Harriet Forbes' *Gravestones of Early New England, and the Men Who Made Them, 1653–1800*, originally published in 1927, was one of the first studies to recognize the potential that gravestones had for revealing cultural ideals. Forbes noted that gravestones reflected the spirit of their creators and taught moral lessons to the living. She also realized that the spatial patterning of gravestones was important. Their location in graveyards outside Puritan meetinghouses served as a comfort to those attending church services, while at the same time reminding the congregation of the fate that awaited them someday. Forbes' key insight was that gravestones are placed with an audience in mind, and that one of their functions is to communicate cultural values to that audience. Forbes also emphasized the need to view gravestones "with the eyes of the past," an early statement on the importance of understanding the cultural context that produced the artifacts.[47] On the other side of the Atlantic, Katharine Ada McDowall Esdaile and Mary Désirée Anderson were among the first to point out the potential that churches and graveyards held for learning about English social history.[48] Both agreed that memorials could be used to glean information about people who were often left out of historical sources. The usefulness of gravestones for understanding lower social classes also attracted the attention of folklorists. In his examination of southern U.S. cemeteries, Fred Tarpley noted that epitaphs on memorials record "the grass-roots archives of folk fact and sentiment."[49] Early studies such as these pioneered the idea that memorials had much to tell about cultural beliefs, setting the stage for an explosion of gravestone studies beginning in the 1960s.

More than any others, historical archaeologists James Deetz and Edwin Dethlefsen popularized the study of memorials. Their work combined sound archaeological methodology with an awareness of the symbolic meanings of memorials.[50] While their work dealt mainly with understanding religious change, Deetz and Dethlefsen also recognized that gravestones contain information about other aspects of societies. By studying epitaphs on the gravestones, they noted, it is "possible to arrive at some statement concerning values regarding death."[51] They also wrote that changes in gravestone symbolism that occurred from the seventeenth to the nineteenth centuries reflected "a wholly new way of looking at the world."[52] These statements are important because they are among the first times that archaeologists articulated the idea that memorials encode a society's core beliefs.

Since the groundbreaking work of Deetz and Dethlefsen, scholars have used memorials to examine numerous issues relevant to archaeology, including social status, ethnicity, and gender.[53] Such studies continue to focus on the ways that memorials encode values and worldview. Dickran and Ann Tashjian follow Deetz and Dethlefsen in asserting that gravestones are the product of a "network of ideas, attitudes, and values."[54] Several studies have dealt particularly with memorials created by groups that can be considered folk groups. Terry Jordan's *Texas Graveyards: A Cultural Legacy* was one of the first studies outside of New England to examine gravemarkers. Jordan demonstrates that patterns of ethnicity stand out clearly in gravestones. His work shows that different cultural groups employ distinct gravestone symbolism and wording, and that what they choose to include on the stone conveys information about the group. Two key volumes edited by Richard Meyer, *Cemeteries and Gravemarkers: Voices of American Culture* (1992) and *Ethnicity and the American Cemetery* (1993) contain numerous studies devoted to the memorialization traditions of various groups. Meyer has also studied the gravestones of pioneers and loggers in the Pacific Northwest.[55] In accordance with the concept that the folk group is part of a larger culture, the markers of both groups fit into the broad pattern of nineteenth-century American memorialization. Most gravestones have the same shapes as those found in other nineteenth-century American cemeteries, and they also feature many of the same symbols and inscriptions. Within this broad pattern, however, the gravestones reflect ideas unique to each group. Such studies show that memorials can also be useful for studying tensions between different social groups. Immigrant groups, for example, often use ethnic symbolism and language as indicators of identity when moving into new areas. J. Finch, Randall McGuire, and LouAnn Wurst have used memorials to examine how groups construct and negotiate social class identity.[56] The latter are particularly valuable because they bring the theme of power relations into memorialization studies. As we shall see later, maritime memorials can also contribute to our understanding of power relations. All of these studies provide useful comparative data for the maritime folk group.

Recent approaches to gravestone analysis have gone even further into the cognitive realm. Death and memorialization are two of the most emotionally charged of human experiences, yet so far, archaeologists have produced few studies interpreting emotion from archaeological data. This is probably due to the belief that such interpretations are too subjective. One exception is the work of Sarah Tarlow. In *Bereavement and Commemoration: An Archaeology of Mortality*, Tarlow uses a material culture approach to study the ways that residents of the Orkney Islands commemorated their dead over the past five hundred years. Tarlow's thesis is that archaeologists need to study funeral monuments not only as indicators of social or economic status, but also as emotional relics left behind by grieving loved ones. By doing so, one can begin to understand the meanings that memorials held for the people who erected them. In her words, "if certain emotions correspond with the values of a society—grief at death, fear of ancestors, love of country, for example—then they will be created and recreated through, amongst other things, material practice."[57] A willingness to address emotion sets Tarlow's work apart from other archaeological studies of burial and mourning. Instead of merely studying memorials as vehicles of cultural ideas, she attempts to understand the feelings behind them, which gives a much more human voice to the people of the past. I include Tarlow's work here because I believe that emotion played a key role in maritime memorialization. To modern ears, the sentiments expressed on memorials, especially those from the nineteenth century, often sound trite or overly emotional. But they were, in fact, the products of real human feelings. To judge earlier peoples by modern standards does them a disservice. Instead, we need to listen to what they were trying to tell us, and that is what I try to do throughout this book.

Seafaring peoples, like other cultural groups, used memorials to express their conception of the world. Although the usefulness of memorials for addressing cultural questions is now well established, scholars have not yet paid much attention to maritime memorials. Henning Henningsen included death and burial in his list of topics for research into sailors' lives, and Westerdahl noted that "mortuary rituals" might provide information about maritime culture.[58] Until now, however, publications of maritime memorials remain few in number. Prehistorians have explored the meanings and landscape contexts of ancient monuments, but those have come from cultures far removed from seafarers of the Age of Sail and thus provide little in the way of useful comparative data.[59] For Age of Sail memorials, David Saunders' *Britain's Maritime Memorials and Mementoes* provides a fine overview of British monuments, including much useful information on maritime and naval history, but is not designed to provide interpretations of cultural meanings. Most other studies consist of descriptive collections of memorials from particular regions or churches.[60] Others examine monuments dedicated to specific individuals or historical events.[61] These tend to focus on the celebrated and extraordinary to the exclusion of the commonplace and everyday. It is the latter, however, that tell us most about a group's beliefs and therefore shape the focus of this book.

Types of Maritime Memorials

Memorials exist in a wide variety of forms. Anything that commemorates a person or event, from a headstone in a cemetery to a highway named after a war hero, can be considered a memorial. For the purposes of this study, maritime memorials were divided into three classes: state, community, and individual—a classification system based on the group or person who commissioned the memorial. Dividing the data this way allows one to compare the different "voices" and see what each group considered worthy of expressing. Within each class, numerous forms exist.

State-sponsored monuments commemorate persons or events of national significance. Examples include Trafalgar Square, London, and monuments at Portsmouth, Plymouth, and Chatham commemorating Royal Navy seamen lost during both World Wars. State memorials are almost always the largest and most expensive, although many, including Nelson's Column, were paid for by private donations in addition to public funds. Despite this fact, it is important to keep in mind that state-sponsored memorials do not typically reflect the beliefs of the maritime folk group. Rather, they highlight the values that the nation-state wishes to perpetuate. In order to learn about the belief systems of maritime peoples, it is necessary to examine memorials created at the community and individual levels.

Community memorials commemorate individuals or events that are significant at the local level (figure 1.2). In communities that maintain an active maritime tradition, these memorials can remain in use—and be added to—over long periods. The Fishermen's Memorial in Gloucester, Massachusetts, for example, was dedicated in 1925 and still serves as the site of a yearly commemorative service. Ships' crews practiced a similar form of communal memorialization. Around the middle of the nineteenth century, it became common for ships' crews to erect collective monuments to lost shipmates upon returning from voyages. Crews erected monuments in churchyards and cemeteries and also placed mural plaques inside churches (figure 1.3). Whether outside or indoors, the form the memorials took was always similar. Each one recorded the name of the vessel, the names of those who died, the circumstances of death, and the dates of death. Royal Navy crews were also in the habit of including the name of the overseas station to which the vessel was assigned and the dates of the cruise's duration. In addition to these common details, additional information such as the sailor's age at time of death and position aboard ship were often included. Some feature epitaphs as well. Community memorials reflect the values considered important by maritime communities, be they a village or a ship's company. Not all community members, however, shared the same beliefs. Different views are present in all social groups, and it is at the individual level that the diversity of beliefs becomes most apparent.

Individual memorials were commissioned by seamen, maritime families, and other members of seafaring communities. Many honor a single

Figure 1.2. Community monument in Cedar Grove Cemetery, New London, CT, commemorating the sinking of the steamer *Atlantic*. Photo by author.

Figure 1.3. Crew monument from the Seamen's Bethel, New Bedford, MA, commemorating two sailors who never returned. Photo by author.

mariner, though family gravestones often commemorate more than one seafarer from the family. In addition to sailors, members of shore-based maritime professions such as shipbuilding were commemorated as well. The variety of beliefs among those who commissioned them produces a wide range of views expressed on such memorials. This diversity of views makes individual memorials the most useful for learning about the beliefs of the maritime folk group. They are also the most numerous, and are found both inside churches and outdoors in churchyards and cemeteries. Typical forms within churches include mural plaques on walls and ledger slabs set into the floor (figure 1.4). Less numerous memorials within churches include stained-glass windows and furnishings donated in memory of a sailor. In general, commemoration within churches tended to be for higher-status individuals, so one finds more memorials for officers than for ordinary seamen, whose memorials are more often

Figure 1.4. Ledger slab for Master John Varrall, who was killed by falling into the hold of his fishing smack in 1846. St. Mylor, Cornwall, U.K. Photo by author.

placed outside, in churchyards and cemeteries. Headstones are the most common outdoor memorial (figure 1.5), but forms such as obelisks and columns are also plentiful, particularly in the nineteenth century.

While memorials to sailors and maritime tragedies can be found in many locations, several areas feature the greatest concentrations. Ports or other locations with ties to seafaring naturally have the greatest number of maritime memorials. People also possess a strong tendency to mark the sites of tragedies, and so maritime memorials are often located at places where a vessel wrecked or in a community close to the scene of the disaster. Churches, churchyards, and cemeteries in coastal cities offer the best locations for recording maritime memorials. Churches dedicated to St. Nicholas are often associated with seafaring, and were the focus of votive activity as far back as the Middle Ages. Other churches can have strong maritime affiliations as well. These commonly include churches in close proximity to harbors or those dedicated specifically to sailors, such as the Seamen's Bethel in New Bedford, Massachusetts (figure 1.6). Likewise,

Figure 1.5. Read family gravestone, Portland St. George, Dorset, U.K. Among other family members, the stone memorializes three men who were lost in two different shipwrecks. Photo by author.

most ports contain one or more cemeteries where large numbers of mariners are buried. Although rare, there are entire cemeteries, such as the Royal Navy Cemetery at Haslar, Hampshire, or sections of cemeteries, such as the Fishermen's Rest in Beechbrook Cemetery near Gloucester, Massachusetts, dedicated to seamen.

Figure 1.6. Bow-shaped pulpit in the Seamen's Bethel, New Bedford, Massachusetts, the famous "Whaleman's Chapel" from Melville's *Moby Dick*. The pulpit is not original, but was instead constructed to fit the expectations of tourists, who had seen the popular 1956 film version of *Moby Dick*. The wall plaques, however, are original, and commemorate many sailors who lost their lives at sea. Photo by author.

Limitations of Memorials

While maritime memorials speak with many voices, not all voices are equally represented. Memorialization studies face two major limitations. The first involves differential representation among social groups. Prior to the eighteenth century, the high cost of memorials usually precluded all but the wealthy from creating permanent monuments. Scholars of death generally agree that, in addition to economic considerations, beliefs regarding memorialization played a part in the dearth of permanent gravemarkers prior to the eighteenth century.[62] Western attitudes toward death changed in the eighteenth century, when the idea that each person deserved a permanent grave and gravemarker took hold in Europe and in the American colonies. The availability of cheaper, mass-produced memorials by the late eighteenth century, coupled with changes in attitudes toward death, resulted in a marked increase in the number of permanent memorials from that time onward. In addition to an increase in the overall number of graves, a broader range of social classes are represented.

The timing of this event varies from region to region, but by the mid-nineteenth century, large numbers of the middle and even lower classes were commemorated with permanent memorials. Before the eighteenth century, then, most maritime memorials honored wealthy elites or were state- or community-sponsored. By the end of the nineteenth century, all maritime social classes were represented. However, memorials for middle- and lower-class seafarers were still not proportional to their numbers in society because the cost of a permanent marker remained beyond the reach of many.

The second limitation of memorials involves the issue of preservation. Like all artifacts, memorials and the sites at which they are found are subject to formation processes. At the artifact level, weathering defaces monuments, rendering inscriptions and symbols unreadable. Weathering has varying effects depending on factors such as the types of materials used (most commonly stone and metal), the quality of the original workmanship, climate, and exposure to the elements. These factors have two main results. First, in general, the farther back in time, the fewer memorials survive, especially in outdoor contexts. There are exceptions to this rule, as for instance in New England, where many colonial gravestones were manufactured from high-quality slates that are superbly resistant to weathering. It is not unusual to find well-preserved seventeenth- and eighteenth-century gravestones in New England cemeteries, whereas many contemporary stones in English coastal cities are now illegible. Second, weathering skews the sample toward state and upper-class memorials because these tended to feature better workmanship or were more likely to be located inside churches.

In addition to formation processes that operate at the artifact level, churches and cemeteries are subject to site-level formation processes as well. A complete discussion of the processes that can result in the movement or eradication of memorials is beyond the scope of this book, but several of the major processes deserve mention.[63] By the early nineteenth century, English churchyards had become so crowded that there was no longer sufficient room to inter new bodies. Concern arose that the vast numbers of decaying corpses were creating health problems for those living and working in the vicinity of churches. Due to these concerns, most urban churchyards in England were cleared of gravestones during the nineteenth and twentieth centuries. In addition, bombing during the Second World War destroyed numerous British churches, especially in

Figure 1.7. Broken headstone of Master Mariner William Walliss, now part of the car park at Hull Holy Trinity, East Yorkshire, U.K. Photo by author.

urban maritime centers. Some of these were removed rather than rebuilt, so most of their associated memorials are now gone. The United States was spared wartime bombs, but twentieth-century development has resulted in the clearance of many Historic-period cemeteries.

Clearance did not always result in complete destruction of memorials. In Britain, gravestones were sometimes lined up along the edges of churchyard walls or pathways. Functional uses were sometimes found for them as well: at Holy Trinity church in Hull, for example, old gravestones were used to pave over the churchyard, which is now a car park (figure 1.7). While stones such as these cannot be used to analyze spatial relationships, they still provide details such as circumstances of death and expressions of beliefs.

The Anglo-American Maritime Memorials Survey

The variety of forms and locations makes a comprehensive survey of maritime memorials a challenge. Variety is also the greatest strength of maritime memorials, however, because it means that memorials represent many different points of view. To get the widest possible perspective, one needs to examine state-, community-, and individual-level memorials. Of these, state and community memorials are the easiest to locate and research, as they are often well documented. Recording individual level memorials is more difficult, but these are the ones that provide the best information about the beliefs of ordinary sailors and maritime families. While many gravestones and monuments from the Age of Sail have succumbed to the ravages of time, thousands still dot the landscape and serve as a largely untapped resource for scholars of maritime culture.

In the chapters that follow, I explore what gravestones and monuments can tell us about British and American maritime culture during the Age of Sail. The primary data set consists of 2,182 maritime memorials, primarily from England and the United States. Seafaring is a worldwide phenomenon, however, and English and American sailors found themselves in every corner of the globe that could be reached by ship. They died in all of these places too, and so the data set includes memorials from throughout the world. Many of these were recorded by the Anglo-American Maritime Memorials Survey, an archaeological project begun by the author in 2002 and which continues to the present day.[64] Others come from published sources.[65] Data collected by the survey has been encoded and analyzed using the Anglo-American Maritime Memorials Database (AAMMD). For the purposes of this study, I have grouped the memorials according to the decade that they were erected. One of the great advantages of studying memorials is the tight chronological control that is possible. Unlike prehistoric archaeology, which typically deals with date ranges in terms of centuries, memorials usually record the year, and in some cases the exact day, that they were erected.[66] Micro-chronological control is not really needed, however, and grouping the memorials by decade makes it possible to track changes easily over the entire period under study. The memorials provide data from the seventeenth century until the end of the Age of Sail, but due to the limitations discussed above, most come from the eighteenth and nineteenth centuries. A date for the end of the Age of Sail is impossible to pin down; although steamships were in general use by the mid-nineteenth century, sail-powered craft continued to be used well into the twentieth century. Even after sailing ships went out of use, those who manned them often lived well into the twentieth century, and so maritime memorials up to the start of the Second World War are included. My interpretations will be concentrated on the period from the mid-eighteenth through early-twentieth centuries. Some recent memorials were recorded as well so that the beliefs of modern seafarers can be compared to their Age of Sail forebears.

From the data, five main themes in maritime memorialization were identified, each of which is explored in a separate chapter. Chapter 2 describes the ways in which fear of death from both natural and manmade forces was expressed in the memorials. Chapter 3 illustrates the values that the maritime folk group developed to deal with the ever-present possibility of death. Chapter 4 demonstrates how the ritual of burial at sea was used to separate the dead from the living and how it reflected the unique traditions of maritime culture. The ways in which sailors and maritime communities dealt with the loss of so many of their comrades at sea and in far corners of the world are discussed in chapter 5. Chronological analysis of maritime memorials reveals a significant increase in religious sentiment in the mid-nineteenth century, in the form of both religious inscriptions linking seafarers to God and symbolism involving the association of Jesus Christ with the anchor. This development forms the basis for chapter 6, the final interpretive chapter. Finally, chapter 7 summarizes the main themes, develops the idea of maritime memorialization as a living tradition, and gives some suggestions for further research into maritime memorials.

2

"Death Stands Ready at the Door"

THE DANGERS OF MARITIME LIFE

On a pleasant afternoon in March 1878, a small boy walked along the cliffs of the Isle of Wight. Though the day was cool, early spring sunlight brought with it the promise of warmer days to come. The boy loved walking about the island, surrounded by verdant greens on one side and the slate-gray sea on the other. Lifting his gaze to the English Channel, he spied "a great splendid ship with all her sails set, passing the shore only a mile or two away."[1] Ships were a common sight in the Channel and had been for thousands of years. Julius Caesar wrote about the native craft of the region during his campaign in northwestern Europe in the first century B.C., and archaeologists have excavated examples of the types of boats he described.[2] Today the English Channel remains one of the world's busiest shipping lanes. On this occasion, however, the promising early spring day quickly turned tragic.

> All of a sudden there were black clouds and wind and the first drops of a storm, and we just scrambled home without getting wet through. The next time I went out on those cliffs there was no splendid ship in full sail, but three black masts were pointed out to me, sticking up out of the water in a stark way. She was the *Eurydice*. She had capsized in this very squall and gone to the bottom with three hundred soldiers on board.[3]

Winston Churchill was only a child when he witnessed the storm that sent *Eurydice* to the bottom, but he never forgot the sight of its masts sticking out of the water like gravemarkers. He later described the horrors that followed. "Divers went down to bring up the corpses. I was told—and it made a scar on my mind—that some of the divers had fainted with terror at seeing the fish eating the bodies. . . . I seem to have seen some of these corpses towed very slowly by boats one sunny day. There were many people on the cliffs to watch, and we all took off our hats in sorrow."[4] In addition to this mark of respect, a monument to *Eurydice* was erected in the nearby Royal Navy cemetery at Haslar. The monument includes an anchor salvaged from the ill-fated vessel (figure 2.1), and lists the names of the 317 men who were lost.[5]

A ship under full sail, with its bow knifing through the waves and spray flying, presents a stirring sight, and one that undoubtedly accounts for much of the romance of sailing ships. As Churchill's story shows, however, life at sea can turn tragic in an instant. A sailor lived constantly, in the words of one seventeenth-century chronicler, with "the breadth of an inch-board. . . . betwixt him and drowning."[6] Constant exposure to danger had a great effect on the worldview of the maritime folk group

Figure 2.1. Monument for HMS *Eurydice*, which foundered in a sudden storm off the Isle of Wight in 1878. Photo by author.

and was expressed on its memorials. Descriptions of death on maritime gravestones often show a marked difference from those of non-mariners. Gravestones for non-seafarers usually employ simple phrases such as "died" or "departed this life." While those phrases do appear on maritime memorials, many go on to describe the circumstances of death in detail. The dangers of the natural world, especially shipwrecks due to storms and rocky shores, figure prominently in those descriptions. Other memorials speak of the hazards of the shipboard work environment: drowning, falling from aloft, and the mariner's great fear of fire have all been depicted on memorials. These testaments to tragedy underscore the importance that danger held in maritime life. This chapter discusses forms of death commonly found on maritime memorials and explores the meanings that these motifs held in maritime culture.

Rocks and Storms: The Hazards of the Natural World

The dangers of the natural world make up one of the most prominent themes on maritime memorials. Among these dangers, two related phenomena are represented in great numbers: rocks and storms. By "rocks," I mean the reefs, shoals, and shores upon which so many sailing vessels met their end. When thinking of shipwrecks, we often visualize a vessel slipping beneath the waves far out at sea, but in actuality, most vessels sink because they run into the land. During the Age of Sail, many more vessels were lost through wrecking on shore than by foundering in deep water or through hostile action. The term "storms" covers everything from monster hurricanes and gales to the much more common thunderstorms. Storms can materialize in an instant and last for minutes or days. Storms present a double threat to vessels, as they have the power to sink ships or drive them onto the land.

Running aground was a constant threat to mariners' lives, and because of this, the "rocks" motif is common on maritime memorials. Typical is the monument for British seaman James Jeffery, who was "shipwrecked on the coast of Northumberland" in 1857.[7] Surgeon William Gray was killed when HMS *Weazle* was "lost on the rocks of Baggy" in 1799.[8] Certain areas were notorious navigational hazards, and it is no surprise that they appear on shipwreck memorials. A monument in a Cornish church commemorates the transport vessel *Despatch*, which wrecked on Cornwall's notorious Manacle Rocks in 1800.[9] Boston's Granary Burying Ground contains the grave of Captain John Mackay, "who was Shipwrecked at Baker's Island," which lies squarely athwart the approaches to Salem harbor.[10] Long recognized as a threat to shipping, the residents of Salem erected a navigational beacon on the island in 1791, and the federal government appropriated funds for a lighthouse five years later. A much updated version of the lighthouse remains active to this day.[11]

Prior to the advent of modern navigation, a vessel's position could not be fixed with great accuracy. The compass was in use in Mediterranean waters by the late fourteenth century, and the ability to navigate by following lines of latitude was known by the fifteenth century. The ability to calculate longitude, however, proved a more difficult problem, as it necessitated the ability to keep time, a difficult task due to the motions of a ship at sea. This problem was not solved until the mid-eighteenth century, when Englishman John Harrison discovered how to successfully adapt clocks for use aboard ships.[12] With the navigational tools available during the Age of Sail, a good navigator could pinpoint his ship's position to within a few miles—provided that the sky was clear enough to observe sun or stars. Overcast weather reduced the navigator to dead reckoning, sailing on a given compass bearing for a certain amount of time. Such methods worked well enough when the vessel had plenty of sea room—that is, sufficient open water to keep from being blown onto the land—but proved a much more dangerous prospect in the vicinity of shore, due to the margin of error. Even when the position was known, the charts and pilot books of the time were not necessarily accurate. Many vessels ran ashore either because their crews mistakenly believed that they were safely away from land or because they piled upon uncharted rocks.

Another problem when it came to avoiding rocks relates to an inherent characteristic of sail-powered craft. Even with correct charts and a known position, a sailing ship remains very much at the mercy of the weather. While an engine-powered vessel can motor against the elements, wind and tide can force a sailing vessel ashore despite all of the crew's efforts to maneuver out of harm's way. This is still true today, and it is one of the reasons why many modern sailing vessels carry auxiliary engines.

Even after the development of reliable navigation, human error could still cause vessels to run ashore. Such a fate befell British sailor Charles Lee, whose cenotaph states that he "was lost in HMS *Serpent*" in November 1890.[13] The case of the *Serpent* provides a horrific example of the deadliness of small navigational errors. On the night of November 9,

1890, *Serpent* was near Cape Villano, Spain, on her way to South Africa. Compass error caused the ship to stray off course by about 10 miles, and it struck a rock in Punta Bay. A heavy sea was running, and an attempt to launch lifeboats resulted only in the boats being torn to pieces on the rocks. Some crewmen went into the water in an attempt to swim ashore, while others found temporary respite by climbing into the ship's rigging. Both measures proved fruitless. Men who went into the water drowned in the towering waves or were dashed to their deaths on the rocks. Those who escaped to the rigging found shelter for a time, but the relentless seas soon dislodged *Serpent* from her perch, whereupon the vessel staggered into deeper water and foundered. The unlucky men clinging to the rigging then met the same fate as their comrades. Charles Lee and 146 of his shipmates died that night, leaving only three survivors to struggle ashore.[14]

Storms presented their own terrors. As I write these words (August 2007), the Earth is engaged in its yearly hurricane cycle. Hurricane Dean, which grew to category-five strength, has just ravaged a path across the Caribbean, causing widespread destruction on the island of Jamaica before devastating coastal Mexico. Hurricanes represent the most extreme form of weather that affects shipping and coastal regions. Hurricanes have been responsible for the worst natural disasters in U.S. history, both in terms of loss of life and in the dollar amount of destruction caused. The hurricane that obliterated Galveston, Texas, in 1900 (an anonymous storm before the advent of our modern naming system) killed some eight thousand people.[15] Hurricane Katrina, which devastated New Orleans and the Gulf Coast in August 2005, caused at least $81 billion in damage, making it the costliest natural disaster in U.S. history (to say nothing of the more than fifteen hundred lives lost and millions more displaced).[16] Far more common than hurricanes are thunderstorms, thousands of which occur each day. It is safe to say that at any given moment, hundreds of storms are raging across the surface of the planet.

Very strong storms such as hurricanes and gales can overwhelm vessels, causing them to founder. Ships are made to ride upon the waves and withstand raging winds, however, so a vessel at sea stands a fair chance of surviving a storm intact. As long as a vessel has adequate sea room, storms can usually be weathered. Problems occur when a vessel loses the ability to maneuver, typically because of the loss of motive power. A vessel with no driving force of its own, be it from engines or sails, lies at the mercy of the elements. Ships are shaped to move through the water efficiently when under power, but when no driving force is present, their shape and mass leave them wallowing in the water. In a storm, a powerless vessel will usually quickly turn to present its broadside to the waves, an extremely vulnerable position from which it can easily be forced onto its side—onto its beam ends, in nautical parlance—swamped, and sent plunging to the bottom. The effects of loss of driving power during the Age of Sail cannot be overstated. Sailing ships were at the mercy of wind, tide, and current to a far greater degree than modern engine-powered vessels. If a storm carried away sails or spars, a crew could quickly find themselves with no way to make headway or even turn the ship's bow into the waves. In such cases, the ship was in grave danger of being sent to the bottom.

The threat of storms loomed always at the back of a sailor's mind. Mariners knew that a life at sea meant encountering storms on a regular basis. They feared them too, because squalls, like the one that sent *Eurydice* to the bottom, could strike in an instant. Caught unprepared, a ship could be dismasted, founder, or be driven ashore. A sudden squall claimed two American schooners, *Hamilton* and *Scourge*, on Lake Ontario one night during the War of 1812. Awakening to the feel of raindrops on his face, sailor Ned Myers of *Scourge* decided to go below for a bottle of liquor that he and a shipmate had hidden in their mess chest. Myers had just reached the companion ladder "when a flash of lightning almost blinded me. The thunder came at the next instant, and with it a rushing of winds that fairly smothered the clap."[17] Within a minute, the squall had laid the vessel on its side, creating a scene of chaos.

> The flashes of lightning were incessant, and nearly blinded me. Our decks seemed on fire, and yet I could see nothing. I heard no hail, no order, no call; but the schooner was filled with the shrieks and cries of the men to leeward, who were lying jammed under the guns, shot-boxes, shot, and other heavy things that had gone down as the vessel fell over. The starboard second gun, from forward, had capsized, and come down directly over the forward hatch, and I caught a glimpse of a man struggling to get past it.[18]

Scourge filled with water and sank within the span of a few minutes. Myers was among the lucky few who survived the disaster: as he swam blindly away from the sinking vessel, he came by chance upon the ship's boat and managed to heave himself aboard. Fifty-three other seamen were not so fortunate. When the wrecks were discovered in the 1970s, underwater surveys revealed that the bones of many of the ill-fated sailors still lie scattered around the hulls three hundred feet (ninety-one meters) below the surface.[19] On warships, being blown on their beam ends was especially dangerous because it could cause cannon to break loose and plunge through the opposite side. Although Myers' account states that one of *Scourge*'s cannon broke free, archaeological investigation revealed that all of the guns are still in their original positions.[20] In this case, it appears that the passage of time embellished the events of that night in Myers' memory. Nevertheless, his account of the sinking of *Scourge* provides a vivid description of the pandemonium that could occur when a ship was struck by a sudden storm.

Prudent mariners constantly scanned the horizon for the approach of dangerous weather. The phrase "to keep a weather eye out" reflects the sailor's preoccupation with constantly being in tune with his surroundings, in particular looking to the weather side (i.e., the side from which the wind is blowing, and therefore from which danger, in the form of storms or enemies, will appear). Concern with weather also translated into a large body of lore dealing with signs relating to the weather, with the object being to predict the weather so as to be prepared for its effects.[21]

Just as storms represent a key feature of maritime life, so too did they often figure prominently in commemoration after death. Captain N. F. Sayre's vessel "sank in a gale of wind" while traveling from Sag Harbor to New York.[22] The Denison family monument in Stonington, Connecticut's Evergreen Cemetery provides stark testimony to the power of storms (figure 2.2).[23] Ezra Denison was only twenty when he signed aboard a U.S. privateer to fight the British in the War of 1812. On December 5, 1812, Ezra and several shipmates went aboard a captured British vessel as a prize crew. The following night, all "perished in the tremendous storm" that sent their vessel to the bottom. Almost four years to the day later, Ezra's older brother Amos Jr. was "swept from the deck of the schooner *Nancy*" in the West Indies by another storm. Two other older brothers, Charles and Edward, died ashore in distant ports; their stories will be told in chapter 5. Like the Denisons, thousands of other mariners lost their lives due to the power of storms, and their stories are described on maritime memorials throughout the world. "Billow on billow roll a trying scene/Till forc'd at last to the tremendous verge/At once she sinks" is how the epitaph for Connecticut mariner Thomas Robinson describes the

Figure 2.2. Denison family monument, which records the loss of four seafarers from that family. AAMMD #287, Evergreen Cemetery, Stonington, CT. Photo by author.

loss of his vessel in a storm in 1795.[24] Billow, derived from the Old Norse *bylgja*, means a surge of water produced by wind, and is typically applied to large waves produced by high winds.[25] This word links wind and wave together, and first appears in the English language sometime around the middle of the sixteenth century. It is probably not a coincidence that this date corresponds with the Age of Exploration, when European nations began creating global seaborne empires. Other common ways to express the motif of wind and waves include the similarly worded "stormy wind and tempest," the "wild stormy deep," and the "stormy blast."[26]

Rocks and storms go hand in hand. Each can cause destruction on its own, but when combined they are at their most deadly. The chief danger of storms lies in their ability to drive ships onto land. One of the greatest fears of sailors is a lee shore, a situation where winds blow from the sea onto the land. Engine-powered craft could use their own motive power to claw off the land, but ships at the mercy of the wind did not have that option. To be trapped against a lee shore in a rising gale was a recipe for disaster. Among the pleasant rolling hills of the West Country of England, the church of St. Mylor, Cornwall, sits only a stone's throw from Falmouth harbor. Heavily maritime in character, St. Mylor churchyard contains an archetypical memorial depicting the deadly combination of rocks and storms. This marker records the loss of the *Queen*, a troop transport that was driven ashore at Trefusis Point near St. Mylor in 1814 with the loss of more than two hundred lives.[27] Mariner John Béchervaise witnessed the *Queen*'s tragedy from the deck of his vessel anchored nearby. Despite several close calls, Béchervaise's ship managed to ride out the storm. The *Queen* was not so lucky.

> From 11, P.M., the *Queen* had fired guns, and when flashes of lightning threw a gleam around, it was evident from her position, that she had drifted, and was fast approaching the rocks on which a long rolling sea was dashing itself into a foam.
> At 5, A.M., during a dreadful squall, the *Queen* parted first from one, and then the other of her cables, and fell on shore just across a rock about forty yards from the beach; and such was the pressure amidships, that she parted, and both parts swinging round brought her bowsprit nearly over her taffrail.[28]

Terrified survivors clung to the wreck, hoping for succor, but rescue vessels could not approach due to the ferocity of the storm.

> When daylight came I could see the ill fated ship on shore, heeling well over on her broadside, and the weatherside of her covered with sufferers, almost entirely naked, exposed to the pelting of the pitiless storm; and by their gestures imploring that aid, I could not give. Many threw themselves off the wreck towards shore, but few of those escaped being beat on the rocks; they were all nearly spent before daylight appeared. It was a heart-rending scene.[29]

The *Queen* monument features elements mentioned by Béchervaise in his account. The illustration shows the *Queen* in her moment of tragedy, dismasted and wallowing in a heavy sea as waves crash over the deck (figures 2.3 and 2.4). Above, lightning arches across the sky. These motifs—storm, raging winds, mountainous seas, and most importantly the vessel herself at the moment of destruction—are repeated over and over again on maritime memorials from the Age of Sail.

Vivid depictions of natural forces such as storms and lightning on late-eighteenth- and nineteenth-century memorials were likely also due

Figure 2.3. Memorial for the *Queen* transport. St. Mylor, Cornwall, U.K. Photo by author.

Figure 2.4. Detail of the *Queen* memorial, illustrating the vessel's tragic last moments. Photo by author.

in part to the impact of the Romantic movement, in which natural phenomena played a prominent role. Likewise, many inscriptions draw upon Romantic imagery as well. A good example is the memorial to the loss of the ship *Alexander* at All Saints Church, Wyke Regis, Dorset, which dramatically states:

> Sudden destruction rear'd his great form
> Black with the horrors of the midnight storm
> And all convuls'd with elemental strife
> Dissolved the throbbing nerves of hope and
> [unreadable] Triumph past. May angels guide you
> to the blest regions of eternal day.
> Where no rude blasts provoke the billowy roar
> Where virtues kindred meet to part no more.[30]

The prevalence of rocks and storms on maritime memorials matches their prominence in other forms of maritime lore. Virtually every sailor's account from the Age of Sail includes numerous descriptions of storms and rocks. In fact, a man who made it through a career at sea *without* having a few close encounters with shipwreck was the exception. Master Mariner Alfred Green spent many years at sea without serious incident, a fact that somewhat disappointed his children.

> Many a time when young folks—and older ones too sometimes—have gathered around me and wheedled me for a jolly racy story of sea adventure, they have brought me up all standing by asking for a nice horrible tale of shipwreck! Then I have had to lamely explain that somehow I never met with any adventures so thrilling.[31]

Green finally experienced one, though, and it was not a pleasant adventure.

> Well, my little folks, greedy for something horrible that has actually been experienced by the real living person now actually telling it, I can at last gratify your morbid, though quite natural taste, for I have just passed through a shipwreck, and under God's mercy alone, am alive to tell of it.[32]

Green went on to describe the loss of his vessel *Mertola*, using the type of imagery described in this chapter. He speaks of *Mertola* "rushing wilding before the blast" of the "overwhelming tempest of wind."[33] Green and his crew were only saved by the providential arrival of another vessel, which took them off the doomed *Mertola* moments before it went down.

Furious winds and mountainous seas were popular motifs in sea songs as well. "Sometimes on Neptune's bosom our ship is tossed with waves / And every minute we expect the sea must be our graves / Sometimes on high she mounteth, then falls again as low / With waves, with waves, when stormy winds do blow," proclaims the song "Sailors for My Money," written in the early seventeenth century and popular with mariners throughout the Age of Sail. Songs that described the loss of individual vessels were mainstays at sea. "The Wreck of the Rambler" tells the story of the loss of HMS *Ramillies* and more than seven hundred of her crew in a great storm in 1760. The song recounts the "dreadful gale" in which "the rain pouring down was a dismal sight / the sea running high over our foretop." "The Loss of the *Amphitrite*" tells how "the raging sea ran mountains high" and destroyed that ship in 1833, killing all but three of the 136 souls on board. Not all such songs commemorated sailors. In the British song "Grace Darling," the title character, a lighthouse keeper's daughter, saves a ship's crew by rowing her rescue boat through "seas like mountains" even though her father pleaded that it was folly "to face that raging sea."³⁴ This song is based on a real incident, and its heroine became famous for this and other rescues in which she risked her life to save sailors. Her American counterpart, Ida Lewis of Newport, Rhode Island, was likewise renowned for saving lives, and it is not surprising that her epitaph describes her as "the Grace Darling of America."³⁵ Throughout maritime lore, from memorials to ballads to literature, nature's fury appears time and time again.

Accidents

Ships are complex technological objects, and like all industrial workplaces, they present a variety of hazards to those who work on them. Among the causes of accidental death, drowning ranks among the most prominent on memorials and in the historical literature. Although they made their living upon the sea, many sailors during the Age of Sail did not know how to swim. The lack of swimming ability meant that sailors drowned in what would today be highly survivable accidents. Such a fate befell Joseph Purdie, who fell overboard and drowned off the Cape of Good Hope.³⁶ Alfred Nicholls, an officer aboard the ship *Moss Glenn*, "was accidentally drowned in the China Sea in the presence of his parents," an event that must have been horrible for them to witness (figure 2.5).³⁷ Small-boat operations conceivably carried the greatest risk of drowning. Small craft were commonly employed to transport goods and people between anchored vessels and the shore. Such voyages could be dangerous in heavy seas or along shores where the boats had to make their way through the surf.³⁸ Memorials for Edward Hawk and Edward Bourchier state that both men drowned in small-boat accidents.³⁹ Friends Robert Golding and Edgar Eagles drowned together off Britain's south coast. The two were buried side by side, with the epitaph "they were comrades in life and in death not divided" split between their two gravestones.⁴⁰

In the days of sailing ships, one of the most dangerous jobs aboard ship was working aloft in the rigging. The rigging was especially deadly for newcomers. Sailing rigs consisted of complex systems of masts, spars, ropes, and tackle. It was easy to lose one's concentration and fall from aloft. Doing so had two possible outcomes, both undesirable: plunging into the sea or crashing onto the deck. If a man fell into the sea, he typically drowned before help could arrive. The description of such an event by Richard Henry Dana Jr. is typical of many such stories.

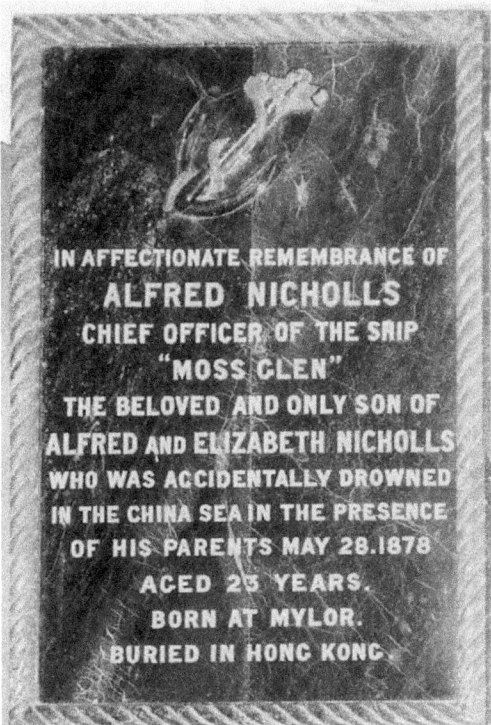

Figure 2.5. Mural plaque for British mariner Alfred Nicholls, who drowned in the China Sea. St. Mylor, Cornwall, U.K. Photo by author.

[The sailor] was going aloft to fit a strap round the main top-masthead, for ringtail halyards, and had the strap and block, a coil of halyards, and a marline-spike about his neck. He fell from the starboard futtock shrouds, and not knowing how to swim, and being heavily dressed, with all those things round his neck, he probably sank immediately.[41]

A boat was quickly launched, but no trace of the man was found. Even those who knew how to swim might be knocked unconscious and drown. Those sailors who fell into the sea, however, had at least some hope of treading water and being picked up. A fall onto the deck, on the other hand, was almost always fatal. Even if a man survived, he was likely to be maimed for life.

It is not surprising that falls from aloft were often recorded on maritime memorials.[42] Connecticut sailor Benjamin Ewen fell from the rigging of his vessel "while in the act of furling the Main top gallant sail."[43] Ewen sank beneath the Pacific and was never seen again (figure 2.6). A similar level of detail is given on the stone of British mariner John Bullen, who "by the hand of Providence was taken from the world of woe by falling from the Main Top Gallant Yard" of HMS *Crane*.[44] British seaman William Andrews tragically died "by falling from aloft while manning yards in honour of the visit of HRH Prince of Wales" at Fortuneswell in 1872.[45] Others are not as detailed, typically stating that the deceased fell from aloft and listing the name of the vessel and location where the accident occurred. Working in the rigging was not the only place where a sailor could suffer a fatal fall. Men who tumbled down open hatchways suffered broken bones or even death. John Varrall, master of the fishing smack

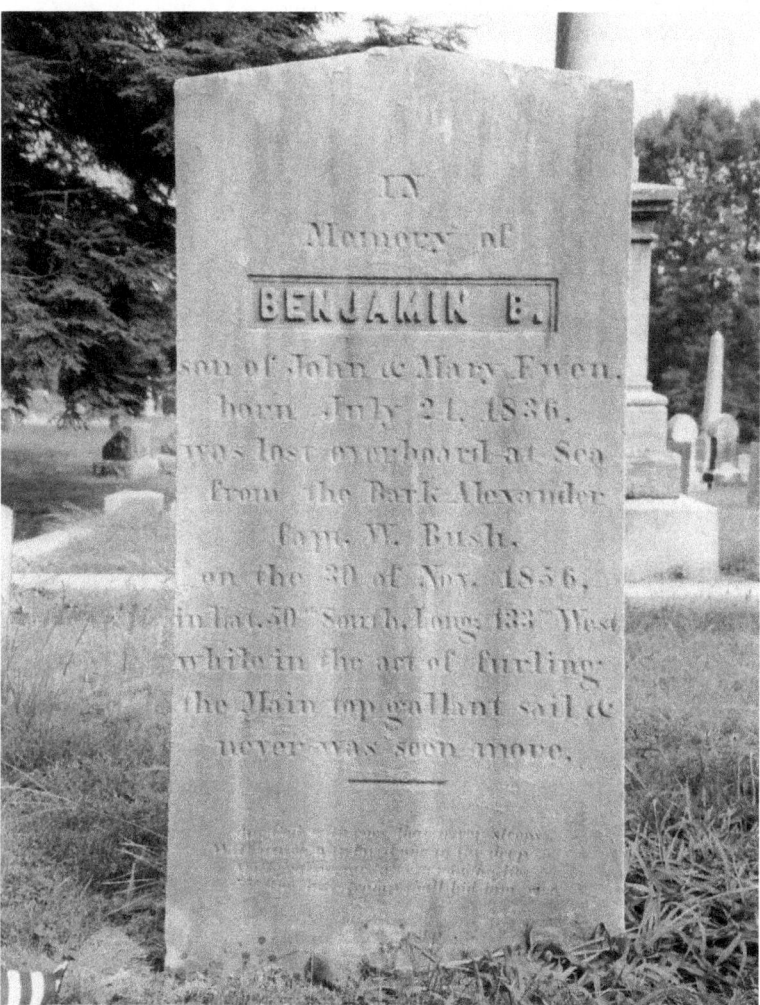

Figure 2.6. Cenotaph for Benjamin Ewen, who fell from the rigging of his vessel into the sea and was lost. Cedar Grove Cemetery, New London, CT. Photo by author.

Ebenezer, was "unfortunately kill'd by falling down her hold"; fellow sailor John Humphreys of the brig *Cheviot* perished in the same manner.[46]

Fire ranked among the greatest fears of seamen in the days of wooden sailing vessels. Not only were vessels made of wood, but deck seams and rigging elements were coated with highly flammable pitch and tar as protection against the elements. Both naval and civilian vessels carried gunpowder, which demanded extreme caution in the use of fire aboard ship. Although fire was greatly feared, ship losses from it seem to have been relatively rare, as only a few memorials commemorate accidents involving fire. Captain Colin Campbell's monument describes his actions during a fire that destroyed HMS *Bombay* in 1864.[47] The monument includes a bronze plaque that shows *Bombay* in flames. Fire could result in catastrophic explosions if the flames reached gunpowder magazines. A monument in Winchester Cathedral commemorates HMS *Doterel*, which foundered after its magazine exploded in the Straits of Magellan in 1881.[48] Seaman William Bean was killed "by some powder taking fire in his Majesty's ship *Torbay* in Portsmouth Harbour" in 1758.[49] Captain Joseph Fitch of the whaler *Superior* lost his life "by the accidental explosion of gunpowder" in 1835.[50]

The bursting of a cannon killed British seamen Thomas Oddy and Charles Stewart on board the *Constantine* while "celebrating the birth-day of our Royal Sovereign George the Third" in June 1793.[51] Other mishaps involving gunpowder include men who were accidentally killed by firearms. Benjamin Scriven was "accidentally shot" while his ship was in port at London.[52] In 1822, British sailor William Lewis' wife commemorated her late husband with a gravestone describing that he was accidentally "killed by a shot from the *Pigmy* schooner."[53]

Deaths by Hostile Action

For more than five thousand years, ships have been used as instruments of warfare, and warfare at sea has been a shaping force in maritime technology and culture. The cannon, missiles, and torpedoes of modern warships are only the latest incarnations of a form that dates back more than five thousand years.[54] The Age of Sail, a time of colonialism and imperialism, was a particularly violent period in the world's history. Even those on vessels not engaged in military action, such as merchantmen or fishing craft crewmen, could find themselves under attack by armed vessels, be they enemy warships or simple pirates. Civilian craft of this period commonly carried weapons for defense. However, according to the available statistics, deaths in action accounted for only a small percentage of maritime casualties, even during wartime. Michael Arthur Lewis estimated that only 6.3 percent of British naval deaths during the Napoleonic Wars were a result of combat.[55] Christopher McKee's study of the U.S. naval officer corps rates the danger somewhat higher. McKee found that 20 percent of officer deaths were combat related.[56] Although this number is higher than Lewis,' it is still smaller than deaths due to illness or the natural dangers of the sea. Despite the small numbers, however, being killed in action was one of the most horrific ways to die during the Age of Sail, as the weapons used during this period were extremely brutal. Cannon shot, meant to crash through wooden planking or disable rigging, could tear a man to pieces. Grapeshot and canister shot were also fired from cannons. These consisted of iron or lead balls that could sweep the decks of enemy vessels, killing or wounding many with one discharge. Perhaps the greatest danger cannon posed, however, came from splinters. A cannon ball striking the side of a wooden vessel with enough force could tear through the frames and planking, filling the air with hundreds of jagged fragments.

Personal weapons were equally deadly. Muskets and pistols, although crude by modern standards, were deadly at close range. In combat, sharpshooters would be posted in the fighting tops to snipe at enemy officers and sailors. The deadly effectiveness of this tactic is perhaps best illustrated by the fate of the British Admiral Horatio Nelson. While in command of the British fleet at the Battle of Trafalgar, Nelson was felled by a shot from a sharpshooter aboard the French ship *Redoubtable*. Nelson was not killed instantly, but the musket ball lodged in his body. Taken belowdecks, he succumbed some three painful hours after being wounded. Many other sailors met a similar fate in combat. Even when not killed outright, the gaping wounds caused by the weaponry of the period were beyond the skill of most surgeons. Lacking adequate medical care, many sailors died of wounds or from infection.

Details of deaths in battle were often included on a seaman's memorial; this was especially true if death occurred during a famous battle. Lieutenant William Buller "died of his wounds received on the Glorious 1st June 1794" while serving aboard HMS *Impregnable*.[57] The marker commemorates the famous battle in which a British fleet destroyed six French vessels and captured another.[58] American sailor John Peirce's memorial states that he was killed "on board the U.S. Frigate *Cumberland*, in the naval engagement at Hampton Roads," a reference to the federal ship sunk by the CSS *Virginia* before its famous battle with the USS *Monitor* in March 1862 (figure 2.7).[59] The twilight of the Age of Sail saw the development of ever deadlier naval weapons. Royal Navy seaman Henry Fittock was killed in the torpedoing of the *Royal Edward* in 1915, a ghastly event that took more than one thousand lives.[60] The Rosser family lost two of its sons and a son-in-law to U-boats, the sons in the steamship *Thames* and their daughter's husband in the *Aigburth*, both of which were torpedoed

Figure 2.7. Gravestone of John Peirce, who was killed aboard USS *Cumberland* during the battle with CSS *Virginia*. Rural Cemetery, New Bedford, MA. Photo by author.

in 1917.[61] Hostile nations were not the only threats; U.S. seaman Isaac Pendleton "was killed with his Boat's Crew by the Savages" when he went ashore on a Pacific island whose name cannot now be read.[62]

The forms of death described on maritime memorials provide stark evidence of the dangers of seafaring life. But these descriptions of death do more than simply chronicle the many ways that sailors could meet their end. The motifs employed in descriptions of death provide insight into the worldview of the maritime folk group.

Danger and Maritime Group Worldview

When hazard and hardship are part of daily life, it affects the group's worldview and becomes reflected in its folklore. Memorials, as the primary manifestation of a group's traditions that deal specifically with the effects of danger, are a natural place for these concerns to be expressed. In his comprehensive study of historic period gravemarkers, Mytum observed that "the trauma of the unexpected event" is often seen as noteworthy and therefore included on monuments.[63] While this is certainly true, it is also true that everyday traumatic events are worthy of commemoration as well when one works in an occupation in which danger and death are commonplace.

This phenomenon has been noted by other scholars studying groups in dangerous situations. In his studies of mining folklore in Utah and California, Wayland Hand described the prevalence of dangerlore among hardrock miners. In Hand's words, "lore centering about accidents and deaths in the mines is common; in fact there is little folklore underground that is not in some way connected with the fears and apprehensions of miners for their welfare and safety while in the bosom of the earth."[64] Meyer's studies of Oregon pioneers and Pacific Northwest loggers show that danger was a primary theme on their gravestones and monuments.[65] The frontier was a dangerous place; many pioneers died on the trail without ever reaching Oregon, while others succumbed to disease, accidents, attacks by hostile Native Americans, and other dangers accompanying early settlement. It is no surprise that early Oregon gravestones often provide "a careful chronicling of the hazards of daily life."[66] Like seafarers, loggers face daily dangers, and many of the loggers' memorials studied by Meyer feature elements of danger such as depictions of working on log rafts, a task where men were frequently injured or killed.[67]

The *Eurydice* story told at the beginning of this chapter shows how suddenly death could strike at sea. Mariners knew that the sea was fickle and that even the kindest day could quickly turn deadly. The motif of death striking suddenly appears frequently on maritime memorials. This motif was sometimes expressed through epitaphs, as in the case of two seafaring brothers from Massachusetts. The elder brother, Benjamin Pitman, was lost at sea in 1815, while his younger brother John drowned twelve years later. In choosing a memorial for their sons, the Pitmans chose to emphasize the fragility of life.

> The rising morning can't assure
> That we shall end the day
> For death stands ready at the door
> To snatch our lives away.[68]

The brevity of life and the possibility of sudden demise is also expressed on the gravestone of British seaman Robert Smith of Hull, who died suddenly from unstated causes at age twenty-seven. Smith's simple epitaph states, "Life how short! Eternity how long."[69] Seafaring was largely a young man's profession, so those whose lives were snatched suddenly away were often young. The motif of the youthful life suddenly cut short was expressed in several ways, as on the gravestone of Connecticut sailor Franses Holmes, who died aboard ship in 1801 at only fourteen years of age. Holmes' epitaph describes the impact of sudden death.

> Whilst sailing on the briney
> deep stern death
> Approach'd the blooming
> youth & stop'd his breath.[70]

The "life cut short" motif was also expressed in maritime mortuary symbolism. In Anglo-American funerary practices, broken columns, wilted flowers, and cut logs typically symbolize a life cut short. Anglo-American mariners used some of these same symbols. Flowers, for instance, were noted on many maritime gravestones. Other forms were more dramatic. The churchyard of Plympton St. Mary's near Plymouth, England, holds a monument to three local brothers, all Royal Navy sailors, who died in separate incidents in various parts of the world (figure 2.8).[71] The monument is in the form of a broken column standing on a pedestal, a type common in late-nineteenth-century cemeteries, which symbolizes the three lives cut short.

Figure 2.8. Broken column monument commemorating three seafaring brothers who died in three separate incidents. Local lore holds that the broken column represents a ship's mast, shattered by a storm. Plympton St. Mary's, Plymouth, U.K. Photo by author.

In addition to using symbols common in Anglo-American mortuary practice, sailors used maritime symbols to express prevailing mortuary ideas. One of the best examples of this practice is the memorial for Bowyer Hamilton Guy Freer, a Royal Navy cadet who died in 1908, just six days shy of his fourteenth birthday.[72] Cadet Freer's monument takes the form of an anchor resting against a pile of rocks, with the anchor chain looped up and over the top of the pile. One end of the chain is attached to the shank of the anchor, while the other end features a broken link hanging in space (figure 2.9). Examination revealed that the broken link was original rather than the result of damage. The end of the chain had been

Figure 2.9. Monument for Cadet Bowyer Hamilton Guy Freer, who was killed six days before his fourteenth birthday. The broken anchor chain symbolizes Freer's life cut short. Royal Navy Cemetery, Haslar, Hampshire, U.K. Photo by author.

intentionally carved as a broken link, most likely to represent the way that Cadet Freer's life was tragically cut short.

The ever-present spectre of sudden death resulted in the development of a fatalistic worldview among mariners. Such an attitude can be seen in many genres of maritime lore from the Age of Sail. In his article "Faith and Fate in Sea Disaster Ballads of Newfoundland Fishermen," Kenneth S. Goldstein demonstrates that fatalism forms a major theme in the folksongs of Newfoundland maritime communities. Goldstein also notes, however, that this fatalistic attitude did not mean that sailors submitted passively to fate. Rather, "the fatalism of Newfoundlanders is based on the idea that it is their lot to live with, fight with and to otherwise deal with the sea and related elements—not to give in to them but to recognize their force and power."[73] Marcus Rediker has also noted the fatalism of mariners.[74] Sailors accepted that they might die at any moment but did not submit meekly. Ned Myers' messmate Tom Goldsmith eloquently expressed this never-say-die attitude moments after escaping from the foundering schooner *Scourge*. "'Ned,' says Tom, 'she's gone down with her colours flying, for her pennant came near getting a round turn about my body, and carrying me down with her. Davy [Jones] has made a good haul, and he gave us a close shave; but he didn't get you and me.'"[75] Close calls were simply a part of life at sea, and seafarers expected their shipmates to accept the possibility of sudden death without complaint. Richard Henry Dana wrote that "whatever your feelings may be, you must make a joke of everything at sea; and if you were to fall from aloft and be caught in the belly of a sail, and thus saved from instant death, it would not do to look at all disturbed, or to make a serious matter of it."[76] Dana's statement implies that to complain would lessen one's stature in the eyes of the group. Francis Olmsted witnessed this attitude during a whaling voyage in the 1840s. One day, a sailor fell from the fore topsail yard arm, but the fortunate man suffered only scrapes and bruises. Though initially shaken, the man soon joked about the incident with his shipmates, leading Olmsted to comment, "Though compelled to undergo the severest toils and privations, which almost always terminate his life before he has reached its natural limit, yet the sailor is a light-hearted, careless fellow, forgetting all sober reflections when danger has passed by."[77] In the maritime mind, life was a constant struggle against the forces of nature and a hazardous workplace environment, with many narrow escapes. Sailors learned to live day by day, and valued a shipmate who could endure hardship without complaint. A worldview that accepted the possibility of sudden death allowed sailors to function in their dangerous environment. When possible, sailors took precautions to reduce threats. While procedures could be developed to minimize some forms of danger, such as shipboard accidents, the forces of nature were beyond humans' ability to control. For this reason, the struggle of humans versus nature, exemplified by the many memorials that detail deaths from rocks and storms, was a common motif on maritime memorials.

Humans vs. Nature

The natural world has played a fundamental role in human development from the time of our earliest ancestors. Before civilization, humans were much more reliant on the natural world for survival, and they were also more susceptible to its whims. Awed by natural phenomena, early humans assigned it supernatural power. Cultures worldwide anthropomorphized natural forces into deities, from the Norse Thor the Thunderer to Choc, the Mayan god of rain and lightning. Like the weather itself, such deities were often capricious.

The nature versus culture struggle seems to be a fundamental part of the human psyche. Nature is the outsider, and is therefore foreign and fearsome. We clear land and build towns in an attempt to tame nature, but the battle can never truly be won. A host of natural phenomena, including storms, fires, and floods, can wipe out humanity's incursions in an instant. The primary purpose of ships is to venture upon the natural element, with the ocean representing perhaps the most powerful natural force of all. Symbolically, ships represent culture in a constant battle against the forces of nature. It is small wonder that this primeval struggle figures prominently on memorials and in other forms of maritime lore.

It should likewise come as no surprise that the climactic point of the struggle—when nature overcomes culture and the waves send a ship to the bottom—should be depicted as well. The motif of the "moment of loss" is charged with meaning. It emphasizes the moment when the forces of nature overcome human life and symbolizes the exact point when hope is lost as humanity succumbs. The *Queen* monument described above is an example of this theme in graphical form. William Palmer's gravestone in the churchyard of St. Thomas à Becket in Warblington, England provides another example.[78] Palmer was killed when his vessel sank while entering the port of Dublin, Ireland, in 1759. Although the inscription does not specify the cause of the sinking, a carving on the top of the stone depicts the event in stark detail (figures 2.10 and 2.11). The carving shows Dublin harbor, with a cityscape surrounding the water. Palmer's vessel seems to be either on its beam ends or in the act of capsizing, and is depicted hard against a structure that may be a quay. The carving captures the moment of disaster, as Palmer's vessel still has its sails set, and another craft approaches as if to render assistance. This theme is repeated on other monuments, such as Edward Hawk's gravestone, which includes a depiction of his boat on its side to reinforce the moment when Hawk's boat capsized, leading to his death by drowning.⁷⁹ A variation of this motif depicts broken parts of a vessel to express the idea that life has been extinguished. One example of this is a cenotaph from Evergreen Cemetery in Portland, Maine, which commemorates Captain Samuel Tucker, who was lost with his vessel in 1882.⁸⁰ The top of Captain Tucker's cenotaph is elaborately carved in the representation of a broken mast and topmast, with rigging still attached, floating on the waves (figure 2.12). While illustrations of vessels at the moment of destruction symbolize the victory of nature over humanity, this form of the motif represents the acknowledgment of nature's victory. Shattered timbers represent proof that nature has won. Like life itself, a broken mast floating on water is ephemeral. For a time, it exists upon the surface of the waves, a stark reminder of nature's power. If the wreck took place far out at sea, the vessel's timbers soon slip beneath the waves, leaving no trace of humanity and causing loved ones at home to

Figure 2.10. Gravestone of mariner William Palmer at St. Thomas à Becket, Warblington, Hampshire, U.K. The stone depicts Palmer's vessel wrecking at Dublin in 1759. Photo by author.

Figure 2.11. Detail of the stone, showing harbor scene and Palmer's vessel. Photo by author.

Figure 2.12. Cenotaph for Captain Samuel Tucker, Evergreen Cemetery, Portland, ME. Photograph courtesy of James C. Bradford.

forever wonder what fate befell their sailor. Almost mockingly, however, the sea sometimes casts parts of vessels upon the shore to bear testimony to its power. Debris scattered along the shoreline indicates that nature has won.

The "moment of loss" motif is woven through maritime songs, literature, and memorials. At the conclusion of *Moby Dick*, Captain Ahab is dragged into the depths by a line bound fast to the whale. The disappearance of the end of the line beneath the surface signifies that Captain Ahab's vendetta has finally come to an end. The topmasts of the *Pequod*, holed and sinking, protrude for a few moments above the surface, before the waves close over them and "the great shroud of the sea rolled on as it rolled five thousand years ago."[81] Nature conquers; no trace of humanity remains. Melville's description, although fictional, echoes the way that the sight of *Eurydice*'s masts was ingrained in Churchill's boyhood mind. The effect of wreckage cast upon shore can be seen in Béchervaise's description of the aftermath of the *Queen* tragedy.

> The scene on the beach beggared description: it struck to the very heart, and would have roused the most hardened to sympathy. The ship in two parts was laying as nearly as possible on her broadside, her hull, in parts, resting on her own spars, rigging, and gear of all sorts. Strewed about the beach lay casks of provisions, cases, chests, arms, &c., and here and there a dead body whose hand or whose face only was visible amid the ruins of the wreck.[82]

Another example comes from the sea song "Three Score and Ten," whose title refers to the seventy fishermen from Hull and Grimsby who were lost in a terrific gale in 1889. This song provides an excellent rendition of the way that broken timbers symbolize death, loss, and grief.

> October's night was such a sight was never seen before
> There was masts, there was yards; broken spars came floating to our shore.
> There was many a heart of sorrow, there was many hearts so brave;
> There was many a hearty fisherlad did find a watery grave.[83]

The sight of broken timbers along the shoreline caused sorrow because they provided proof of the tragedy. A memorial to James Stephenson, a Hull fisherman killed in this gale, echoes the motifs discussed in this section. Stephenson's heavily worn gravestone shows his fishing smack, *Olive Branch*, dismasted in heavy seas (figure 2.13).[84] This illustration combines the broken mast with the moment of loss, and his epitaph reinforces the theme.

> He has gone, oh how hard not a friend to be near
> To hear his last sigh, or watch his last tear;
> No parting, no farewell, no kind words of love,
> To cheer his last moments, or point him above.

The final line, with its phrasing "last moments," reemphasizes the importance of the moment of loss. These motifs symbolize the defeat of humans by the sea, which ends with the banishment of humanity from the realm of nature.

If this interpretation has merit, then we should expect that the opposite case—when a ship successfully makes port, representing the triumph of humanity over nature—to be important as well, and therefore also to be represented. And indeed it is. In the city of Hull, East Yorkshire, once

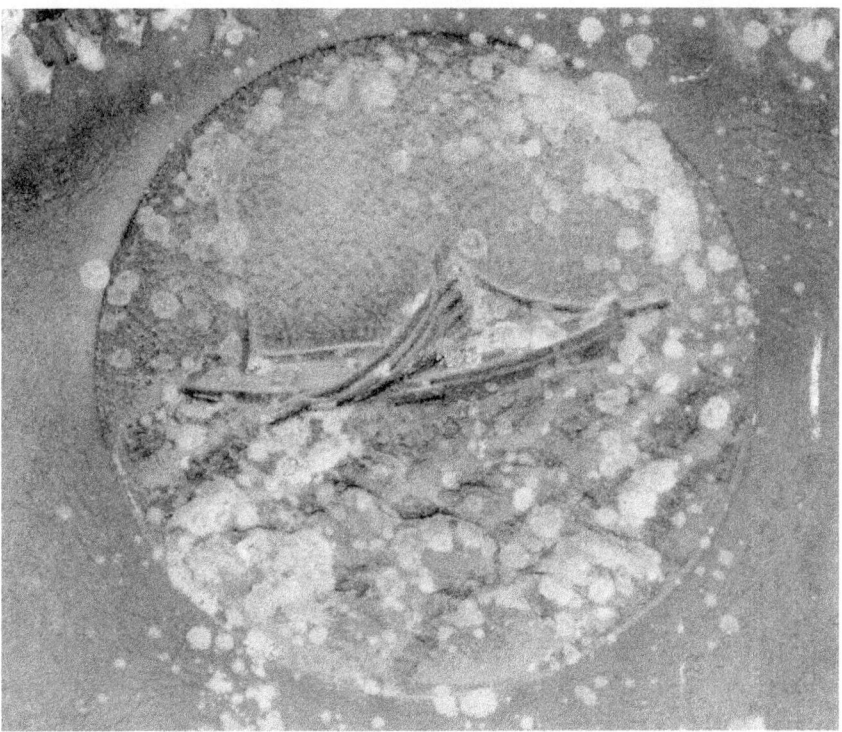

Figure 2.13. Detail of James Stephenson's gravestone, showing his fishing smack *Olive Branch* sinking in the great gale of 1889. Sculcoates Lane Cemetery, Hull, U.K. Photo by author.

one of England's foremost whaling ports, the former graveyard of Holy Trinity Church has been turned into a parking lot, with many old gravestones serving as pavement. Despite this bizarre treatment, the gravestone of eighteenth-century sailor John J. Powell, who died in 1785, can still be read.[85] Powell's epitaph nicely summarizes the sentiments of many a mariner who had survived a life of battling nature.

> from storms and rocks
> from sea and tide
> I safely here at
> anchor ride.

Note that storms and rocks are the first two dangers mentioned, with two other natural forces, sea and tide, immediately following. Powell's epitaph is by no means unique. The gravestone of Captain Edward Russell in Salem, Massachusetts' Old Burying Point graveyard celebrates the fact that he survived "the battering storm the hurricane of life."[86] Across town at Broad Street burial ground, his contemporary Captain Addison Richardson, in an epitaph "inscribed by himself," notes that he "weathered life's wintry storm and its fervid pestilential summers."[87] Powell died at only twenty years of age, but Russell lived to the ripe old age of seventy-six, and Richardson reached seventy-two. Small wonder that epitaphs emphasizing the motif of safely reaching port seemed fitting for both of these men, since over the course of their careers, they probably faced dire situations many times. These sentiments expressed in stone echo sailors' words from their autobiographies. Nearing the end of his life, John Nicol wrote that "[I] now only look for the time when I shall enter my last ship, and be anchored with a green turf upon my breast."[88] Examples such as these highlight the importance that the motif of safely reaching journey's end held for mariners in the Age of Sail. As we shall see in chapter 6, the "safe in port" motif had religious significance as well.

The emphasis on the dangers of the natural world calls attention to a significant omission on Age of Sail maritime memorials. Few memorials mention disease, despite the fact that it was probably the greatest killer of mariners before the advent of modern medicine. Scurvy, a disease caused by vitamin C deficiency, became a threat to sailors with the advent of global seafaring in the fifteenth and sixteenth centuries. Scurvy was easily preventable by providing fresh food, especially citrus juice. This fact was known among mariners as early as the first half of the seventeenth century, as evidenced by its inclusion in John Smith's *Seaman's Grammar* of 1627.[89] In addition to calling for better provisions to improve the health of sailors in general, Smith specifically stated that lemon juice should be carried to prevent scurvy. However, navies and merchant services were slow to supply citrus juice due to financial considerations. In addition, it was impossible to keep a supply of fresh produce on hand during extended sea voyages. Scurvy therefore remained a problem until the nineteenth century. Typhus, often called "gaol fever" on land but known to seamen as "ship fever," could also decimate seamen.[90] Typhus was spread by a louse that lived in dirty conditions, especially filthy clothing and bedding. In the early days of global seafaring, little attention was paid to keeping vessels clean. Most men slept on the decks, and bedding soon became filthy and infested. Also, there was no standard uniform for sailors. When a sailor signed aboard a merchant ship or was pressed into a naval vessel, he came aboard dressed in whatever clothing he possessed. In the cramped conditions aboard ship, a seaman infected with typhus could easily spread it to the entire community. Preventing typhus was a matter of maintaining a clean ship. Hammocks made their appearance in English naval vessels in the late 1500s, and became standard issue during the seventeenth century.[91] With hammocks, it was no longer necessary for sailors to sleep on damp or filthy decks, so sanitation improved. Captains also began employing other measures to keep ships clean. The practice of scrubbing the decks every morning became a maritime tradition. Ships were also fumigated periodically to kill rats and insects. Such measures helped alleviate the problems of pests and disease aboard vessels but never entirely prevented them.

In addition to diseases such as scurvy or typhus that occurred aboard ship, sailors were also in danger of taking ill when in port. As they began to explore the world, Europeans discovered that they had no immunity to a variety of exotic diseases. Sailors, in the vanguard of discovery, were especially hard hit by these new threats. In particular, hot, humid, tropical climates proved deadly for Europeans. Yellow fever, a mosquito-borne disease endemic to tropical climates, killed thousands. The "yellow jack" or "black vomit," as it was variously called by sailors, was prevalent in West Africa and the Caribbean. In his memoirs, Commander James Anthony Gardner of the British Royal Navy described his experiences with yellow jack in the Caribbean in 1801. At Port Royal, Jamaica, Gardner dined with friends aboard HMS *Elephant*, in celebration of that ship being ordered to return to England. Gardner's friends were joyous at the prospect of leaving the disease-ridden Caribbean, but unfortunately not all of them made it. "Poor fellows, little did they think that instead of going home their bones would be left at the Palisades. I am grieved to say that out of the whole mess only two or three returned," lamented Gardner.[92] Soon, the fever made its appearance aboard Gardner's ship, HMS *Brunswick*, as well. Within days "the *Brunswick* had 287 men on the sick list, and buried a great many."[93] The situation was so bad that the vessel was rendered unfit for service: "On our sick list being shown to the admiral he seemed astonished at the number, and when he found it was so swelled with yellow fever patients he ordered our boat off immediately and would not suffer any communication with our ship."[94] The admiral's actions make it clear that he understood the highly contagious nature of the disease and feared for the safety of the entire British fleet.

Many other deadly diseases existed, although these may not have killed as many sailors as scurvy, typhus, and yellow fever. When ashore, sailors often frequented prostitutes, and complaints of venereal disease were common among sailors returning from shore leave. Although treatments for venereal disease existed, many sailors did not seek them because it was customary for their wages to be docked to pay for the treatment.[95]

In contrast to other memorials, which often contain graphic descriptions of the events that led to tragic death, few memorials to victims of disease include anything beyond cursory details. One that does is the mural plaque for British mariner John Warren.

SACRED
TO THE MEMORY OF
JOHN RICHARD WARREN, R.N.
SECOND MASTER OF H.M.S. RANGER, WHO WHEN IN
COMMAND OF A SLAVER, WHICH HE WAS TAKING
TO ST. HELENA FOR CONDEMNATION, CAUGHT A FEVER
FROM THE NEGROES, OF WHICH HE DIED ON THAT
ISLAND ON THE 18TH DAY OF JANUARY 1862,
AGED 23 YEARS.[96]

Warren's memorial, commissioned by his shipmates, is an exception. Even in this case, the epitaph is more about Warren's role in the fight against the slave trade, rather than the fever itself, which is essentially reduced to the unfortunate byproduct of his attempt to help others.

Other memorials to sailors who died of disease follow the same pattern, mentioning few details about the actual disease itself. The crew of HMS *Boadicea* erected a monument to their shipmates "who were killed in action or died of wounds disease or accident" during the ship's time on the Cape of Good Hope and West Coast of Africa Station from 1878 to 1882.[97] Of the forty-seven names listed, twelve perished in an "epidemic of smallpox," eleven others died of "fever" and one succumbed to an unspecified "illness." The crew of HMS *Archer* also dedicated a monument to their fellows "who died of fever" upon that ship's return from West Africa in 1866.[98] Likewise, HMS *Racer*'s crew memorial was specifically dedicated to shipmates "who died by accident and of yellow fever" from 1858 to 1862 during that ship's service.[99] None of these memorials, however, provide more than cursory details about the diseases.

It is probable that many of the sailors whose fates are listed merely as "died at sea" perished from disease. New Bedford sailor John Sanford "died at sea" in March 1842 "after 7 days sickness of Fever," but this is the only gravestone I have seen that specifically links these two concepts.[100] Nevertheless, disease was the greatest killer of sailors in the days of wooden ships, and it is therefore probable that many who died at sea of otherwise unspecified causes succumbed to various forms of illness. Disease, like storms or rocks, is an element of the natural world. Why then does it not figure prominently on memorials, which so often emphasize the theme of humans versus nature?

Several reasons probably account for the lack of maritime gravestones that mention disease. From a purely practical standpoint, diseases do not lend themselves to depiction in the way that storms or shipwrecks do. How would one illustrate malaria or yellow fever on a gravestone, especially in a time before the germ theory of disease, when the physical appearances of bacteria and viruses were not known? This in itself cannot account for the lack of disease-themed memorials, however, as most memorials rely on text rather than imagery to tell their stories. Why, then, are there so few memorials that describe the debilitating effects of diseases? I think the answer lies in the ability of the forces of the elements to overwhelm the human mind. Disease simply does not possess the same power to awe the senses that the forces of elemental wind, water, and rocks do. In addition, the lack of references to disease on maritime memorials accords with nineteenth-century attitudes toward death. In his study of Victorian children's monuments, Snyder examined the themes that parents chose to emphasize on memorials to those who died in childhood. Although disease killed more young children than any other cause, memorials emphasized childhood innocence in a rapidly changing and industrializing world.[101] As with children, it seems that memorials for mariners were chosen to emphasize themes other than disease. Statistically, disease was probably the leading cause of death, but other issues occupied the minds of those who created the memorials. For sailors, those issues included shipboard accidents and the forces of the natural world, particularly rocks and storms.

Why does nature have such a hold on the human psyche? It seems that the answer is: simply because nature is unpredictable and uncontrollable. In a classic interpretation that has stood the test of time, anthropologist Bronislaw Malinowski explained how humans respond to the unpredictable forces of nature. While conducting ethnography among the Trobriand Islanders of the South Pacific, Malinowski noted that certain tasks were accompanied by more ritual activity than others. Activities that were associated with danger necessitated the use of magic rituals designed to protect the Trobrianders from harm. In particular, Malinowski noted a clear difference between lagoon fishing versus deep-sea fishing: "It is most significant that in the lagoon fishing, where man can rely completely upon his knowledge and skill, magic does not exist, while in the open sea fishing, full of danger and uncertainty, there is extensive magic ritual to secure safety and good results."[102] Based on these observations, Malinowski formulated the anxiety-ritual theory, which holds that humans develop magic rituals to ensure that dangerous or uncertain tasks are completed safely and correctly.

Although postulated in the early part of the twentieth century, the key tenets of the anxiety-ritual theory have been borne out by numerous studies. It has been applied by anthropologists in cultures around the world, from traditional societies to professional baseball.[103] Several studies have dealt specifically with how the anxiety-ritual theory applies to seafarers. John Poggie and Carl Gersuny compared magic ritual among commercial fishermen and textile mill workers in New England.[104] They concluded that the high-risk fishermen, whose lives entailed experiencing danger and uncertainty on a daily basis, utilized more magic than the low-risk textile workers. A related study provides additional support for Malinowski's ideas.[105] This study examined ritual taboos among southern New England fishermen, and concluded that taboos were much more prevalent among fishermen whose work took them to sea for days at a time rather than among those fishermen who only went on day trips. Fishermen who spent the most time at sea faced more personal danger, because they were out of sight of land for extended periods of time. Thus, they developed taboos that were designed to keep the vessel and crew safe from the elements. Mullen, in his study of the folklore of Texas commercial fishermen, noted that "danger and economic uncertainty are the most important factors in analyzing fishermen's folklore."[106] While the prevalence of danger lore among Texas fishermen supports the anxiety-ritual theory in and of itself, Mullen also noted another factor that calls to mind Malinowski's distinction between lagoon and deep-sea fishing. An analogous situation existed among commercial fishermen in Texas, where one group fished the protected bays that line the Texas coast, while a second group ventured far out onto the Gulf in search of their catch. In keeping with the anxiety-ritual theory, the lore of Gulf fishermen included much folklore of danger at sea, which was virtually absent from the lore of bay fishermen.[107]

The data from maritime memorials are completely in keeping with the anxiety-ritual theory. Just as those workers who face the most danger and uncertainty develop the most rituals to deal with it, so too does the prevalence of danger spill over onto memorials. While memorials that emphasize the dangers and hardships of life at sea are prevalent, they are not spread evenly across the spectrum of occupations that make up the maritime folk group. Memorials for shore-based members, such as dockyard workers and shipbuilders, never mention the travails of rocks and storms. This is logical, as these workers did not face the threat of storms and shipwreck on a daily basis. Instead, the dangers mentioned on their memorials tend to focus on accidents in the workplace. Shore-based maritime workers did not have to brave uncharted reefs and sudden squalls, but shipyards and docks had their share of dangers. Loading and unloading heavy equipment and supplies called for a great deal of care and was an environment in which a worker could be injured or killed in an instant. Such a fate befell Thomas Atwill, who was "accidentally killed" while working at the Devonport Royal Navy dockyard, near Plymouth, in 1901.[108] Atwill's stone does not specify the exact circumstances of the accident that killed him. The gravestone is typical of those for shore-based maritime workers who died under tragic circumstances. In most cases, the cause of death is stated simply as accident, with little or no detail to tell the story of what happened. Such stones still fulfilled an important teaching function, which will be discussed in the following chapter, but these types of tragedies did not bring forth the detailed descriptions or vivid imagery that one encounters on the memorials for those who died at sea in dramatic circumstances. Instead, memorials with striking illustrations and stories of tragedy are concentrated among the mariners who spent the most time braving the elements upon the sea, primarily bluewater sailors and fishermen.

By contrast, accidents such as gunpowder explosions and falls from aloft are much more subject to human control. Accidents can and do happen, but procedures can be developed to mitigate them. In the Age of Sail, for example, access to the compartment where gunpowder was stored was strictly controlled. Aboard Royal Navy warships, only the gunner and his mates were allowed inside, and they donned cloth slippers when entering so that their iron-nailed boots did not generate sparks. No lights were allowed into the powder storage; instead, a dim light filtered in through a leaded glass window from a specially sealed compartment adjacent to the powder room. Just as these procedures helped prevent accidental explosions, so too did customs for working aloft in the rigging. Going aloft was typically a job for young, agile men. Older sailors worked on deck and were not sent into the high-risk environment of the rigging. Accidents still happened, but the danger was minimized by having the most capable men assigned to the task. All of these systems of control served to curtail the possibility of accidents and contrast markedly with the dangers of rocks and storms, which could destroy a vessel in an instant despite all of the care taken by its crew.

Conclusions

The maritime folk group worked in a dangerous and fickle environment, in which sudden death could strike with little warning. Prevailing Western cultural attitudes considered a "good death" to be one in which the individual died at home, in his or her old age, surrounded by family and friends. A "bad death," by contrast, was the type that killed the young, happened unexpectedly, occurred through some tragic means, or killed a person far from home, with no way for family or friends to be present.[109] The nature of seafaring meant that bad deaths—whether in the form of natural forces or industrial accidents—constantly stalked sailors. This had a great impact on the group's worldview.

When one works in an occupation in which danger and death play a prominent role, these concerns seep into group consciousness and manifest themselves in, among other things, mortuary traditions. Consciously and unconsciously, group members wove the theme of danger into the tapestry of maritime memorialization. Although every manner of maritime death was described in memorials, the struggle of humans against the forces of nature figures especially prominently. Malinowski's anxiety-ritual theory offers a useful paradigm for interpreting the prevalence of the human versus nature theme on maritime memorials. Unpredictable and uncontrollable, nature's power loomed large over maritime life. To cope with this constant threat, the maritime folk group developed a distinctive set of group values.

3
Values for a Dangerous World

Memorials not only chronicle the many hazards that mariners faced; they also record the group values that sailors developed to deal with these threats. By "values," I mean the core standards and beliefs that a group holds to be true and important. Values guide actions by providing standards of behavior for members to follow. Dangerous environments cause group members to develop strong bonds and a shared set of values and worldview. The hazardous nature of their work environment caused sailors to develop a set of shared group values that emphasized attention to the performance of duty and the need to watch out for other group members. These values are directly expressed on maritime memorials and in other forms of maritime folklore. The values of the folk group provide an interesting comparison to those seen on "official" memorials erected by nation-states. Maritime folk group values mirror some of the ideals espoused on memorials erected by nation-states, but also differ markedly from them in several key ways.

Maritime Folk Group Values

Bravery and Duty

Doing one's duty was one of the chief values for coping with the dangers of life at sea. Aboard ship, the safety of all hands required that every man do his job, and this value appears over and over again on maritime memorials. Nowhere is this more poetically expressed than in the 1879 epitaph of Adam F. Vannarp in Cedar Grove Cemetery, New London, Connecticut.

> While we are securely and peacefully sleeping
> He stands at the helm his duty performs
> Now walking the deck and his painful watch keeping
> Or sits at the masthead mid perils and storms.[1]

The epitaph acknowledges the dangers of maritime life, and makes it clear that the proper response to such challenges is the carrying out of one's duty, however difficult or painful it may be. The image of the sailor standing courageously at the helm is a familiar one in maritime memorialization, and is repeated in both text and iconography (figure 3.1). The symbolism of this image is very clear cut; the helm is the control center of the ship, and to remain at the helm during danger is to remain in control. A man who did so not only helped keep the ship under control but also inspired others to perform their duty. Mariners shared this value in common with other groups in dangerous occupations. Duty is a common theme on military gravestones, and has also been recorded on the stones of stagecoach drivers and railroad firemen.[2] When Casey Jones, the greatest of railroad folk heroes, died trying to prevent his freight train from slamming into a passenger train, his body was reportedly found with one

Figure 3.1. Statue at the Fishermen's Memorial in Gloucester, MA. Photo by author.

hand on the throttle and the other on the brake.[3] Whether factual or not, the symbolism is of Jones dying at his post, performing his duty to the end.

Such notions were not entirely fanciful. We have archaeological evidence of a helmsman staying at his post in the face of disaster. In August 1628, the Swedish royal warship *Vasa* sank in Stockholm harbor on its maiden voyage. The disaster was caused by a sudden gust of wind heeling the vessel over, allowing water to pour in through *Vasa*'s open lower gun ports. As the ship began to heel, *Vasa*'s helmsman attempted to turn the ship into the wind, hoping that this would allow the ship to right itself. The attempt proved unsuccessful, but the helmsman remained at his post to the end, where his body was found by archaeologists more than three hundred years later.[4]

Returning to Vannarp's gravestone, its epitaph is also notable for listing "storms" among the dangers faced. As we have seen, storms were one of the natural hazards that loomed large in maritime group consciousness. Like Vannarp's tombstone, a nearly contemporary memorial in Liverpool also illustrates the theme of performing duty in the face of the dangers of the sea. One entire face of the Newlands family monument is dedicated to three sons, all of whom drowned in separate incidents between 1865 and 1870.[5] The epitaph for the lost brothers states:

> FROM DUTY THEY WERE CALL'D AWAY
> TO WHERE THE STORMS OF LIFE ARE OE'R
> AND MAY WE WITH SUBMISSION SAY
> THEY ARE NOT LOST BUT GONE BEFORE.

Like Vannarp's gravestone, the Newlands memorial emphasizes mariners performing duty in the face of peril. In addition, it also includes the view of death as a release from the hardships of maritime life.

Attention to duty in the face of danger forms the theme of the memorial to Royal Navy Captain Colin Andrew Campbell. In this case, Campbell's actions during a fire at sea formed one of the significant events of his life, as described in the inscription:

> HE SERVED WITH DISTINCTION IN THE
> CRIMEAN, CHINESE, AND ABYSSINIAN WARS
> HE COMMANDED HMS BOMBAY WHEN SHE WAS
> BURNT OFF THE COAST OF BRAZIL
> 14TH DEC^R 1864,

AND BY HIS PROMPT AND JUDICIOUS MEASURES WAS THE MEANS OF SAVING THE LIVES OF THE GREATER PART OF THE SHIP'S COMPANY[6]

In addition to the epitaph, Campbell's monument in Highland Road Cemetery, Portsmouth, includes a bronze panel depicting the fire aboard HMS *Bombay* (figures 3.2 and 3.3). The illustration shows the ship engulfed in flames and smoke, while crowded boats lie close alongside rescuing survivors. On the boat in the foreground, one sailor can be seen hauling a shipmate from the water. The fact that Captain Campbell's family chose this incident to depict on his memorial illustrates the importance it had in his life. Fire ranked among the greatest fears of the crews of wooden sailing vessels. Not only were vessels made of wood, but deck seams and rigging elements were coated with highly flammable tar as protection against the elements. In addition, naval vessels carried large stores of gunpowder, which demanded extreme caution in the use of fire aboard ship. The outbreak of fire could easily result in panic, as described by Edward Coxere's account of a fire aboard his ship in Spithead in 1648, not far from the spot where Campbell's monument would be erected two centuries later. Shortly after anchoring in Spithead,

> ... the powder took fire in the gun-room and a sad blow was given, so that we seemed to be nothing but fire and smoke and expected to have been blown up into the air in a moment. So dreadful was it that the men which could swim leapt over board into the sea to swim to the boats that were at the stern of the ship. Everyone shifting for their lives, among the rest I was not a little concerned, but sufficiently scared, for my life lay at stake and it was 'Everyone shift for himself'; the captain was then no more regarded than the cook.[7]

Upon reaching the boats, panicked sailors rowed away from the ship as fast as possible, leaving many seamen trapped aboard with no means of escape. Fortunately, those left behind managed to get the fire under control before it could reach the powder magazine. Other accounts from the Age of Sail show that this response to fire was not unusual. Eighteenth-century seaman Jack Cremer records a similar incident in Plymouth harbor.[8] In this case, a fire broke out in the boatswain's storeroom, resulting in panic among the crew. Many sailors jumped overboard and swam for shore, while two naval vessels anchored close by cut their cables and sailed away

Figure 3.2. Monument for Captain Colin Andrew Campbell. Highland Road Cemetery, Portsmouth, U.K. Photo by author.

as quickly as possible. Disaster was averted by a brave midshipman who entered the room and extinguished the blaze. Edward Barlow witnessed a fire aboard the *St. Michael* in 1691 in which the sailors exhibited the same behavior.[9] Panicked men leaped overboard, while a few stayed behind and fought the fire. According to Barlow, several of those who jumped into the sea drowned before they could be picked up by other vessels. Given these descriptions, it is easy to see why Captain Campbell's family chose to emphasize the fire aboard HMS *Bombay* on his monument. A captain who could attend to duty and save most of his crew when faced with the horror of fire at sea deserved recognition for his actions.

Figure 3.3. Detail from Campbell's monument, depicting the burning of HMS *Bombay*. Photo by author.

Many memorials express the bravery shown by mariners during battle. At St. Mylor, a plaque commemorates Edward Bayntum Yescombe, commander of the *King George* packet, who "lost his life in bravely defending his ship against the enemy" in August 1803.[10] Another wall plaque in the same church describes the courage of Captain John Haswell, RN, who died in July 1811.[11] Although Haswell did not die in action, his memorial emphasizes his bravery in several engagements. American sailors also valued courage. Old Burial Hill in Marblehead, Massachusetts, contains the grave of Captain Joseph Lindsay, USN, who died in 1826. Lindsay's family chose to emphasize his service to his country in the War of 1812. His epitaph emphasizes the "coolness, skill, & bravery" that Lindsay exhibited as sailing master of the schooner *Ticonderoga* during the Battle of Plattsburg Bay on Lake Champlain in September 1814.[12] Old Burial Hill is also the final resting place for another U.S. Navy veteran of the War of 1812, James Dennis Hammond, who was wounded when the USS *Constitution* defeated HMS *Java* in December 1812.[13]

While seafaring could be a harsh and dangerous career, it also provided some of the most memorable events of a sailor's life. Despite the difficulties they endured, men sometimes looked back on their seafaring days with a certain sense of nostalgia, and chose events from this period to highlight on their memorials. Events singled out for inclusion were often a particular incident of which the person was most proud. Nowhere is this better shown than on the simple gravestone of Able Seaman William Bolton in St. James' Cemetery, Liverpool. Bolton died in 1850 at age 67, and his family chose to emphasize an event from Bolton's younger life when they erected his gravestone. The inscription proudly proclaims, "deceased was one of the British Seamen who fought at the Memorable Battle of Trafalgar on Board of H.M.S. *Timerara* [sic]."[14] No doubt Bolton had regaled his family over the years with tales of his service in the Navy and his account of his part in the battle. Bolton had every reason to be proud, as HMS *Téméraire* was one of the ships engaged in the thickest of the fighting. Major General Elias Lawrence of the Royal Marines, whose grave lies in the churchyard of St. Budeaux, Devonport, also noted his presence at Trafalgar.[15] Both of these men chose this battle because it formed a crucial part of their identities.

Taking Care of Other Group Members

High context folk groups, such as sailors, place particular emphasis on loyalty to other group members. Memorials illustrate several ways in which group loyalty could be expressed in memorial practices. In situations where a sailor died far from home and family, it was common for his shipmates to erect a memorial to him. In Liverpool, fellow American ship masters and English friends erected a monument to commemorate Elisha Halsey of Charleston, South Carolina, who died aboard his ship in the Bay of Biscay.[16] Halsey's monument stands out in St. James' Cemetery because it includes American flag and American eagle motifs.

Providing a grave for other mariners applied even in the case of enemies. The British gave a proper burial and erected a headstone to honor William Henry Allen, commander of the U.S. brig *Argus*, who died of wounds received when his vessel was captured by the British brig *Pelican* during the War of 1812 (figure 3.4).[17] The gravestone also commemorates U.S. Navy midshipman Richard Delphey, who was killed in the same engagement. Allen's stone, while erected during a time of war between Great Britain and the United States, later came to symbolize the unity of the two countries. In 1930, the United States Daughters of 1812, in appreciation of the respect shown to Allen and Delphey by the British, restored the doorway of the chapel. As part of this process, Allen's headstone was

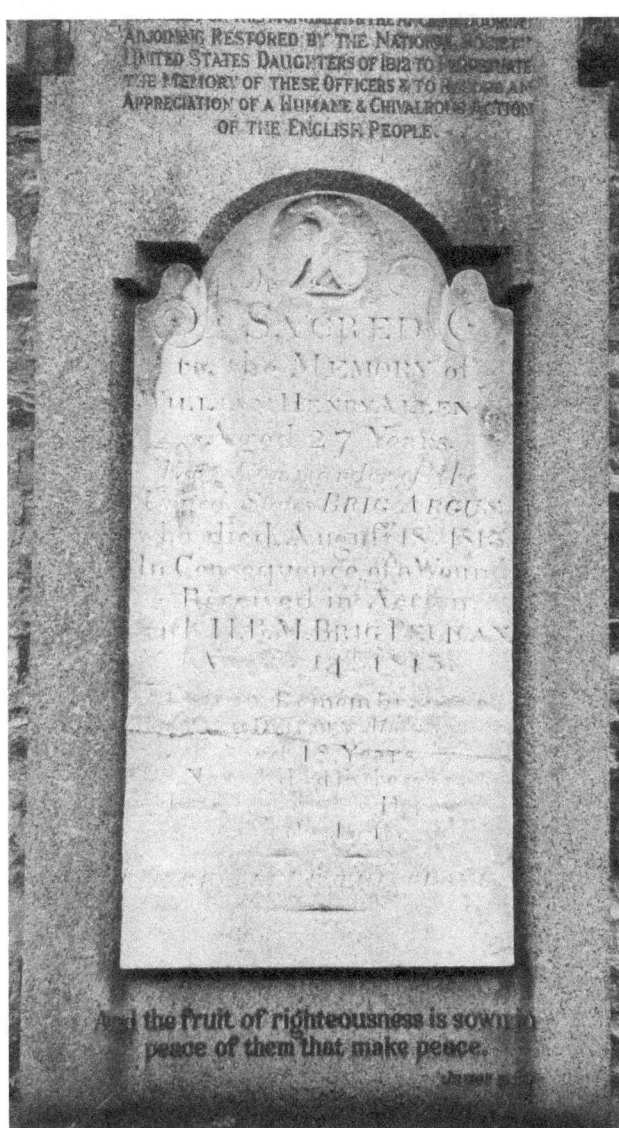

Figure 3.4. Gravestone of William Henry Allen, an American naval officer killed during the War of 1812. St. Andrews, Plymouth, U.K. Photo by author.

remounted and became part of a new monument.[18] A similar memorial is the monument for Royal Navy Midshipman Thomas Barratt Powers of HMS *Superb*, who was killed in action during a British attack on Stonington, Connecticut, in July 1814.[19] The memorial was erected by the captain and officers of Powers' ship, who dedicated it as a "tribute of respect and esteem"—an idea that has not dimmed with the passage of time. When the Maritime Memorials Survey recorded Powers' monument in August

Figure 3.5. Monument for midshipman Thomas Barratt Powers, RN, who was killed in the War of 1812. Evergreen Cemetery, Stonington, CT. Photo by author.

2002, we noted that a pair of flags, one British and one American, had recently been planted at the base of the monument, possibly in celebration of Independence Day (figure 3.5).

Memorials show that the group value of taking care of shipmates crossed ethnic lines. On crew monuments, the dead were listed in rank order, reflecting the shipboard hierarchy that formed a fundamental part of maritime life. However, such monuments do not discriminate on the basis of socioeconomic class or ethnicity: all who died were included. The obelisk dedicated by the crew of HMS *Boadicea* in the Royal Navy cemetery in Portsmouth, for example, notes the deaths of "Kroomen" during that vessel's tour on the Cape of Good Hope and west coast of Africa station between 1878 and 1882.[20] Kroomen were Africans, often freed slaves, in the service of the Royal Navy.[21] A similar example from the United States comes from the Seamen's Bethel in New Bedford (figure 3.6).[22] This plaque is dedicated to three men who were drowned by the capsizing of their boat while pursuing whales in the Ochotsk Sea in 1854. Two of the men have Anglo-American names, but the third, listed as "Frank Kanacka," was likely a native Hawaiian islander. Pacific islanders were often employed on whaling vessels (recall Queequeeg from *Moby Dick*), and were known as "Kanackas" by Americans. While in some sense a racial epithet, the crew nevertheless felt it was important to record the death of their shipmate upon their return to New Bedford, even though the man commemorated had probably signed aboard in

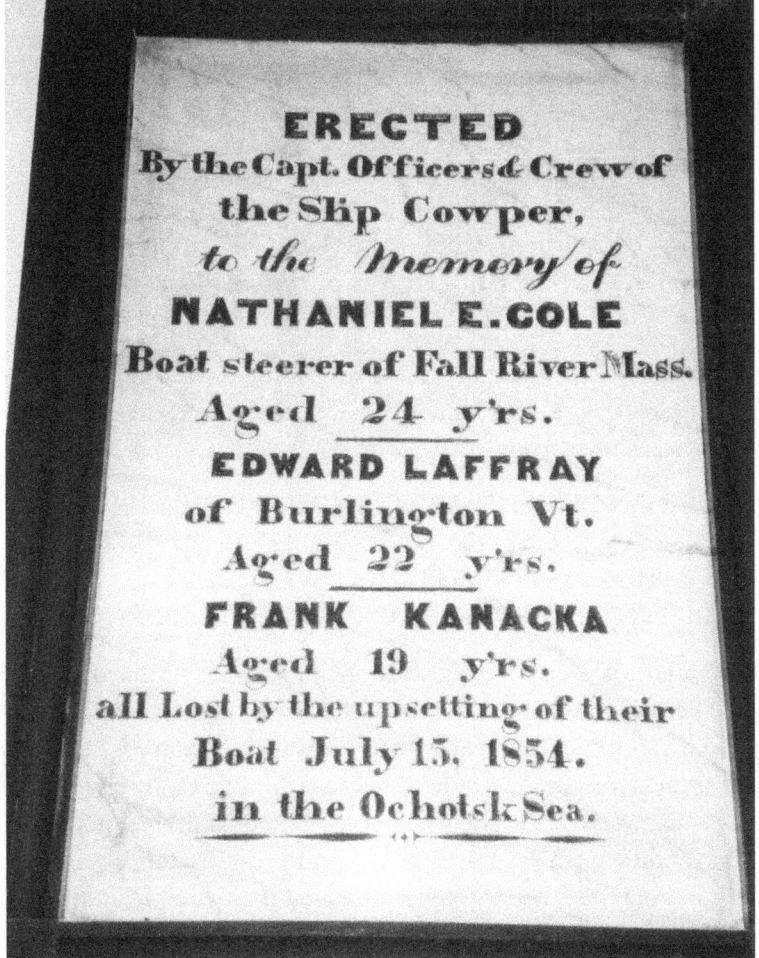

Figure 3.6. Monument to three sailors, including a native Pacific Islander. Seamen's Bethel, New Bedford, MA. Photo by author.

the Pacific, might never have been to Massachusetts, and almost certainly had no family there. Likewise, the Royal Navy sailors described above felt it was necessary to include the Kroomen, who probably had no ties to England. This reflects a feeling of cohesion among members of the maritime folk group that transcended ethnic boundaries.

Another way that sailors took care of one another was to pay for memorials for a deceased shipmate's family. The churchyard of All Saints church in Wyke Regis contains the gravestone of British seaman John Henry, sail maker aboard HMS *Danae*, who died in Cuba in December 1873. The stone was dedicated "in loving remembrance" by Henry's parents, who lived in nearby Weymouth, but it was erected by the officers and crew of the *Danae*.[23] In Plymouth, the officers and workmen of Devonport dockyard erected a gravestone for Thomas Atwill, who was accidentally killed there in 1901.[24] The two stanzas of Atwill's epitaph express the sentiments of both colleagues and his wife. The first stanza reads:

> YES WE MISS HIM O HOW SADLY
> NONE BUT ACHING HEARTS CAN TELL
> EARTH HAS LOST HIM, HEAVEN HAS FOUND HIM:
> JESUS DOETH ALL THINGS WELL.

This stanza, with its sentiment of "yes we miss him," could indicate a tribute from both colleagues and family, but the sentiment expressed in the second stanza is clearly from Atwill's wife.

> SLEEP ON DEAR HUSBAND AND TAKE THY REST
> FOR GOD HAS CALLED WHEN HE THOUGHT BEST.
> THE LOSS IS GREAT THAT WE SUSTAIN
> BUT IN HEAVEN WE HOPE TO MEET AGAIN.

A similar pattern is seen on the gravestone of Thomas Arthur Bennett, First Class Petty Officer, RN, who died at the Royal Navy Hospital Haslar in 1915 and was interred in the nearby Royal Navy Cemetery.[25] Bennett's stone stands out from those around it because it is of a shape commonly found in civilian cemeteries, and yet it is placed in the middle of a section of standard military-issued gravestones (figure 3.7). It seems that Bennett's widow wanted something more personal than an official military stone, but did not possess the financial means to pay for it. The bottom of the stone states that it was erected by "His late shipmates, HMS

Monarch," but the dedication and epitaph are clearly from his wife. The stone is dedicated to "my devoted husband," while the epitaph mournfully states:

> SAFELY AT NIGHT THE STARS ARE GLEAMING,
> OVER A SILENT GRAVE,
> ONE I LOVED BUT COULD NOT SAVE,
> DEEP WITHIN MY HEART CONCEALED.

When a man died aboard ship, it was common practice to take up a collection to help his family. Part of the burial at sea ritual involved selling the deceased's possessions, an act that served the dual purpose of separation and taking care of the group by helping the deceased's family. Maritime memorials show that some of this money could also be used to provide permanent commemoration. In this manner, the maritime folk group took care of its own.

Figure 3.7. Thomas Bennett's civilian-style gravestone set amid standard military stones. AAMMD #10, Royal Navy Cemetery, Haslar, Hampshire, U.K. Photo by author.

Self Sacrifice

Looking out for other group members included putting one's own life in danger if necessary in order to save a brother tar. A monument in Plymouth commemorates Edward F. Tucker of HMS *Jackal*, who "died by drowning in attempting to save his shipmate" in 1895.[26] This characteristic of British seamen is shown most eloquently by a monument in Kingston Road Cemetery in Portsmouth. This cross is prominently situated next to one of the main paths near the entrance to the cemetery, and yet today it is easily overlooked because it is so heavily overgrown with ivy (figure 3.8). It is worth taking the time to push back the tangle and read the inscription, however, for this monument records a story of exceptional gallantry in which eleven sailors from HMS *Ariadne* died trying to save one.[27] After listing the names of the eleven who were lost, the inscription provides the full story of the tragic event:

> ON THE 8TH MARCH 1872 OFF THE COAST OF PORTUGAL,
> WHEN THE SHIP WAS PROCEEDING TO GIBRALTAR,
> WERE CAPSIZED
> IN THEIR CUTTER AND DROWNED WHILST BRAVELY
> ATTEMPTING IN A HEAVY SEA TO RESCUE AN
> UNFORTUNATE SHIPMATE WHO HAD FALLEN
> OVERBOARD

Sacrifices such as this were not uncommon. The grave of Lieutenant William Graves in the Royal Navy Cemetery, Haslar, also records his act of sacrifice to save his shipmates.[28] Lieutenant Graves

> LOST HIS LIFE BY DROWNING
> IN THE DISASTROUS COLLISION IN THE SOLENT
> APRIL 25TH 1908
> HIS LAST ACT WAS TO CARRY OUT SINGLE
> HANDED HIS CAPTAIN'S ORDER, TO LET GO THE
> STARBOARD ANCHOR, THEREBY SAVING THE
> LIVES OF MANY AT THE SACRIFICE OF HIS OWN.

Willingness to sacrifice one's own life for the sake of shipmates was a value held in common by American sailors as well. Two examples provide evidence of this value among American seamen. In New London, Connecticut, the gravestone of B. F. Skinner describes his loss off Cape Hatteras, North Carolina, in March 1865 while attempting to rescue survivors from

Figure 3.8. Crew monument for eleven sailors form HMS *Ariadne* who drowned while attempting to save a shipmate who had fallen overboard. Kingston Road Cemetery, Portsmouth, U.K. Photo by author.

the sinking steamer *General Lyon*.[29] A similar fate befell seamen Fredric A. Akin. Akin, whose gravestone is in the Rural Cemetery in New Bedford, Massachusetts, was "one of the Heroes who was drowned at Cuttyhunk while trying to save the lives of the crew of the Brig *Aquatic*" in February 1893.[30]

National Ideals: Victory, Glory, Patriotism

At this point it is useful to compare values expressed on memorials erected by the maritime folk group with ones put forth on memorials created by nation-states. Monuments and memorials created by nation-states to commemorate significant persons or events are designed to perpetuate the ideals that the state wishes to associate with itself and the values that it claims to champion. Such monuments thus represent a conscious attempt to interpret history in the way that the nation wants it to be seen. Common themes on state memorials include victory, glory, patriotism, and honoring the dead who gave their lives to the national cause. The following examples illustrate typical ways that these themes are depicted on state-level naval monuments.

Victory and Glory

Many nation-state memorials celebrate victory and the attendant glory that it brings to the nation, its leaders, or naval heroes. In fact, victory and glory form the theme of the earliest known memorial that includes a maritime component. The Egyptian Pharaoh Ramesses III commissioned a relief for his mortuary temple at Medinet Habu depicting his victory over the Sea Peoples, a group of nomadic raiders who devastated the eastern Mediterranean near the end of the Bronze Age. The battle, which took place around 1176 B.C.E., was both a naval and land engagement. The portion of the relief depicting the naval battle shows Egyptian ships ambushing and defeating those of the Sea Peoples on the Nile.[31] On the relief, Ramesses III is depicted much larger than other figures, in the midst of the battle shooting a bow at the invaders. His size and warlike posture emphasize personal glory. It seems likely that Ramesses III chose this as one of the events he wished to be remembered by because the battle represented the glory he earned by defeating a group of invaders and preserving the Egyptian state.

Classical Greek and Roman war monuments were also designed to celebrate victory and glorify the nation and its rulers. One such naval monument commemorates a sea battle that played a decisive role in ancient history. The Roman ruler Octavian rose to power thanks in large part to his victory over the fleet of Antony and Cleopatra at Actium in northwestern Greece in 31 B.C.E. This battle took place between fleets of oared warships armed with rams. When it was over, Octavian celebrated his victory by commissioning a monumental wall on a hillside overlooking the battle site. Octavian ordered that rams from the captured warships be removed and mounted in sockets along the wall (figure 3.9). The exact number of rams originally present is unknown but is estimated to have been thirty-three to thirty-five based on the size of the wall and the spacing between remaining sockets.[32] The resulting monument provided graphic testament to a defeated and broken enemy. In addition to glorifying Octavian's victory, it served as symbolic placement of Roman power in Greece by marking the spot near Actium as Roman. Indeed, it is not too much of a stretch to say that Actium marks the point where the Roman Republic ended and the Roman Empire began, as Octavian went on to become Caesar Augustus. Octavian's campsite memorial at Actium served as both a physical embodiment of the genesis of his power and a reminder for future generations of his lasting glory.

Many state-sponsored naval memorials in modern times follow the same themes first seen in ancient Egypt and the classical world. Classical elements such as columns and triumphal arches remain popular. Nelson's Column in Trafalgar Square, London, arguably the most famous

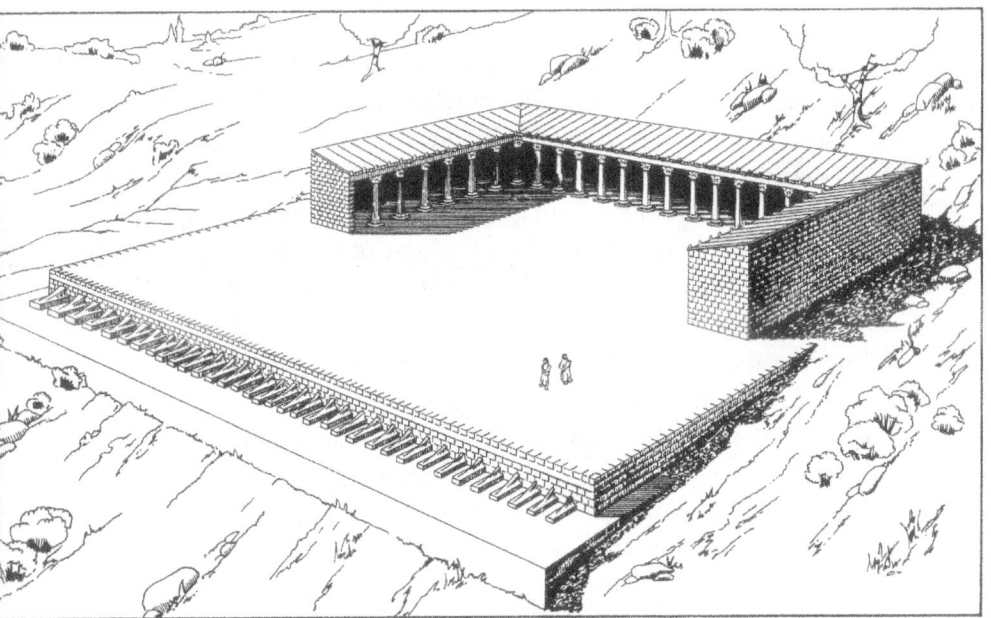

Figure 3.9. Reconstruction of Octavian's campsite memorial for the Battle of Actium. Courtesy of the American Philosophical Society.

naval monument of the modern era, hearkens back to Roman victory monuments such as Trajan's Column. Victory over a defeated enemy also served as the theme for many of the monuments erected in northern cities following the American Civil War. The Soldiers and Sailors Memorial Arch in Brooklyn, New York, incorporates a Roman-style triumphal arch symbolizing victory. Statues of northern sailors on the monument are guarded by a protective sea goddess, symbolizing the northern belief that their cause was divinely protected and therefore just.[33] The Indiana Soldiers and Sailors Monument in Indianapolis consists of a tall column rising from a pedestal base. The form and size of the monument denote triumph, which in this case is made even more explicit by a statue of Victory atop the column, facing toward the defeated South.[34] The monument also includes depictions of watercraft and weapons, further illustrating its warlike nature and bringing to mind the captured enemy rams featured on Octavian's campsite memorial.

Other naval memorials make this connection even more explicit. The Macedonian Monument, built to honor Stephen Decatur's capture of HMS *Macedonian* during the War of 1812, incorporates cannon taken from the captured British warship. Decatur's victory, along with those of other American naval forces in that war, served as an important catalyst of American national identity, because such victories symbolized that the fledgling nation could emerge victorious against its powerful former rulers. Like Octavian's campsite memorial, the Macedonian Monument serves as a permanent physical marker for the creation of a new national identity. As noted by Mayo, the monument's placement on the grounds of the U.S. Naval Academy in Annapolis, Maryland, training site for naval officers, also serves as an example of the type of conduct that the nation expects from its future naval leaders.[35] This is a common function of military memorials.[36]

Warships themselves, the most visible symbols of naval power, can also serve as floating monuments. Despite the high costs involved in maintaining wooden or steel warships, numerous examples are preserved by nations throughout the world. Not surprisingly, the vessels chosen are typically those that symbolize an important naval victory. Of these, the most famous in the Western world are probably HMS *Victory*, Nelson's flagship at Trafalgar, and the USS *Constitution*, celebrated for its victories against the British in the War of 1812.

Patriotism

Closely related to victory—and often found on the same monuments—the theme of patriotism is also an important ideal that nation-states wish to perpetuate. In times of war, patriotic slogans are often used to stir emotions and rally support for the national cause. In U.S. history, two famous patriotic slogans, "Remember the *Maine*" and "Remember Pearl Harbor," stemmed from disastrous naval tragedies. Slogans, however, have a limited life, and phrases soon fall out of use once their associated wars end. Memorials, on the other hand, provide a permanent focal point at which to perform patriotic activities. Unlike words, monuments provide a place in the physical world at which performances can be conducted over and over again, on significant dates such as anniversaries.

Patriotism is often symbolized by commemorating a heroic individual who is put forth as an exemplar for those in naval service as well as the nation at large. Like slogans, the memory of these individual heroes can serve as rallying points in times of war. The British naval hero Admiral Lord Horatio Nelson provides probably the best example of this phenomenon. Nelson died hours after being wounded by a sniper while standing on the quarterdeck of HMS *Victory* at the Battle of Trafalgar on October 21, 1805. The battle, in which a smaller British force captured or destroyed twenty-two French and Spanish vessels while losing none of their own, was the most famous in a string of victories by Nelson. The fact that he did not return from it only cemented his legacy as the foremost British naval hero. Public happiness over the victory at Trafalgar was tempered by despair over Nelson's loss, resulting in a great public outpouring of memorials that included the construction of arches, columns, and other monument forms.

While many of the early memorials that served as sites of public patriotic commemoration during the Napoleonic Wars were torn down soon afterward, two important symbols are still used today to mark Nelson's legacy. HMS *Victory*, preserved at Portsmouth Historic Dockyard, and Trafalgar Square in London provide places where national pride and patriotism continue to be celebrated. Ceremonies are held annually at both sites on the anniversary of the battle. Bicentenary celebrations at Trafalgar Square in October 2005 included a wreath-laying by the Duke of York, a parade of six hundred Sea Cadets, and a show of Royal Navy history called

"Spirit of Nelson." Aboard *Victory*, Queen Elizabeth II and the Duke of Edinburgh attended the annual Trafalgar dinner.[37] The widespread celebrations attended by state officials demonstrate the continuing importance of Nelson's legacy on British national identity.

The annual commemorations of Nelson illustrate the way that a national hero can be used as a continual resource for patriotic commemoration. In contrast, the memorialization of American naval hero John Paul Jones illustrates how long-forgotten symbols from the past can be revived when necessary to assist with the construction of naval and national identity. Jones, best known for his defeat of HMS *Serapis* while commanding the *Bonhomme Richard*, was the foremost hero of the Continental Navy during the American Revolution. Unlike Nelson, whose death during a time of war and at the height of his fame ensured a lasting legacy of memorialization, Jones faded from the American psyche after the Revolutionary War ended and American independence was won. He served for a time as an admiral in the Russian Navy before dying in obscurity in Paris in 1792. At the time of his death, the U.S. government had no interest in bringing Jones' body home or indeed even in paying for his funeral. French authorities, showing more foresight than their U.S. counterparts, anticipated that there might come a time when America would want to honor its forgotten hero. The French arranged for Jones to be buried in a sealed lead coffin filled with alcohol so that the body would stay preserved and could be easily transported back to the United States at a future date.[38] Buried in Saint Louis Cemetery in Paris, Jones was all but forgotten by the U.S. Navy for more than one hundred years. At the turn of the twentieth century, however, the United States and its military were searching for heroes to commemorate. In 1905, American ambassador to France Horace C. Porter located Jones' grave and exhumed the body, which was positively identified by the lead coffin and Jones' features, which had been remarkably preserved. With great fanfare, Jones' remains were returned to the United States aboard USS *Brooklyn*, accompanied by ten other warships. He was to be interred beneath the new chapel at the U.S. Naval Academy in Annapolis. The strange odyssey of Jones' body did not end with his return, however. Because the chapel was not yet complete, it was not immediately possible to inter the body. President Theodore Roosevelt, Admiral Dewey and members of Congress attended an official ceremony of commemoration in April 1906, on the anniversary of Jones' capture of HMS *Drake* in 1778.[39] Unfortunately, there was no place to inter the body because construction of the chapel was not yet complete. The body was placed in a temporary vault in the meantime. Jones was not interred for good until 1913, and his resting place now serves as a permanent memorial to one of the founders of the American naval tradition.

In addition to individuals, memorials that commemorate important events can be used to focus national feelings of patriotism. A good modern example of this is the USS *Cole* memorial, whose purpose is to honor the seventeen sailors killed when that vessel was damaged in a terrorist attack while in port at Aden, Yemen, on October 12, 2000. The *Cole* memorial was dedicated in the destroyer's home port of Norfolk, Virginia, on the first anniversary of the attack. The dedication ceremony probably would have garnered little national press coverage except for the fact that it took place just one month after the devastating September 11, 2001 terrorist attacks. As it was, the ceremony was covered by major television news networks, including CNN and Fox News. In this manner, the *Cole* memorial, while designed to honor only the seventeen victims of that tragedy, served for a time as a proxy memorial for all those who had lost their lives in the recent terrorist attacks. The dedication, which included such patriotic symbols as a military color guard and American flags, also served as a forge for patriotic feelings in the wake of the tragedies of the previous month.

Honoring the Lost

Another important function of nation-state maritime memorials is to honor the sacrifice of those who lose their lives while in service, whether during war or peace. While this function has been present in nation-state war memorials since at least the nineteenth century, the tradition of honoring the lost became widespread following the First World War. There is no doubt that the horrific scale of death in that conflict accounts in large part for the wave of memorialization that followed in its wake.[40] Monuments were erected on many battlefields to honor those who fell there, while numerous communities built public monuments to honor their dead. Such commemorations, whether on battlefields or in villages, typically included lists of names of the fallen. This tradition also dates back to at least the nineteenth century, but as mentioned above, the great scale of death in the First World War magnified it, resulting in larger monuments with many more names than their nineteenth-century predecessors.

Three famous British naval memorials exemplify the tradition that became widespread following the First World War. The Royal Navy, like other branches of the service, wished to honor its dead, but faced the problem that many of its fallen lost their lives at sea, where their bodies were either buried or lost and could not be recovered. With no way to create markers at the site, it was decided to erect monuments at Portsmouth, Plymouth, and Chatham, the three principal Royal Navy manning ports.[41] The three identical monuments are in the form of tall columns rising from pedestal bases. The corners of the bases include buttresses supporting lions, much like those at Nelson's Column in Trafalgar Square, while the top of each column includes a similar treatment, with four sculpted ships' prows representing the four winds. Each column is topped by a copper globe, which can symbolize both the global reach of the Royal Navy as well as those who died in the seas around the world. Brass plaques mounted on the pedestals record the names of all of the sailors who died during the war. The memorials were completed in the 1920s. Following the Second World War, additional space and plaques were added to record the names of those lost in that conflict. The dedicatory inscription included on each monument reads:

> In honour of the Navy and to the abiding memory of those ranks and ratings of this Port who laid down their lives in the defence of the Empire and have no other grave than the sea.

The phrase "to the abiding memory" coupled with the inclusion of the names of all the men—some sixty-six thousand from both World Wars among the three monuments—demonstrate the importance of the need to remember those who sacrificed their lives in national naval service as individuals, not just through monuments that celebrate victory or patriotism. Listing the names of the dead has become so much the accepted way of memorialization, in fact, that it would now be virtually unthinkable to create a national memorial, whether maritime or not, that did not list names. In the United States, for instance, the Vietnam Veterans Memorial consists of a simple black granite wall inscribed with the names of some fifty-eight thousand who died in that conflict.

Ideals such as victory, glory, patriotism, and honoring those who served are the dominant themes found on maritime memorials commissioned by nation-states. In some cases, the values expressed by the maritime folk group mirror those of national governments, while in other cases different values are celebrated. The maritime folk group, like the nation-state, valued bravery, attention to duty, and self-sacrifice. The chief difference between the two types of memorials comes in the area of group maintenance. Nation-state memorials put forth the values that the nation believes necessary to maintain its ideology. In contrast to state-level memorials, the maritime folk group placed more emphasis on values pertaining to the maintenance and protection of the group in the face of the hardships and difficulties inherent to their profession. Chief among these was the idea of taking care of those who died, both through providing burials and memorials for them and by helping out their families.

Teachings Writ in Stone

Nation-states erect memorials to perpetuate national ideals. National memorials are a conscious attempt to display ideas that the nation holds dear. Citizens and outsiders alike learn the values that the nation espouses by viewing its memorials. Memorials, however, can also perform a teaching function at the folk-group level. They can be used to show newcomers group values, and to warn newcomers about the hazards of their profession.

A new member learns the ways of his or her folk group through interacting with other group members. When a man went to sea for the first time, he learned his duty on the job. Seamanship skills were acquired in a hands-on manner. New sailors learned how to handle lines, work sails, steer a course, and a myriad of other skills by performing these tasks under the guidance of experienced shipmates. Similarly, a sailor learned the group's traditions—how to *be* a sailor—by interacting with other group members. Dana's description of life in the forecastle provides a glimpse into this process. In the forecastle,

> [Y]ou hear sailors' talk, learn their ways, their peculiarities of feeling as well as speaking and acting; and moreover pick up a great deal of curious and useful information in seamanship, ship's customs, foreign countries, &c., from their long yarns and equally long disputes. No man can be a sailor, or know what sailors are, unless he has lived in the forecastle with them—turned in and out with them, eaten of their dish and drank of their cup.[42]

Notable in this passage is that Dana specifically states that he learned about both "seamanship" and "ship's customs." In other words, interaction taught newcomers both practical job skills as well as the group's traditions. Dana also names two of the mechanisms by which information was passed along: "yarns," or narratives, and "long disputes." Veteran sailors used both narratives and debate to teach new members proper group knowledge and behavior.

Oral traditions are one mechanism for passing on group knowledge, but as we have seen from the discussion of state memorials, monuments provide a physical place to promote ideas. Memorials provided a material culture forum to teach novice sailors the group values that they were expected to perpetuate. For this interpretation to be plausible, of course, sailors had to visit memorial sites, and there is good evidence to show that they did. Through the eighteenth century, most memorials were located inside churches or in the grounds immediately adjacent to churches. This is where the dead were buried and monuments commemorating them were placed. At least as far back as the medieval period, it was customary for mariners to visit a church and offer thanks at the conclusion of a successful voyage. Such devotions were sometimes accompanied by gifts such as money or votive ship models.[43] Many churches in Europe still possess votive models donated by thankful mariners. Visits and offerings were concentrated in churches located in the places where sailors naturally found themselves; they tend to cluster in churches close to the waterfront rather than in ones more distant from the water. Over time, such churches became heavily maritime in character as generation after generation of seafarers left offerings and buried their dead there. A. J. Parker has discussed votive offerings gifted to Bristol churches by mariners, and also noted the way that church spires could serve as landmarks.[44] Churches that serve as landmarks are naturally those that are highly visible from the water, and so it is easy to see why mariners were drawn to them. Other examples of maritime churches include St. Budeaux in Plymouth, where Sir Francis Drake was married in 1569 and which continued to be used for maritime commemoration into the twentieth century; St. Mylor in Cornwall, home to the *Queen* monument and hundreds of sailors' graves; and the Old North Church in Boston. Mariners did not visit churches only to offer thanks. Sailors were also tourists, often visiting interesting locations in the ports where their ships called. Eighteenth-century British mariner Samuel Kelly, for example, described touring Westminster Abbey, noting in particular the monument for Admiral Sir Cloudesley Shovell.[45] Kelly also visited the grave in the Scilly Islands, where Shovell had originally been buried following the tragedy that claimed his life. Charles Nordhoff took advantage of a stopover at Mauritius to tour the island. One of the locations he visited was a cemetery, where he wandered among the graves and read the inscriptions on gravemarkers. He found a wooden gravemarker rudely carved "with a sailor's jack knife" that marked the grave of a fellow seaman. Its inscription read, "Here, a sheer hulk, lies poor Tom Bowling."[46] Nordhoff noted that it was customary for the local people to clean the graves regularly.

By the nineteenth century, many older churches remained in use, and specialized sailors' chapels were built. In *Moby Dick*, Melville sends Ishmael on a visit to New Bedford's Seamen's Bethel before the *Pequod* embarks for the South Seas. This church was built in 1832, and the scene of whalemen and their families gathering there no doubt has a basis in fact. Among the many tablets that line the Bethel's walls are those that speak of mariners killed by drowning, lost in vessels that foundered, and even one who was killed by a shark. Like churches, nineteenth-century cemeteries were meant to be visited. In the nineteenth century, many churchyards were closed to new burials because they had become unhygienic or had simply run out of space. The new rural cemeteries offered beautifully landscaped parks for the living to enjoy in addition to serving as a final resting place for the dead. People visited these new cemeteries to walk, meditate, and view the monuments. Monuments were meant to be seen and their messages were meant to teach.

Sailors who visited churches and cemeteries to give thanks for successful voyages, bury their dead, or remember shipmates who never returned would have seen memorials for other sailors. These memorials helped teach them the proper forms for commemorating the maritime group's dead. This is suggested by the fact that many memorials feature similar, or in some cases identical, phrasing, suggesting that they were drawn from a common source. Pattern books for both symbols and inscriptions were in use by the eighteenth century, and this no doubt accounts for some of the similarity. Pattern books, however, tended to contain commonly used symbols and epitaphs, but did not typically include standard forms for commemorating maritime tragedies and accidents. Instead, it seems likely that maritime group members used other maritime memorials as a source of inspiration. Three monuments from Falmouth, Cornwall, illustrate how this process may have occurred. The earliest, from St. Mylor church, commemorates maintopman John Bullen of HMS *Crane*, who "was taken from the world of woe by falling from the Main top Gallant Yard of that Ship, when on duty, the 17th day of January 1846, off the Isles of Scilly; Aged 23 Years."[47] Of importance here is the fact that Bullen's gravestone was erected by his shipmates, who chose to emphasize that he died "when on duty." Two decades later, a pair of memorials was dedicated at Falmouth; the memorials contain wording very similar to Bullen's stone. Both commemorate cadets who were killed while serving aboard HMS *Ganges*, a Royal Navy training vessel stationed at Falmouth between 1866 and 1899. The first is located inside St. Mylor church, close to the spot of Bullen's gravestone. This ledger slab memorializes John W. Griffin, boy of the second class, who died in August 1867 "from injuries received by a fall when in discharge of his duty."[48] Several miles away, Falmouth Cemetery contains the grave of John Barry, another boy of the second class, who fell to his death almost exactly a year after Griffin. The phrase "from injuries received by a fall when in discharge of his duty" is repeated on Barry's stone, indicating that it may have come from the same source as Griffin's.[49] The formal tone suggests that official death notices sent to the families may have been the original source for this phrase. Once set in stone—literally—the wording of gravemarkers could have served as a template for notifying other families who had lost a son in similar circumstances. When searching for the proper wording, Griffin and Barry's shipmates may well have drawn inspiration from nearby maritime gravestones.

I suggest that memorials such as these may have fulfilled two functions. First, they taught new members group values. All three monuments emphasize duty, which we have seen was an important maritime group ideal. Duty was undoubtedly drummed into the heads of the *Ganges* cadets during their training. In addition, the emphasis on duty could also have been influenced by the earlier gravestone, that of John Bullen, which lies in a prominent position on the floor of St. Mylor church and would have been seen easily by cadets visiting the church. That the *Ganges* cadets had a connection with St. Mylor church is shown by the fact that when they decided to erect a monument to all of their comrades who had died while in training, the obelisk was placed in St. Mylor churchyard (figure 3.10).[50] Cadets who saw Bullen's gravestone would have learned the lesson that one must perform his duty, even at the cost of his own life. By the same token, I believe that the numerous other memorials commemorating sailors who died on duty, sacrificed themselves to save others, or

Figure 3.10. HMS *Ganges* monument, St. Mylor, Cornwall, U.K. Photo by author.

remembered their fellows by creating monuments to them likewise taught subsequent generations of sailors proper group behavior. Such ideals were instilled by oral tradition as well, but material culture is particularly suited to providing a sense of permanence that oral genres lack. Memorials were, quite literally, teachings writ in stone. In conjunction with oral forms of lore, they helped to both express group values and to perpetuate them.

Memorials may also have performed a second teaching function. A key function of folklore dealing with danger is that it teaches how to prevent accidents or death from occurring. Folklorists have documented the ways that workers in dangerous occupations use folklore to teach critical information to newcomers. Superstitions, for example, function as taboos against actions that are thought to bring about disaster. Mariners in the Age of Sail held numerous superstitions, some of which survive among their modern comrades. Mullen found that Texas commercial fishermen retained, for instance, a host of beliefs that were thought to bring about bad luck. Sailing on a Friday, a hatch cover turned upside down, or bringing a suitcase on board, among others, were all proscribed actions in the minds of Texas fishermen.[51] Implicit within each superstition are rules for avoiding trouble: never begin a voyage on a Friday, make sure that all hatch covers are right-side up, do not bring a suitcase aboard. Superstitions likewise performed a teaching function in other occupational groups whose members worked in dangerous situations. Like sailors, miner folklore included many superstitions that functioned to ensure safety.[52] Some of these were in fact the same superstitions transferred to the mining environment. Rats deserting a ship and rats fleeing a mineshaft both foreshadowed imminent disaster. Miners also relied on hunches that were thought to save lives as well. In one story from Colorado, the wife of a Cornish miner had a dream about ocean waves pounding on the coast of Cornwall. Fearing that it foretold disaster, the woman persuaded her husband not to go to work the next morning and thereby saved his life; a mineshaft flood drowned many of his coworkers.[53] Bancroft recorded this story in 1945, but it was connected to a real incident that occurred in 1895. Whether the story of the dream is factual, however, is not the point. What matters is that the tale served to teach miners to listen to hunches and watch out for signs of coming trouble.

Like superstitions, narratives can be used to teach. Occupational safety has improved dramatically since the nineteenth century, but modern workers still use stories as teaching tools. In his comparative studies of railroad, telephone, and airline industry workers, Santino found that safety was a chief concern for all three groups.[54] Stories that emphasized the proper performance of tasks in order to minimize or prevent workplace accidents formed a common part of the lore of all three. Santino dubbed such stories "cautionary tales" because workers tell them in order to teach other workers how to avoid accidents. Santino documented one cautionary tale, for example, about a telephone lineman who was in a hurry to finish a job, was careless about the placement of a pot of molten solder, and ended up stepping into it and burning himself badly.[55] When workers swap such tales during storytelling sessions, inexperienced workers learn not to repeat the mistakes that led to the accident. Building on Santino's work, Gargulinski found "accident and cautionary narratives" to be the most common form of lore among New York City subway workers.[56] The stories revolved around preventing the type of accidents common in a subway environment, such as falling in front of trains or stepping on the high-voltage third rail.

Songs can also serve as cautionary instruments. In the song "Don't Go Down in the Mine," a miner heeds his child's prophetic dream and stays away from work. That day, a mineshaft fire kills a score of his fellows.[57] Songs as cautionary instruments were not limited to the pre-industrialized past; they are also found in modern occupations. The 1940 ballad "The Dying Truckdriver" by Alton Delmore tells the story of a young truck driver killed by a drunk driver, while "Tombstone Every Mile" describes a road in Maine that is known for its dangerous icy conditions.[58] Both songs serve to remind truck drivers, another high risk occupational group, to pay heed to the hazards of the road.

Superstitions, sea songs, and shipwreck tales probably functioned as cautionary tales in the manner described by Santino and Gargulinski. Wherever sailors gathered, be it in the forecastle or in seaport taverns, sailors sang songs and swapped yarns. Many of these songs and stories describe the hazards and hardships of maritime life. As such, they both warned others about dangers and also described the proper precautions to take to avoid accidents.

Memorials may also have played a role in teaching sailors about the dangers of their occupation. Providing a description of the event on a memorial was another way of preserving the memory so that others could learn from it. The mechanism by which this occurs can be understood by examining the way that disaster sites function in oral tradition. It was common in mining lore for places where death occurred to be remembered and pointed out to newcomers. The process by which this took place has been documented by Hand in his study of Utah silver miners. According to Hand, "New miners are casually informed of such places, but gradually come into possession of all the known facts about the accident and any and all lore that may have sprung up."[59] Such lore taught new workers two things: dangers that they might encounter and proper actions to avoid accident. Like the lore surrounding accident locations, memorials to accident victims can perform a similar function. As we have seen, numerous memorials for maritime tragedies include the date and name of the place or vessel involved, while others provide a detailed description of the event. Like the fledgling miners described by Hand, new sailors who saw the memorial would learn about the tragedy, either directly from the memorial itself or by inquiring into the lore associated with it. In learning about the tragedy, they would also learn proper procedures to either avoid the accident entirely or minimize risk.

Two memorials from New London, Connecticut, may illustrate this idea. The monument for Robert Smith tells that he "was drawn from his boat by a whale in the Pacific Ocean and drowned" in 1828, while James Skinner "was drawn from his boat while fast to a whale off Desolation Island in the Indian Ocean and drowned" in 1860.[60] Whales were hunted from small boats, and when a whale was harpooned it would sound, or dive for the bottom. The harpoon was connected to hundreds of fathoms of line. When the whale sounded, this line played out at a rapid rate, which was dangerous in the crowded confines of a whaleboat. While on a whaling voyage, Francis Olmsted heard one cautionary tale about what could happen in this situation. In this story, the crew harpooned a whale, which immediately sounded. The line became wrapped around one man's foot; he was pulled overboard and drowned.[61] Stories such as this, and inscriptions such as those on the Smith and Skinner memorials, informed other whalemen about the dangers involved with hooking onto a forty-ton leviathan and reminded them to take care when they found themselves in similar situations. In these examples, the specific lesson was to stay well clear of the line attached to the whale. Likewise, memorials that describe death by "falling from aloft," could have reminded sailors to take care while working in the rigging. The outcome of this process was that other group members learned about the circumstances of the accident and what went wrong, and therefore gained an appreciation of the right way to perform shipboard tasks.

When Values Fail

Memorials express the values that the group holds as ideals, but that does not mean that every group member practices these ideals at all times. Values on memorials represent the ideals that the group cherishes and the way that it wants to see itself. To believe that the values expressed on maritime memorials always represented reality, however, would be to present an overly romanticized view of maritime life. What was idealized and what actually occurred were sometimes two entirely different things. Anthropologists have long recognized this dichotomy, and use the term *real vs. ideal* to describe this phenomenon.[62] In this concept, *ideal* represents the core beliefs and values that the culture wants to believe it possesses and practices, and that members of the culture will describe when asked about the group's beliefs. The *real*, on the other hand, refers to what actually happens in any given situation, and what might be observed by an outsider viewing the culture. To cite a modern example, most U.S. citizens would claim that in the United States, people can become whatever they wish to be if they are only willing to work hard enough. The idea of the "self-made man" is one of our most cherished national beliefs, but in reality, unequal opportunity continues to exist.

The maritime occupational group is no different than any other group in this respect. While espousing a lofty set of values, reality sometimes took a different turn. A core group value held that sailors should come to the aid of their fellows, but there are examples of mariners refusing to aid others, even if the man's life was in jeopardy. The panicked behavior of sailors during fires has been noted above. John Nicol witnessed an incident where a seaman fell overboard, and the ship's bosun refused to go in after the drowning man.[63] Seaman Charles Newhall related a story in which the cry of "Man overboard!" rang out on his boat. Upon inspection, the crew determined that the captain's dog, not one of the sailors, had fallen overboard. The captain immediately ordered the ship to put about. The dog was rescued, but the captain claimed that he would not have turned back for one of the men.[64]

The notion of sailors "going down with the ship" and bravely sacrificing themselves to save others is largely a romanticized idea that appears to be based on the popularization of one real-life event. In January 1852, the *Birkenhead*, a British troop transport carrying soldiers and their families, struck a rock off the African coast. Soldiers and sailors remained aboard while women and children were sent off in the ship's three lifeboats. When the stricken vessel sank, it took most of the men down with it. Their act of self-sacrifice was justly lauded by the public. There is, however, another way to view this incident. The *Birkenhead* story, with soldiers and sailors bravely sacrificing themselves so that helpless women and children might live, was probably also popularized by the press because it fit the value system of nineteenth-century imperial Britain. During the *Pax Britannica*, the media was a willing participant in the growth of the British Empire, and fed the public a steady diet of stories and iconography that played up the virtues of imperialism while downplaying its costs.[65] Stories of British sailors and soldiers laying down their lives for others fit the prevailing imperial worldview, but according to B. R. Burg, the behavior of *Birkenhead*'s men represented the exception rather than the rule in such situations. Burg analyzed major nineteenth-century passenger ship disasters and determined that ships' crews usually attempted to save themselves rather than helping passengers.

> The "women and children first" axiom held true only where there was a presumption that all would eventually be rescued and when ample time was available to effect their evacuation. . . . When officers, crewmembers, and male passengers were faced with the stark choice between saving their own lives or the lives of women and children, there was no hesitation. They moved decisively. In almost all such cases, it was "every man for himself."[66]

"Every man for himself" runs contra to the ideal of self-sacrifice that formed one of the core values of maritime culture. In some ways, then, incidents such as those chronicled by Burg represent times when values fail. On the other hand, they may also tell us something about sailors' conception of group boundaries. Passengers—men, women, and children alike—were outsiders. Since they were not members of the maritime folk group, sailors may not have seen as much reason to help them.

Another area in which historical data does not match the values portrayed in memorials is in the area of racial and ethnic relations. Sailors memorialized their shipmates, whatever their race or ethnicity, and yet the historical records show a mixture of tolerance and discrimination in maritime society. Sailors, who valued freedom and independence, did not typically approve of slavery or other forms of servitude.[67] British sailor John Nicol, for example, pitied the plight of slaves in the West Indies. On one island, he witnessed female slaves being brought aboard to sell fruit to the sailors. One of the slave masters

> was flogging one on our deck, who was not very well in her health. He had struck her once as if she had been a post. The poor creature gave a shriek. Some of our men, I knew not which—there were

a good many near him—knocked him overboard. He sunk like a stone. The men gave a hurra! One of the female slaves leaped from the boat alongside into the water and saved the tyrant, who, I have no doubt, often enough beat her cruelly.[68]

Regarding the treatment of slaves, Nicol also states that "no stranger can witness the cruelty unmoved," and claims that "I esteemed them in my heart."[69] An attitude of tolerance toward black sailors seems to have been present in the eighteenth-century Royal Navy, as N. A. M. Rodger reports that, on the whole, black sailors received decent treatment aboard British warships.[70]

Other sailors, however, did not subscribe to such liberal views as Nicol. For black sailors, discrimination was often a part of life. Creighton's examination of diaries of nineteenth-century American mariners revealed that officers typically gave harsher punishments to black sailors than to white ones.[71] Blacks were also more likely to be relegated to menial jobs such as stewards and cooks.[72] It is important to remember, however, that such discrimination was a product of the times. As W. Jeffrey Bolster points out, blacks faced equally bad or worse treatment on land.[73] Racism was part of the attitude of most whites of the period. Whites believed themselves inherently superior to other ethnic groups. Eighteenth-century English mariner William Spavens, for example, exemplifies this attitude in his comments about the Chinese. While in China, Spavens spent time wandering about the countryside and observing the people, who were "industrious, lively, and active."[74] Notwithstanding these positive comments, Spavens went on to say:

> Their whole nation, a few excepted, are a set of the most accomplished thieves upon the face of the earth, the Russians and Tartars not excepted; they steal, and encourage others to do so; they buy stolen goods, and take every advantage in buying, selling, &c. to cheat, go beyond, and defraud any person they have concern or dealing with: Knavery is so prevalent and habitual among them that they will plead custom for it instead of law.[75]

Such attitudes simply formed part of the Anglo-American worldview during the eighteenth and nineteenth centuries. Aboard ship, the extent of the racism that a black sailor faced depended to a large degree on his position. Cooks and stewards were more likely to be treated badly, but blacks who became able-bodied or ordinary seamen were generally treated with more respect. These men had proven themselves and were treated by and large the same as other sailors.⁷⁶ This included, at least some of the time, recognition on memorials erected by shipmates.

Maritime communities often helped survivors of vessels that wrecked on their coasts. Local residents were known to provide food, clothing, and shelter for survivors who struggled ashore. They also provided decent burials for the dead and erected memorials to commemorate tragedies. The monument for the *Queen* transport, which wrecked near Falmouth, Cornwall, is one such memorial, and Béchervaise's eyewitness account of the tragedy tells that the local community "interested themselves to a great degree in aid of the sufferers," including providing a new set of clothing to each of the approximately one hundred survivors.⁷⁷ Community actions such as these were common, and they represent the values of maritime culture at its best.

Another form of community action represented the antithesis of those values. This was the practice known as wrecking, in which individuals used false signals to lure ships ashore, whereupon the vessel would be looted while any survivors were subjected to robbery, rape, and murder. The actions taken by the residents of Falmouth following the *Queen* disaster were admirable, and yet Cornwall had the reputation of being home to the most dreadful wreckers of all. The phenomenon of wrecking has been explored by Bella Bathurst in her entertaining book *The Wreckers*. In it, she sheds light on the apparent conundrum of maritime communities saving shipwreck victims on some occasions while actively working to wreck vessels on others. Bathurst concludes that the number of people involved in actually luring vessels to their destruction was probably very small. Most wreckers were actually salvagers, perfectly willing to steal the goods that a shipwreck offered, and yet often equally willing to help rescue the ship's crew first.⁷⁸ In Bathurst's words, "Shipwrecks bring free loot, and people like free loot. A rare few of those people will provoke a wreck, some will plunder an existing wreck at the expense of the crew or passengers, but the majority will only take things from a ship or a shoreline when they are sure that they are not doing so at the expense of other people's lives."⁷⁹ Most residents of maritime communities understood the terrors of the sea and chose to help those in need. If this entailed making a little profit by purloining a few items temporarily left without an owner, then all the better. Those few who decided to make a career out of destroying vessels were criminals, and their actions went against the group value of assisting other group members in need.

Maritime group values were important, and memorials and other maritime lore abound with descriptions of courage, attention to duty, and self-sacrifice. However, the values expressed on memorials should be viewed as a set of guiding principles. They describe the behaviors that sailors wanted their group to possess. Reality, however, sometimes took a different turn. Still, if some failed, others truly believed in the group's principles. Their memorials stand as a testament to the importance that these values held in maritime life.

Conclusions

We live in an age in which the term "values" is used by some to assert moral superiority, and others cynically wield it as a bludgeon to coerce the populace into following a particular political ideology. Values are not, however, the exclusive province of any one social, religious, or political group. All groups have values, and all groups use them to express and perpetuate group ideals. Memorials, as tangible products of the memory of group experiences, offer one of the key material culture forms through which groups display their value systems. Nation-states like the United States and the United Kingdom use memorials to display core beliefs such as honor and patriotism. These are abstract concepts, however, in which the effects on individuals can be lost in the collective display. Folk groups such as mariners, on the other hand, focus on more personal values. All groups seek to perpetuate themselves, and therefore taking care of group members is a key value. Among sailors, this took the form of commemorating those who died in their dangerous profession, and helping family members to provide memorials if they could not afford to do so. Group maintenance also involves the proper performance of group tasks, and therefore attention to duty likewise formed a core maritime value. This was extremely crucial for sailors, who worked in an extremely dangerous environment and had to work as a team to survive. Attention to duty went so far, in fact, that a man was expected to sacrifice his own life if need be in order to save his fellows.

Words like group loyalty, duty, and self-sacrifice may sound trite today, but they were nevertheless important to mariners in the Age of Sail. Their prevalence on maritime memorials illustrates how key these values were to the group's conception of itself. Sailors did not always meet these lofty ideals; there are plenty of stories of sailors refusing to help their fellows, and practices such as wrecking caused tangible harm to other group members. Still, the value system provided a set of ideals for which to strive. If they were not always met, it can be said simply that sailors, like all of us, are only human.

Despite a group ethos that stressed teamwork to fight the forces of nature, many sailors lost the struggle. Countless mariners died at sea due to accidents or disease, drowned on vessels that foundered, or perished when their ships wrecked on rocky shores. The rituals that the maritime folk group developed to deal with these types of losses form the subject of the next two chapters. Chapter 4 examines the ritual of burial at sea, demonstrating how it was a performance used to separate the dead mariner from shipboard society and at the same time re-create the social order aboard ship that had been disrupted by death. Chapter 5 looks at the ways that sailors and maritime communities memorialized those who died at sea or in distant corners of the globe. Both of these chapters share a common theme: the unsatisfactory nature of trying to cope with the loss of those who never returned from the sea.

4

"The Natural Sepulchre of a Sailor"

BURIAL AT SEA AS RITUAL PERFORMANCE

In February 1667, as His Majesty's ship *Monmouth* rode at anchor in the Downs, Captain Sir Thomas Allin recorded the following entry in his log: "8 *Saturday*. The wind westerly, handsome weather, inclining to the southerboard. We sent for a boat-load of water. Buried one Stephen Wright."[1] The brevity with which Allin noted Wright's funeral is typical for log entries from the Age of Sail, but it belies the importance of this ritual. Far from being a simple process to remove a body, burial at sea had deep symbolic meaning, but many of its facets remain unexamined.[2] Henning Henningsen, in one of the best scholarly articles on the subject, provides an overview of the history of burial of sailors at sea and ashore.[3] William P. Mack and Royal W. Connell describe the structure of the burial at sea ceremony and relate the history of mourning traditions practiced aboard ship.[4] Other studies have cited examples from maritime lore.[5] While all of these studies provide useful information regarding the history and structure of the ritual, its functions and meanings remain largely unexplored. To those aboard ship, however, the ritual held great symbolic meaning and was a key part of maritime memorialization.

Several detailed descriptions of burial at sea services have been preserved, allowing interpretations to be made about the structure and meaning of the ritual. One of the most detailed comes from Frederick Perry, an officer aboard the American clipper ship *Continental*. In 1876, as *Continental* made its way through stormy seas in the South Pacific, an unfortunate sailor working in the rigging lost his grip and plummeted to the deck below. After clinging to life for approximately six hours, the seaman succumbed to his injuries. Perry described the burial service that was held the following morning.

> At eight bells, in the morning watch, *i.e.* at 8 a.m., all hands were mustered to bury the dead. The ensign was run up half-way to the monkey gaff, the main-yards were backed, and the body of poor Louie, lying on the sliding board covered by the flag, and perched upon the shoulders of four of his watch-mates, was solemnly brought aft to the lee gangway and placed with the foot of the board resting on the ship's rail.
>
> It was a bleak, raw, cold morning. The heavy leaden clouds overhead seemed to have drawn the edges of the dark-hued canopy that enshrouded us closer to the horizon. The sound of the wind shrieking through the rigging and the flapping of sails and creaking of spars as we rolled and tossed in the heavy sea added a weird note somewhat like the wail of innumerable lost souls already gone before.
>
> The rough, hardy crew, standing with uncovered heads in the withering gale, solemnly gathered around the body at the ship's side. The captain, advancing to the break of the poop, with Prayer-book in hand, began in a tremulous voice to read: "I am the resurrection and the life." As these solemn words sounded above the whistling winds which broke in upon the silence of the surrounding crew, you could see an honest tear coursing down the cheeks of most of the rough, rugged faces, tanned by the wind and moist with flying spray. As the captain came to the words: "We commit this body to the deep," the inboard end of the sliding board was raised and the body slid out, feet first, from under the ensign and, with a splash, disappeared beneath the angry waves.[6]

Perry wrote in the twilight of the Age of Sail, but the service performed aboard *Continental* that cold morning would have been familiar to mariners from three centuries earlier. It will never be known when sailors performed the first formal burial at sea service, but it is clear that a developed body of tradition existed soon after the beginning of the age of global seafaring. The earliest monument that I know of depicting a burial at sea is that of James Hales, who died while returning to England from Portugal in 1589. Hales' monument in Canterbury Cathedral shows two men lowering his body over the side of the ship.[7] Because the sculpture is a work of art, it is risky to make any conclusions about the scene, but the men seem to be placing the body carefully into the sea rather than simply heaving it over the side. If this was indeed the case, it would indicate a burial rather than an act of cursory disposal. By the late sixteenth century, Captain Luke Ward described shooting cannon as part of the ceremony for a man who died at sea.[8] In his *Sea Grammar* of 1627, Captain John Smith provided details on the disposal of the dead after battle. "Winde up the slaine, with each a weight or bullet at their heads and feet to make them sinke, and give them three gunnes for their funerals," Smith instructed ship's surgeons, and followed with tasks to be done afterward: "Swabber make cleane the ship, Purser record their Names."[9] Elements that Ward and Smith mention, such as shrouding the corpse, weighting it down, and firing cannon, became part of traditional practice. The 1662 edition of the *Book of Common Prayer* formalized the structure and wording of the burial at sea service. This version became the standard form used aboard English and American vessels throughout the Age of Sail and remains the basis for the burial at sea ceremony as it is conducted today.

The development of a widespread body of tradition, and its incorporation into official religious practice, demonstrates the importance of the burial at sea ritual. At sea, it would have been easy to dispose of a body simply by heaving it over the side. Although this was done at times—notably during the heat of battle or when disease killed many men at once—sailors disliked disposing of a body without proper ceremony. Instead, they considered it their duty to provide a proper burial. The reasons for this are rooted in, and reflect, core beliefs of the maritime folk group. This chapter examines those beliefs, demonstrating how the ritual of burial at sea was designed to lay the dead properly to rest, and also served as a stage for the performance of maritime group worldview.

Burial at Sea versus Ashore

When possible, sailors generally preferred interment on land to burial in the sea. In his *Journal*, Edward Barlow recorded two instances where people were interred ashore even though it would have been easier to bury them in the water. In one instance, the captain's wife, who was aboard with her husband, died while the ship lay in Grimesby Roads near Hull. She was taken ashore and buried at Grimesby church.[10] As wife of the captain, this woman was a high-status individual, but Barlow makes it clear that burial ashore was not necessarily restricted to elites. On a later voyage, the ship's carpenter died in Naples. Laws forbade the burial of foreigners within the city, so the easiest thing for the ship's company to do would have been to bury the carpenter at sea. Instead, Barlow and a party of seamen took the carpenter's body several miles away from Naples and buried him next to the sea.[11] The carpenter, while higher in rank than a common sailor, was only a petty officer. Further evidence that burials on land, when practical, were preferred for all, regardless of status, comes from Sam Noble. Noble describes the elaborate funeral arrangements, procession, and burial service performed for an ordinary seaman who drowned at St. Helena.[12]

The examples described above all deal with vessels in port. Retaining a body on a vessel at sea, however, was another matter. Before the development of embalming and refrigeration in the mid-nineteenth century, it was not possible to preserve a body for an extended period of time. Since the Middle Ages, bodies of wealthy or high-status individuals who died away from home were sometimes transported home for burial. One method of preserving the corpse for its journey was accomplished by opening the corpse, removing the internal organs, treating the cavity with vinegar, and packing it with salt.[13] Such extended preparations were not usually possible aboard ships at sea, nor would they have been done for most common sailors.

Practical considerations aside, maritime superstition held that it was bad luck to have a corpse aboard. Royal Navy Captain Basil Hall claimed that the reason for the superstition was that the corpse reminded sailors of their own mortality, which was never far away at sea.[14] Whatever the reason, it was widely believed that the presence of a corpse on board would cause storms or adverse winds.[15] Hall claims that mariners also believed that sharks would follow any vessel with a dead body aboard.[16] This belief dates back at least to the medieval period, as Fletcher S. Bassett cites numerous references to the belief in medieval Europe.[17] Like any superstition, belief in the bad luck caused by a corpse had its detractors. As far back as 1639, the author of "A Helpe to Memory and Discourse" argued that the belief had no validity.[18] Nevertheless, the belief remained a part of maritime lore well into the twentieth century. Horace P. Beck cites a case in Scotland where a man died on a small offshore island and it took eight days to find a vessel to transport his remains to the mainland for burial because no sailor wanted to set out with a corpse aboard ship.[19]

Despite difficulties regarding preservation and superstitions, there were cases when bodies were kept until they could be buried on land. Usually, these were high-status individuals such as admirals or captains. The most famous of these is probably Admiral Horatio Nelson, who was brought back to England for burial following his death at the Battle of Trafalgar in 1805.[20] Only eight memorials recorded by the Maritime Memorials Survey specifically state that the bodies were brought ashore for burial, and four of these were high-status individuals. The social status of two is unknown. The first of these is a British sailor who died at sea and whose body was kept for twenty-two days until the ship made port.[21] Unfortunately, the memorial does not specify the rank of the deceased. American Charles Fordham died at sea and was buried in Manila, Philippines, in 1850.[22] His cenotaph, in his hometown of Sag Harbor, tells neither his rank nor how long his body was kept before the ship made port. In these cases, the absence of rank probably indicates that these men were sailors rather than officers.

Of the high-status individuals, all four were ship captains. A plaque in St. Budeaux church, Plymouth, memorializes Sir Thomas Byard, who died at sea while commanding HMS *Foudroyant* in October 1798.[23] The inscription on his memorial states that Byard's body was brought home and buried in a vault in the church, next to his teenage daughter who had died four years previously. Byard's wife Susanna joined her family upon her death ten years later. The body of Massachusetts captain Seth Pinkham was returned to Nantucket following his death in Brazil.[24] Fellow captain William Crowell was returned to Martha's Vineyard for burial after he died in Liverpool in 1861.[25] By far the most amazing of the memorials that describes a body being brought home for burial is that of Captain John Norman.[26] Norman's story is one of the nine recorded on the family gravestone in St. James' Cemetery, Liverpool. After detailing the names of four other family members, including his mother, the gravestone states:

> Also CAPT^N JOHN NORMAN,
> son of the above Mary Norman
> who died on board the Ship "John Norman"
> in the China Sea on his homeward voyage
> from Foochow to London,
> August 31st 1861, Aged 52 Years
> His remains were brought to England
> by his Wife and interred here
> February 9th 1862

Captain Norman's wife Frances, the last person to be added to the stone following her death in 1886, must have been an extremely determined woman to bring her husband's body halfway around the world in the face of prevailing maritime superstitions against such a practice. The fact that she was able to do so was most likely due to her husband's position as captain of the vessel. It may also be that Mrs. Norman accompanied her husband to sea and was therefore in a position to prevent him from being buried there.

Only two memorials provide definite exceptions to the general rule that only the bodies of high-status individuals were kept on board until the vessel made port. The first comes from St. Mylor church in Cornwall. A slab marker on the floor of the church marks the grave of John Bullen, a maintopman aboard HMS *Crane*, who died by falling from the rigging of that vessel in January 1846.[27] The gravestone definitively states that Bullen's remains were buried in the church rather than at sea. In this case, however, the accident occurred while the *Crane* was off the Isles of Scilly, a distance of less than one hundred miles from Falmouth. It is likely, therefore, that Bullen's body was kept aboard because the vessel was close to making port. The same probably held true for Massachusetts sailor Thomas Davis, who died aboard ship in the North Atlantic. Davis' stone, located in Nantucket, states that he died at 38° N latitude and 63° W longitude, a position approximately 425 miles southeast of Nantucket.[28] Most likely, the ship was headed for Nantucket at the time, which explains why Davis' body was not buried at sea. In this case, it is interesting that Davis' body was buried at Nantucket, even though he was a native of Dorchester, Massachusetts, only a short distance away on the mainland. It seems that his crewmates decided to bury Davis at the first possible opportunity. The reasons why sailors preferred to bury their dead on land seem rooted in maritime beliefs regarding the dead at sea.

The Dead at Sea

Prevailing beliefs regarding the dead explain why sailors were reluctant to keep a corpse aboard ship. Folk belief holds that ghosts are commonly the spirits of those who die before their time. The spirits of people whose lives are cut short due to violence or accident, it is believed, are not able to rest peacefully. The hazardous nature of seafaring during the Age of Sail meant that all too many sailors met their deaths on the waves. Moreover, seafaring was largely a young man's profession, so many of those who were killed at sea died in the prime of their lives. Thus, the sea represented an environment that was highly conducive to the production of ghosts. At sea, several forms of death typically resulted in restless spirits.

One of the most horrific fates that could befall mariners was to be lost at sea. During the Age of Sail, a staggering number of men were lost at sea and never recovered. Over 20 percent of the memorials recorded by the Maritime Memorials Survey commemorate sailors who were either lost at sea or who were drowned in vessels that wrecked. In the majority of such cases, their bodies were never recovered. Therefore, they did not receive proper burials and were likely to become ghosts.

Even when a body was present, sailors sometimes did not receive proper burials. This was often due to outbreaks of disease that killed scores of mariners at a time. In such cases, bodies were typically thrown overboard with little or no ceremony. Those who were killed in battle were also likely to become restless spirits. British naval officer James Anthony Gardner, who served in the Royal Navy during the late-eighteenth and early-nineteenth centuries, provides one such tale from the Napoleonic Wars. During one engagement, Midshipman Robert Sturges was killed by a cannon ball. Later, Sturges' ghost was reportedly seen haunting the cable tier (a compartment in the bow where the anchor cables were stored) and the midshipmen's berth, which "had such an effect that not one of the midshipman would stay below by himself."[29] During battle, the bodies of the dead were often thrown overboard rather than being kept until a funeral service could be performed. Such victims were likely to become ghosts for two reasons: their lives were cut short violently and they were not properly buried. Sailors abhorred the custom of throwing the dead overboard without burial rites. As he lay dying at Trafalgar, for example, Admiral Horatio Nelson expressed fear that his body would be quickly dumped into the sea. Addressing Thomas Masterman Hardy, captain of HMS *Victory*, Nelson pleaded, "Don't throw me overboard, Hardy!"[30] Nelson's status ensured that his body would not be subjected to such a fate, but the same did not hold true for thousands of others.

Sailors believed that the spirits of those who offended God or nature were often doomed to a life of endless wandering. Of these, the *Flying Dutchman* offers the best-known example. Samuel Taylor Coleridge's Ancient Mariner, who was fated to wander because he had offended the spirits of the deep by slaying an albatross, represents this maritime belief transplanted to literature.[31] Sailors, who lived with danger always present, were loathe to permit anyone aboard who might bring judgment down upon their vessel. Mariners took warning from the biblical story of Jonah, who committed a crime, fled aboard a ship, and caused the vessel to be afflicted with storms. Seamen referred to anyone who was thought to bring bad luck as a "Jonah," and such persons were ostracized.

In all of these cases, the spirit was stuck in a liminal phase, as Turner put it, "betwixt and between": no longer living, but not properly incorporated into the world of the dead.[32] Sailors, like their contemporaries ashore, feared such spirits. Midshipman Sturges' ghost, for example, terrified his shipmates even though it seemed to mean no harm. The chantey "The Ghostly Fishermen," well-known among nineteenth-century fishermen, contains a similar belief. In this case, the spirits of drowned sailors come aboard the vessel that was responsible for ramming and sinking their ship.

> Right o'er our rail came climbing, all silent, one by one,
> A dozen hardy sailors. Just wait till I am done.
> Their faces pale and sea-worn, all ghostly through the night,
> Each fellow took his station as if he had a right.
> They moved about together till land did heave in sight,
> Or rather, I should say so, the lighthouse threw its light;
> And then those ghostly sailors all to the rail as one,
> They vanished like the morning dew after the rising sun.[33]

Although these ghosts caused no harm, they nevertheless produced "a chilly dread" among the crew. Not all maritime spirits were benign. Sailors also feared the dead because their appearance signified disaster or death.[34] Sailors rounding the Cape of Good Hope dreaded the sight of the *Flying Dutchman*, for example, because its appearance was thought to mean that their own vessel might soon be wrecked. Whether destructive or benevolent, sailors feared visitations by the dead.

Fear of spirits upon the sea illustrates a noteworthy aspect of the maritime belief system. Normally, folk belief holds that the dead cannot cross water. Instead, water is supposed to trap spirits. Containers of water would not be placed in a room in which a corpse was laid out, for example, for fear that the spirit might become trapped.[35] The belief that water formed a barrier to the return of the dead resulted in several other folk practices. In Europe it was customary to pour a pitcher of water on the ground between the coffin and the deceased's house once the coffin had been taken outside at the start of the funeral procession. Ruth Richardson notes that funeral processions would cross water to prevent the spirit from returning.[36] The practice of burial on islands, widespread throughout the world, may be a cross-cultural reflection of the same belief.[37]

Since it was believed that water traps spirits, it at first seems strange that sailors feared the return of spirits from the deep. The answer to this apparent conundrum lies in another folk belief: spirits of the dead *can* cross water when they are aboard boats—an idea that dates back to ancient times. The best-known ancient example is probably Charon from Greek mythology, who ferried the souls of the dead across the rivers Acheron or Styx to Hades. Although the belief that dead souls traveled by boat is ancient, it was still current among mariners during the Age of Sail. Rather than remaining in one place, ghost ships from maritime lore traveled far and wide. The *Flying Dutchman*, although traditionally associated with the Cape of Good Hope, could be seen throughout the oceans of the world. While in the North Atlantic, for example, the crew of HMS *Hind* heard a mysterious voice wailing across the sea. According to Gardner, who witnessed this incident, "One fellow said, 'I'll be damned if we were off the Cape but I should think it was the Flying Dutchman.'" A shipmate reminded him that "he has got a roving commission and may cruise where he likes."[38]

A related belief held that witches, who like the dead were normally barred from crossing water, could do so in boats or other craft that mimicked the shape of a boat. In nineteenth-century England, children were taught not to leave eggshells unbroken after a meal, lest witches commandeer them. The poem "Egg-Shells" by Elizabeth Fleming, published around the beginning of the twentieth century, describes this belief.

> Oh, never leave your egg-shells unbroken in the cup;
> Think of us poor sailor-men and always smash them up,
> For witches come and find them and sail away to sea,
> And make a lot of misery for mariners like me.
>
> They take them to the sea-shore and set them on the tide-
> A broom-stick for a paddle is all they have to guide-
> And off they go to China or round the ports of Spain,
> To try and keep our sailing ships from coming home again.

They call up all the tempests from Davy Jones's store,
And blow us into waters where we haven't been before;
And when the masts are falling in splinters on the wrecks,
The witches climb the rigging ropes and dance upon the decks.

So never leave your egg-shells unbroken in the cup;
Think of us poor sailor-men and always smash them up;
For witches come and find them and sail away to sea,
And make a lot of misery for mariners like me.[39]

Legends of ghost ships such as the *Flying Dutchman* and the belief in witches putting to sea in eggshells illustrate the historical context in light of which ideas about corpses aboard ship must be viewed. Sailors believed that harmful spirits traveled the waters of the globe, searching for unwary vessels to attack.

Sailors likewise feared that spirits of the dead who were in the water would attempt to come aboard, either to cause harm or to use the vessel as a means of conveyance back to shore. In the example by Gardner cited above, the mysterious voice heard by the *Hind*'s crew turned out to belong to a sailor who had fallen overboard. A rescue boat was sent to pick him up, but its crew was suspicious that the man was actually a spirit attempting to trick them in order to get aboard their ship. They would not let him into the boat "until he had told his name and answered several ridiculous questions."[40] Beck provides another story that illustrates how sailors feared the return of ghosts.[41] This tale concerns the seal-hunting ship *North Star*. Sealing vessels operated by tying up to ice and sending hunting parties out onto the floes. In this case, inclement weather forced *North Star* to abandon seventy-five crewmen on the ice. When the vessel was finally able to return, it was found that all of those left behind had perished, but only seventy bodies were found. These were given proper burials. On a subsequent trip to the same place, ghosts of the five men whose bodies were never recovered were seen boarding the ship one night. Upon returning to port, *North Star*'s crew deserted. Word soon spread throughout the community, and no one would sign aboard the haunted vessel. The belief that ghosts seek access to vehicles so that they can be transported home prevailed upon land as well, and survives to this day as the contemporary legend "The Vanishing Hitchhiker."[42] Variations abound, but the basic story is that a driver picks up a lone hitchhiker late at night and drives her (the hitchhiker is usually female) home. Upon arrival, the driver discovers that the passenger has vanished. Investigation reveals that the hitchhiker had died in an automobile accident, usually at the location where she was picked up. The theme is a spirit doomed to wander, who can never quite make it home. Likewise, the contemporary legend "The Death Car" incorporates the same theme as the story of the ill-fated *North Star*.[43] In this case, a vehicle where a death has occurred is offered for sale at an unbelievably low price. The car turns out to have a terrible odor, scaring away would-be buyers.

Fear of the sea's restless dead explains why sailors believed that the burial at sea service was so necessary. To the maritime mind, the sea was alive with the spirits of unquiet dead, both on the surface and under the waves. Not all of these ghosts were malevolent, but all were feared. By performing the proper rites, sailors hoped to ensure that the dead would rest peacefully instead of returning to trouble the living. The burial at sea ceremony included numerous elements that were designed to separate the dead from the living and incorporate the deceased's spirit into the afterlife.

Proper Placement of the Dead

The burial at sea ritual, like other funeral ceremonies, functioned primarily as a rite of passage. As defined by Arnold Van Gennep, rites of passage refer to the rituals that accompany changes from one stage of life to another.[44] Scholars have long known that mortuary practices function as rites of passage that separate the dead from the living and incorporate the deceased into the afterlife. The proper rituals are necessary in order to keep the dead person's spirit from returning to haunt the living. As noted by scholars such as Van Gennep, Effie Bendann, and Richard P. Taylor, the belief that proper mortuary rituals are needed to prevent haunting seems to be universal.[45] In Western tradition, the idea dates back at least to Homeric Greece, and remained current through the medieval period.[46] Maritime lore during the Age of Sail, which grew out of earlier Western traditions, was replete with tales of unquiet spirits.[47] Sailors had no wish to add to the number of restless spirits in the depths. They therefore viewed a proper burial service as a critical deterrent to the return of the dead.

The burial at sea service was a ritual that few non-mariners ever witnessed, but one whose elements they would have instantly recognized if they had. Structurally, burial at sea was simply the funeral service used on land adapted to a maritime setting. Most of the elements in the ritual—preparing the corpse, transporting it to the grave site, and holding a graveside service—occurred in the same order as on land. Nevertheless, the ritual also included unique elements that reflected both the maritime environment where the ceremony took place and the unique traditions and beliefs of the maritime folk group.

As on land, the first step in the ritual was to prepare the body for burial. This process began with washing the body. Washing prior to burial is a gesture of respect, but also has symbolic functions. Many cultures view dead bodies as unclean objects. A corpse is an empty shell left behind once the spirit departs, a part of the person still present in the physical world. As such, it represents the deceased in a liminal state, neither living nor properly incorporated into the realm of the dead. Objects in liminal states are sources of pollution and are therefore dangerous to the community.[48] The symbolic reason for washing a dead body is to prevent pollution from spreading to other members of the group. On land, female relatives of the deceased were usually responsible for preparing the body.[49] In the largely male society aboard ship, this was not usually possible. Instead, accounts of burial at sea show that the washing of the body of a deceased sailor was done by his messmates. In *White Jacket: or, The World in a Man-of-War*, for example, Melville describes drawing a bucket of sea water to bathe his dead messmate.[50] The messmates, who were typically the deceased's closest friends aboard ship, took the place of the closest friends and relatives on land. The performance of washing by the deceased's messmates highlights the fact that in the maritime worldview, a man's messmates were considered his closest family. This fact is further illustrated by a common maritime euphemism for death. When a sailor died, it was said that he "lost the number of his mess." As we will see, the departed's messmates performed the role of family throughout the funeral ritual.

After bathing, the dead sailor was dressed. Like washing, the deceased's messmates performed this task. In Perry's account quoted earlier in this chapter, the deceased was dressed in his best suit of clothing. Other accounts make it clear that this was the usual practice. In *White Jacket*, the dead sailor was dressed in a "white frock, trowsers, and neckerchief," which sounds like the shore-going rig of a man-of-war's man.[51] The custom of burying dead sailors in their best clothes mirrors traditional practices on land; even today, it remains customary for the dead to be formally attired. The use of formal clothing is an important aspect of the burial ritual because it marks a rite of separation of the dead from the living. Funeral rites take both the living and the dead from the world of the profane to the realm of the sacred. According to Leach, shifts from the profane to the sacred are typically accompanied by the wearing of formal attire.[52] Dressing the corpse formally, and the use of formal attire by mourners as well, represents another stage in the proper placement of the dead.

With the corpse washed and dressed, the next step was to place the body into some sort of container. By the late seventeenth century, coffins had come into general use on land.[53] Aboard ship, however, coffins were typically reserved for high-status individuals such as officers, well-to-do merchants, and ship owners. When the captain of HMS *Berwick* died in the Mediterranean in 1798, for example, the carpenter constructed a coffin for him.[54] I know of no accounts from the Age of Sail that mention common sailors being buried at sea in coffins, though references were found to merchants or other elites being granted the privilege. Instead of wooden coffins, most sailors were simply wrapped in shrouds. Shrouds had been used on land for the burial of most people until the late seventeenth century, so their use aboard ship was simply the continuation of another land-based tradition. A sailor's shroud might consist simply of a spare piece of canvas, as described by Perry above. Pieces of old sails were also used. The most popular reference, however, is to shrouding the dead seaman inside his own hammock. Hammocks had been a common form of bedding for sailors since the seventeenth century, especially aboard naval vessels, which had large crews and limited sleeping space. In addition to being a practical solution to the need for a shroud, hammocks were likely employed for burial for two other reasons. First, many sailors were superstitious of wearing a dead man's clothes, and it would be natural for this taboo to be applied to a deceased person's hammock as well. Also, the hammock would have been seen as an appropriate burial shroud because of its association with sleeping. Sleep was a popular metaphor for death, especially in the nineteenth century. Gravemarkers in the shape of beds and inscriptions describing the person as "asleep" were common during that time.[55] Sailors also thought of their hammocks as their own private space, a place of comfort and repose, as illustrated by a description in Sam Noble's autobiography. After burying a shipmate on the island of St. Helena, Noble states "we marched away, leaving our shipmate to his long, last sleep in a little hollow of the hill (not unlike a hammock), encompassed on all sides by the broad waters of the Atlantic."[56] Noble's description makes clear the congruence in the maritime mind between sleeping in one's hammock and sleeping in death. It also shows that the hammock was considered a proper place for a sailor to rest until the Resurrection.

The maritime environment required the use of one item that was not necessary on land. In order for the body to reach its proper resting place on the seabed, it had to be weighted down. Two round cannon shot, placed at the foot of the corpse, were the classic weights used for sea burial. During the Age of Sail, it was common for merchant vessels as well as naval ones to carry cannon, so cannon balls would have been found on most ships of the period. In the absence of cannon balls, any heavy object would do. Perry recorded the use of pieces of discarded iron shackles.[57] Other forms of weights were more exotic. For example, the coffin of American naval Lieutenant William Barron, who was killed by the bursting of a cannon aboard USS *Boston*, was weighted with a piece of the gun that had killed him.[58]

The manner of employing weights to bury bodies at sea contributed to the symbolic separation of the dead from the living. Placing the weights at the foot of the corpse would have made the body sink feet first. This seems to be a maritime adaptation of a rite of separation used on land. It was customary in Anglo-American funerary practice to always keep the corpse facing away from its former dwelling as it was being taken to the cemetery.[59] The corpse was always carried out of the house feet first, an orientation that remained the same during the trip to the cemetery. This practice symbolized the one-way nature of the corpse's voyage. In addition to providing symbolic separation of the corpse from its former home and family, the custom was thought to prevent the deceased's spirit from being able to find its way back to its former home. Placing weights at the foot of the corpse in the burial at sea ritual served the same purpose. Weighted at the feet, the corpse would sink feet first, with the head facing outward and away from the vessel. As in the funeral procession on land, the dead would not be able to "see" his former abode, making it less likely that his ghost could return. It may be significant that James Hales' monument shows his body being lowered feet first. If so, this would indicate that the feet-first practice for burial at sea existed at least as far back as the late sixteenth century. In this case, however, it may simply be due to artistic license on the part of the sculptor.

After the shroud was weighted, it was time to sew it up. On land, the coffin lid formed one of the most solid barriers of separation between the living and the dead.[60] A hammock, which lacked the solidity of wood, did not form as substantial a barrier as a coffin. Nevertheless, there is evidence that mariners tried to use the hammock to mask the corpse. Hall stated that it was customary for extra clothes and bedding to be placed inside the shroud before it was sewn up, "apparently to prevent the form being too much seen."[61] Making the shroud look less like a human body was another way of emphasizing the increasing separation between the dead and the living.

Sewing the body in its shroud was usually done by the sail maker or his mates, who sometimes took the last stitch through the nose of the deceased. Various explanations have been advanced regarding the origin and meaning of this custom. G. P. Bradley believed that the tradition derived from the Norse practice of burying bodies with wooden stakes through their breasts in order to prevent the corpse from coming back to life.[62] This practice is probably related to the belief that revenants such as vampires could be laid to rest by driving a stake through the body.[63] Bradley noted a similar tradition among Arab sailors, who would break the bones of a deceased shipmate before putting the body over the side in order to prevent the person's ghost from returning to the ship.[64] I am not suggesting here that the custom practiced by Anglo-American sailors in the Age of Sail can be traced directly to either the Norse or Arab traditions, but that the practices had a similar meaning. All three seem designed to prevent the return of the spirit. In *White Jacket*, two old salts debate the advantages and disadvantages of the nasal stitch.[65] One holds the view that the stitch needs to be taken in order for the dead to rest peacefully. His companion, on the other hand, argues that the dead do not like the stitch through their noses, and that doing so will cause the deceased's ghost to return and haunt the ship. Although Melville included the discussion of the nasal stitch to illustrate the barbarity of the tradition and put forth his view that it should be stopped, it nonetheless seems likely that he has touched upon the main themes involved with the issue. Some saw it as a necessary practice in order to prevent the dead from returning while others believed that the custom itself caused hauntings.

The nasal stitch likely served both practical and symbolic purposes.

On the one hand, the pain of the needle would revive a person who appeared to be dead but who might really only be unconscious. During the nineteenth century, the fear of being buried alive was common in England and America.[66] One of the reasons for conducting a wake or other vigil with the corpse prior to burial was to make sure that the person actually was dead. The term "wake" itself comes from the idea that if the person was not dead, the lights and loud noises that accompanied the proceedings would cause the person to awaken. At the same time, it was believed that the commotion of the wake would help frighten away evil spirits. Like wakes on land, the last stitch probably served dual functions: a practical one intended to ensure that the person really was dead and a symbolic one whose purpose was to prevent the dead from walking.

Once the body had been sewn inside its hammock, it was customary to cover it with the national flag. On modern naval vessels, this is done to show that the person died in the service of his or her country.[67] It is clear, however, that in the days of sail the custom was not limited to warships. Perry recorded the practice aboard the *Continental*, and it is also known from English civilian vessels.[68] In addition to serving as a mark of respect, the use of the flag performed the same function as the pall on land. In both cases, covering the corpse provided another boundary layer between the living and the dead. As such, this practice continued the process of separating the deceased from his former shipmates.

On shore, after the preparation of the body for burial was complete, it was customary for it to lie at rest for a period before burial. The body was usually laid out in the deceased's home, typically in the front room or parlor. The length of time before the funeral varied, but was usually only a few days and rarely as long as a week.[69] During this time, family and friends could gather to pay last respects to the deceased. It was also customary for a family member or friend to conduct an all-night vigil with the body. Candles were burned throughout the night, as it was generally believed that light helped deter harmful spirits.[70] For high-status individuals such as royalty or state officials, lying in state might take place at a cathedral or government building and the period might be as long as a week. During this time, those who wished could visit and pay their respects to the deceased.

Aboard ship, the period before burial mirrored the social structure on land. The bodies of common sailors were usually taken up to the main deck and placed immediately abaft the mainmast to await burial.[71] Having the body in the open air on deck would be agreeable because it would allow the deceased's spirit to fly away from the body. On land, it was customary for a window to be left open in the room of the house where the body lay. The door to the room was also kept open. It was considered bad luck to close the door or window, because that might allow the dead person's spirit to become trapped in the house.[72] For sailors who grew up observing this custom on land, the deck of the ship would no doubt be seen as the best location to place the corpse before burial, because having it in the open air would fulfill the need the give the spirit access to depart. It is also likely that sailors did not want a dead body kept belowdecks in their sleeping area. It was also customary aboard ship for one or more of the deceased's messmates or watchmates to stay with the body until time for the funeral. Once again, the messmates, the people closest to the deceased, fulfilled the function performed by family and close friends ashore.

Unlike on land, however, the period of waiting before burial was usually much shorter at sea. In most cases, burial services were conducted within twenty-four hours of the person's death. There were several reasons for this. As already discussed, sailors had a superstition against having a corpse on board and would have wanted to conduct the funeral as quickly as possible. In addition, the lack of means for preservation would have prevented keeping the corpse for a long period before odors associated with decay became intolerable. Finally, there was no reason for an extended period of visitation, because the relatively small population aboard ship would not need a lengthy period in order to pay last respects and relatives would not need time to travel from distant places.

Exceptions to the rules of having a short lying-in-state period and keeping the body on deck sometimes occurred in the cases of high-status individuals. As on land, high-status persons were sometimes afforded lengthier periods of waiting before the funeral. When the captain of James Gardner's ship died in the Mediterranean, the body was laid out in the great cabin at the stern of the ship. This was an area usually off limits to ordinary sailors. In this case, however, an exception was made.

> The ship's company paid respect to his memory; they divided their black silk handkerchiefs, and wore one part round their hats and the other round their arms, and requested they might see the corpse before the interment; which request was granted, and they walked

through the cabin in ranks and bowed to the coffin while passing, and most of them in tears—a sight truly impressive.[73]

The captain's funeral, with black mourning emblems, coffin, and parade of visitors, mirrored those of important personages on land.

The tolling of the ship's bell and bosun's call signaled all hands that it was time to bury the dead. On land, the funeral began with a procession from the deceased's house to the churchyard or cemetery. The deceased's house and the houses of neighbors were often decorated in black as symbols of mourning. Mourning decorations served to highlight the reversal of the normal order. At sea, symbolic reversals were performed as well. The ship would be stopped for the burial service, which was a reversal of the normal order because a ship at sea was usually moving. The vessel's yards would be cockbilled, meaning that some would have their ends tilted up while others were tilted down. Seamen had an extreme dislike for yards not being in perfect horizontal trim, and any degree of tilting looked unseamanlike to the nautical mind. To deliberately cockbill the yards was thus an important deviation that contrasted sharply with ordinary practice. Finally, the most widely recognized symbolic reversal was to fly the flag at half mast. All of these things emphasized the funeral as an event that was not part of a ship's ordinary routine. It was a period of sacred time.

Funeral processions performed a crucial role in the symbolic separation of the dead from the living. Richardson describes some of the ways that funeral processions fulfilled this function.[74] Processions sometimes took circuitous routes to the graveyard in hopes that the spirit would not be able to find its way back to haunt its former abode. In addition, stops were sometimes made at thresholds such as crossroads and bridges. Prayers and songs would be performed at these locations before the procession continued on its way. The object of such rituals was to seal these thresholds so that the spirit would not be able to cross back over them. Aboard ship, however, it was not possible to conduct a proper funeral procession due to space limitations and lack of distance between the deceased's "home" and place of burial. Therefore, an important element was missing from the funeral service as performed at sea. As discussed below, the inability to conduct a procession and create barriers against the return of the spirit seems to have contributed to a sense of uneasiness among sailors regarding sea burial.

On land, the Order of Burial prescribed by the *Book of Common Prayer* began with the priest meeting the funeral procession at the lych gate, a covered shelter at the entrance to the churchyard. The maritime equivalent of this was for the chaplain, captain, or other officer who was to perform the service to come out onto the quarterdeck when the procession arrived at the lee gangway. During the service, the placement of personnel corresponded to the social hierarchy aboard ship. The crew gathered in the waist or on the booms. Officers stood on the quarterdeck, forbidden territory for ordinary sailors unless they had duties there. Officers and crew showed respect for the deceased by removing their hats. As in other parts of the burial at sea ritual, the dead sailor's messmates played the part of the family, flanking the body as it lay at the ship's side awaiting burial. The service was performed by the ship's chaplain, if the vessel carried one, or by the captain or another officer if it did not.[75]

The service began as on land, usually with the reading of John 11:25–26, Job 19:25–27, I Timothy 6:7 and Job 1:21. This was followed by one or both of Psalms 39 and 90, and a passage from I Corinthians chapter 15. The only difference in the service as performed at sea came during the committal. On land, the committal stated:

> Forasmuch as it hath pleased Almighty God of his great mercy to take unto himself the soul of our dear brother here departed: we therefore commit his body to the ground, earth to earth, ashes to ashes, dust to dust, in sure and certain hope of resurrection to eternal life, through our Lord Jesus Christ, who shall change our vile body that it may be like to his glorious body, according to the mighty working, whereby he is able to subdue all things to himself.[76]

The maritime version of the committal addressed the fact that the body would rest under the waves instead of being buried in the earth:

> Forasmuch as it hath pleased Almighty God of his great mercy to take unto himself the soul of our dear brother here departed: we therefore commit his body to the Deep, to be turned into corruption, looking for the resurrection of the body, (when the sea shall give up her dead,) and the life of the world to come, through our Lord Jesus Christ; who at his coming shall change our vile body, that it may be like his glorious body, according to the mighty working, whereby he is able to subdue all things to himself.[77]

It is not known when sailors first started to substitute this version for the original passage. The above wording was formalized in the 1662 edition of the *Book of Common Prayer*, the first edition of the prayer book to contain a section of prayers specifically for use at sea. It is probable, however, that the phrase "commit his body to the deep" began as a folk process aboard ship prior to its formal adoption by the Church of England.

As the committal was read, the deceased's shipmates tilted the board or grating and the corpse slid feet first into the sea. This was the climactic moment of the ritual. The sound of the shrouded corpse striking the water followed by the sight of it sinking into the depths signified that the body had breached the final threshold and become part of the underworld. Invariably this caused a stir of emotion among onlookers. According to Englishman Robert Young, who witnessed a burial at sea while traveling to Australia in 1853, "a sudden splash in the water produced a powerful thrill in many a heart."[78] American seaman William Leggett also noted the importance of the sound of the splash: "a splash was heard—a deep silence succeeded."[79] Hall commented that aboard Royal Navy vessels the entire grating was sometimes pushed overboard, having been first tethered to the side of the vessel by a length of rope. The reason for doing this is unclear; Hall thought that "there is something solemn, as well as startling, in the sudden splash, followed by the sound of the grating as it is towed along under the main-chains."[80] Samuel Samuels described the moment: "A few ripples from the splash and a few bubbles from the broken water, and all was over."[81] Samuels' words indicate the finality of the body sinking. Seeing the body sink was a powerful experience because it brought home the realization that the person was truly gone. It was also a time of tension, because things could still go wrong. If the body had not been properly weighted, it would float instead of sink. The account of one West Indian captain, who forgot to properly weight down a body, illustrates the distress that this caused among sailors.

> Well, after they let him go he would not go to the bottom. He float. The men kept watching and he kept going and we watched him a while and he was gone. We could do nothing else. That's how he goes.... Whenever you are going to bury a man out at sea you must put a sinker on him and when you let him go he goes. It doesn't matter if he make bottom or where he make. You must put a sinker on

him. We could see him after we gave way to go and that was wrong. We should have put a sinker on him.[82]

This story shows how concerned sailors were that the body penetrate the surface of the sea. Regardless of its final resting position, sailors needed to see that their shipmate had crossed this final threshold, as bodies that floated rather than sank were likely to become restless dead.

After the body was given to the sea, the remainder of the funeral service continued as on land. At the conclusion, all hands were dismissed, yards straightened, and the vessel continued on its way. As Perry's description shows, captains could be quick to get underway again, especially when they had a fair wind. Given the sailors' dread of corpses aboard ship and the fear of lingering at a grave site, it is probable that most sailors shared this sentiment. On land, a meal at the deceased's house following the funeral service typically served as the final act of the ritual. The rigid structure of shipboard life afforded no time for such a practice. The ship's day was divided into standardized periods (watches), and all meals took place at set times. A funeral was not considered an occasion worthy of changing the structure of the ship's day. However, most accounts mention that the ceremony occurred in the morning or shortly before noon. Noon represented the end of the morning watch, and it was the time when sailors were traditionally fed dinner, the main meal of the day. Therefore, in the case of funerals conducted in the morning, sailors would be sitting down to a meal shortly after the conclusion of the ceremony simply as a matter of ordinary practice. Like the funeral meal ashore, this would give the sailors time to reflect on the ceremony and the deceased. As such, the meal would serve as another event that helped to remove the dead from his former world and allow the shipmates to continue the process of creating a new social order.

There was one final aspect to the burial at sea ritual. Aboard ship it was customary to hold an auction of a dead sailor's clothing and other possessions. This auction was usually conducted several days after the funeral, but was sometimes done immediately following death.[83] In cases where a body was present and was given a burial at sea, the accounts almost always describe the auction as taking place between one and three days after the funeral. As such, the auction served as a final part of the burial at sea ritual by bringing closure to the event of the man's death. The dead man's possessions were a constant reminder of a person who was no longer present.

Removing such things from the possession of the dead man and giving them to new owners served as a final act of separation between the dead and the living. When the auction was complete, the dead sailor no longer owned anything aboard ship. From that point on, the deceased existed only in memories. Some of these memories were encapsulated in the dead man's former possessions. Owning one of these, then, was one way of helping to keep the deceased's memory alive.

The auction illustrates another aspect of the maritime worldview. Many accounts state that at these auctions it was customary for sailors to offer more money than items were actually worth.[84] Sailors knew that the proceeds from the auction would be given to the deceased's family at the conclusion of the voyage. By paying extra for the deceased's possessions, they help ease the financial burden on a family that had most likely lost its main source of income. Like contributing money to raise a memorial, this was another way that the maritime folk group looked out for its members.

The Sea: Boundary or Threshold?

Once the body had sunk beneath the waves, the dead sailor should have been properly incorporated into the realm of the dead, enjoying the delights of Fiddler's Green if he had been a good person, or keeping company with Davy Jones if he had not.[85] Unfortunately, performing the proper burial rites did not always ensure that the dead would rest peacefully. In Perry's story, Louie's shipmates gave him a proper burial. Days later, however, several crew members reported seeing Louie's ghost. Beck provides additional examples of this phenomenon.[86] In one case, the ghost of an English captain haunted his former ship despite having received a proper burial. Two other vessels were haunted by the spirits of former owners, who moved items around and tangled rigging lines.

The belief that even those who had received proper burials could return was likely due to the fact that several aspects of the maritime environment prevented the creation of proper boundaries between the living and the dead. Richardson emphasizes that the funeral ritual was designed to turn thresholds into boundaries so that the dead could not return.[87] In Richardson's analysis, two thresholds were especially significant. The first was the coffin lid, which was nailed shut, usually at the deceased's home prior to the funeral procession. Nailing the lid shut turned the coffin into a permanent boundary between the living and the dead. Later, the grave itself became the final boundary when it was filled with earth. This was done at the end of the service, and marked the final separation between the deceased's former life and his or her new home in the realm of the dead. In the minds of the living, the covering of earth over the coffin represented an impenetrable barrier that would keep the dead from returning.

During burial at sea, however, neither of these thresholds could be turned into impenetrable boundaries. The sound of coffin nails being driven home possessed a note of finality that could never be achieved when sewing a body into a hammock. This may explain why coffins were utilized for burial at sea in some situations. More importantly, the sea itself was not as good a boundary as a layer of solid earth. Symbolically, the sea is more of a threshold than a boundary. Although the sea divides nations, it also serves as a highway for transport and commerce. No one understood this better than mariners, who made their living on this highway. As previously discussed, the spirits of the dead could travel across the sea when aboard vessels. In addition to allowing the horizontal movements of spirits across its surface, the permeable nature of water makes the sea conducive to vertical connections between the upper world on the surface and the underworld in the depths. For this reason, folklore holds that water serves as a portal between the realms of the living and the dead.[88]

Vertical connections between the world of the living and that of the dead form a key aspect of ghost lore. Connections between the physical and spiritual worlds almost always take place through some sort of portal, an idea that dates back thousands of years. In the *Odyssey*, Odysseus and his men summon the spirits of Hades by performing sacrifices at the mouth of a cave that leads to the underworld. The cave serves as a portal that the dead use to enter the world of the living. Similarly, staircases serve as the foci for action in haunted house stories. Vertical portals such as caves and staircases physically connect spaces that are on different levels, and allow passage between those levels. Therefore, they are natural conduits for the living to enter the realm of the dead and vice versa. Vertical connectors serve an important symbolic function as well. A person or being traveling along a vertical connector exists in a liminal state, neither on one level nor the other. This helps to explain why staircases serve as a locus of action in haunted house stories; ghosts, which are seen as liminal spirits trapped between worlds, are naturally associated with a physical structure that serves as a connector between two locations.[89]

In maritime lore, two gateways between the surface and the deep stand out: the ship's anchor cables and the shoreline. Objects, humans, and spirits could move back and forth between the upper world and underworld via both of these portals. Ross has examined the ways in which anchor cables served to connect the sky, the surface, and the underworld. Miceal Ross demonstrates that the idea of the anchor as a portal to the depths can be traced back to medieval legends. The earliest tales concerned the theme of undersea creatures such as mermaids luring men down into the depths via anchor cables. However, the connection worked both ways: not only could sailors go down the cables, but denizens of the underworld could also travel up them to the world above.[90] It is clear that the idea of the anchor as a connection to the depths existed in maritime lore during the Age of Sail. In Perry's account, for example, it is significant that the seaman's ghost was seen perched on the cathead. The cathead was the timber where an anchor was secured after being hoisted out of the water. In Gardner's tale, the cable tier was one of the locations haunted by Sturges' ghost. The cable tier, located in the bow of the vessel, was used for storing the anchor cables. Both the cathead and the cable tier served as physical and symbolic portals between the vessel and the deep. It would be natural for sailors to associate spirits traveling up the anchor cable from the depths with these two locations.

The second gateway between the underworld and the surface was the shoreline. Astrid Lindenlauf contends that the ancient Greeks, among other cultures, viewed the sea as a safe place for the disposal of certain objects. This was because the sea was viewed as a "place of no return" that would keep the things that were put into it.[91] I agree with Lindenlauf's argument but believe that it can be taken further. In certain cases, the sea does keep things that are deposited in it. To cite a tragic example, the bodies of those lost at sea are usually never seen again, nor are their resting places known. However, the sea is not always the final resting place for things that enter it.

Far from keeping everything that is deposited within it, the sea has a tendency to send things back. As anyone who has ever walked along a beach knows, the edge of the sea forms a threshold where objects pass back and forth between the depths and the land. Sailors and coastal residents were intimately familiar with the things that washed ashore, including timbers from wrecked vessels, sailors' personal possessions, and the corpses of mariners themselves. The way that this provided symbolic confirmation of loss has already been discussed. It seems likely that the permeable nature of the sea resulted in the uneasiness of the maritime mind regarding sea burial. The burial at sea ritual was designed to emphasize the boundaries between the living and the dead, but a watery grave did not offer the comforting solidity of earth. Although the burial at sea ritual represented an attempt to properly place the dead and erect barriers against the return of spirits, the sea remained a threshold from which the dead could sometimes return.

Because the sea offered no stable grave, sailors were never entirely comfortable with it as a final resting place. As a grave, sailors viewed the sea in two contradictory ways. On the one hand, the sea was considered to be the proper resting place for sailors and vessels. This was typically the case when a proper burial service was performed or when a vessel had completed its useful life. Reminiscing about shipmates who had been buried beneath the waves, Sam Noble described the sea as "the natural sepulchre of the sailor."[92] American sailor Richard Henry Dana agreed. Writing of one former shipmate in *Two Years Before the Mast*, Dana declared, "at least he died as a sailor—he died on board ship."[93] These sentiments seem to be echoed on a memorial for North Carolina sailor Henry Bailyss Howard, who "died and was buried at Sea" in 1851 at age twenty-one.[94] Howard's gravestone states that "He loved the sea 'twas the home of his choice" (figure 4.1). The sea was thus a fitting, although untimely, place for Howard to rest.

On the other hand, the sea was also seen as an undesirable place to spend eternity. Sailors were well aware of what happened to bodies buried at sea. Sewing the corpse up in a hammock was one way of mitigating this problem, but sailors knew that such measures would not last for long. The wording of the Committal used during the burial at sea service acknowledges that the body would be "turned into corruption"—in the maritime case, violated by the effects of water and marine life—but also assured mariners that they would be made whole again at the coming of the savior. Sailors, never particularly religious, remained uneasy.

To make matters worse, the sea was home to a host of beings known to torment the living. Cursed spirits and malicious witches roamed the oceans. Victims of shipwrecks, men lost overboard, and those whose bodies were heaved into the sea without service due to plague or in the heat

Figure 4.1. Gravestone of Henry Howard, who was buried at sea in 1851. Oakdale Cemetery, Wilmington, NC. Photo by author.

of battle never received proper burials. As a result, their ghosts were likely to return. Performing the proper burial service reduced the chance that the dead would walk. Even proper burial, however, was no guarantee. This was largely due to the nature of the maritime environment. Unlike on land, aboard ship it was not possible to perform a funeral procession. Therefore, the maritime service lacked one crucial source of separation. Lack of a procession meant that there were no twists and turns to confuse a spirit that sought to return. Anchor cables, which were viewed as conduits connecting the upper world with the underworld, also facilitated the passage of spirits. It was not only sailors aboard vessels at sea who had to fear the return of ghosts. At the shoreline, tides and storms frequently returned things that had been sunk in the depths.

To the maritime mind, the sea could be "the natural sepulchre of the sailor" provided that the proper forms were observed. Despite the best intentions of mariners, however, the sea remained an untrustworthy grave. The nature of the sea itself prevented a permanent boundary between the quick and the dead. As they roamed the salt seas, mariners were always aware that their passage was marked, and could be interrupted, by the spirits of thousands of shipmates who slumbered restlessly in watery graves.

Conclusions

The burial at sea ritual contained a number of processes designed to separate and place the dead. As noted by Richardson, funeral rites can be viewed as a succession of stages that move both corpse and spirit across a series of thresholds.[95] At various points throughout the funeral, rituals are performed to turn the thresholds into boundaries, thus preventing the return of the spirit. The burial at sea service practiced aboard English and American ships during the Age of Sail was an adaptation of the English funeral service used on land. As such, it also included threshold symbolism. Some thresholds were the same as those on land, while others were unique to the maritime environment. At sea, unfortunately, thresholds could not be turned into permanent boundaries. Because of this, spirits of the dead sometimes returned even after receiving the proper rites.

Burial at sea also functioned as a stage for the performance of maritime group values. A man's messmates, his closest friends, served as proxy family. Sailors took care of the group by contributing money to the families of men who died at sea. This sometimes took the form of purchasing the deceased's clothing at artificially high prices.

For those buried at sea, commemoration did not end when the body slipped beneath the waves. Like the deceased's shipmates, maritime communities mourned the loss of those who were committed to the deep. In addition, maritime communities struggled with the problem of how to cope when men were lost at sea and never received a burial or were buried in distant lands far from home. As demonstrated in this chapter, the sea was not always thought of as an adequate grave. Aboard ship, the burial at sea ritual served as the best way to try to lay the dead to rest properly. On land, maritime communities created their own traditions for dealing with this problem. The creation of memorials to honor those who never returned is the subject of the next chapter.

5
"Was Never Since Heard Of"

REMEMBERING THE MISSING

In the middle of the nineteenth century, Paul and Louisa Ewer erected an obelisk in New Bedford's Rural Cemetery to commemorate their son, Walter (figure 5.1). Its inscription reads:

SACRED
to the memory of
WALTER C.
Only son of
Paul & Louisa G.
EWER
born Aug. 31 1827
who was lost at sea
from Brig Zoroaster
on her passage to
California
Lat 7° 8' North
Long 114° 24' West
March 18, 1850
Aged 22 yrs 7 mos.
and 18 days

He sleeps beneath the blue lone sea
He lies where pearls lie deep
He was the loved of all: yet none
O'er his low bed may weep.[1]

A separate line at the top emphasizes the fact that Walter's body is not present in the grave: "The sea his body, Heaven his spirit holds." In choosing their son's memorial, the Ewers expressed feelings prevalent both in the maritime folk group and in the wider Anglo-American culture of which it was a part. Both the obelisk shape and the motif of the finger pointing heavenward, which symbolized the soul's ascent to its joyful home, were common in mid-nineteenth-century cemeteries. At the same time, the story of Walter's loss, including details such as the name of the vessel and the latitude and longitude where death occurred, illustrates prevailing maritime beliefs about memorialization.

In particular, the emphasis on the absent body highlights a problem that was endemic in maritime society: how to memorialize those who never returned from the sea. Finding ways to commemorate the missing has been a problem for as long as humans have gone down to the sea in ships. On the Baltic island of Gotland, four Swedish Vikings left a runestone commemorating their travels far to the south, in what is now the Ukraine. The monument states that they had also "raised stones in memory of Hrafn," who lost his life in the dangerous cataract Aïfor, whose names translates as "ever fierce, ever noisy, or impassable" on the Dnieper River.[2] Numerous other runestones from Sweden memorialize Vikings who never returned from their southern travels. Others commemorate men who lost their lives closer to home in the Baltic. To quote only one other example, "Sigrid had this stone raised for her husband Svein. He sailed often to Semgali with his fine ship round Domesnes."[3] Sigrid's words, from a wife to her husband, foreshadow the sentiment expressed by many English and American sailors' widows a millennium later.

Despite the similarities of English and American memorials to their predecessors, there is no direct cultural continuity. Rather, mariners in the Age of Sail faced a problem as ancient as seafaring itself, and dealt with it in some of the same ways as their predecessors. Other aspects, however, were unique to their time and place and to the group traditions of English and American maritime culture in the Age of Sail.

Commemorating the missing was not unique to maritime communities. For centuries, soldiers, pilgrims, and other travelers had died and been buried far from home. Nevertheless, with the increase in global seafaring, the problem of memorializing absent loved ones became prevalent to a much larger degree in maritime communities than in shore-based populations. Over 40 percent of the memorials recorded by the survey

Figure 5.1. Obelisk for lost sailor Walter Ewer. AAMMD #308, Rural Cemetery, New Bedford, MA. Photo by author.

commemorate mariners whose bodies are not present at the location of the memorial. As discussed in the preceding chapter, most of those who died at sea were buried there. Likewise, the bodies of sailors who died in foreign ports were rarely returned home for burial. When the deceased was given a burial service, the family at least took some comfort in the knowledge that the proper ritual had been performed. The bodies of those lost at sea, however, were seldom recovered and thus rarely received funerals.

Memorials for the Missing

Cenotaphs had existed in various cultures since ancient times, but in English and American maritime culture a marked increase in memorials for missing sailors took place beginning in the second half of the eighteenth century. The earliest such memorial recorded by the survey is the gravestone of Captain John Hyer in Copp's Hill Burying Ground in Boston (figure 5.2).

>In memory of Capt. JOHN HYER
>Who Died at Cape Franceway,
>March 8th 1742/3 in y^e
>46th Year of his Age.
>
>Here lyes ye Body of two of
>the children of Capt. JOHN
>& Mrs SARAH HYER
>
>SARAH Died Novr 11th 1743
>in ye 13 Year of her Age.
>SAGE Aged 7 Months
>Died Augst 30 1734.[4]

Visually, nothing sets the Hyer stone apart from any of the other monuments at Copp's Hill. Death's head and crossbones motifs were common in Boston during the mid-eighteenth century. By memorializing a person whose body was not present in the grave, however, the Hyer stone marks a new attitude toward maritime dead. This shift in attitude is demonstrated by the introductory phrases employed. The phrase "in memory of" for Captain Hyer, contrasted with the use of "here lyes ye Body" for his two children, emphasizes the fact that the captain's remains are not present in the grave. Although the mid-eighteenth century saw the emergence of absent-body commemoration in Anglo-American maritime culture, memorials for the missing were not common at that time. All follow the same pattern as the Hyer gravestone. Joseph Richards, for example, who "died at Port Mahone" is remembered on his father's gravestone, located not far from the Hyer stone in Boston's Copp's Hill.[5] Richards' death in January 1742 was actually two months before Hyer's, but as discussed below, there is reason to believe that his commemoration did not occur until several years later. Captain John Dennis of Newport, Rhode Island,

Figure 5.2. An early memorial for an absent sailor: the gravestone of Captain John Hyer, Copp's Hill, Boston, MA. Photo by author.

was remembered with a melancholy epitaph stating that after sailing from Newport in 1756 he "was never since heard of, doubtless made his exit in the watery element."[6] Further implications of this phrasing will be discussed later in this chapter. William Palmer, who was lost at Dublin in 1759, was the earliest absent-body gravestone recorded in the United Kingdom.[7] Each of these memorials commemorate lost mariners, but do so at graves containing the bodies of other family members.

The waning years of the eighteenth century witnessed a marked increase in the number of memorials dedicated to sailors who were lost or buried far away. This increase was first noted on memorials dating to the 1790s. Although the overall number of memorials recorded from that decade remained small, nearly half were dedicated to missing sailors. From the 1790s on, a substantial number of memorials to absent sailors were erected in every decade through the end of the nineteenth century. This holds true for both England and the United States, although in England there were fewer such memorials through the first three decades of the nineteenth century. However, this seems to reflect the fact that fewer memorials are preserved in England than in the United States until the second quarter of the nineteenth century rather than a true difference in mortuary practice. The ratio of empty graves in England is comparable to the ratio of such graves in the United States. It appears, then, that the phenomenon of memorializing sailors who were lost at sea or who died and were buried far away became common practice in maritime communities in both England and the United States around the turn of the nineteenth century. Once the practice became a tradition, it continued steadily until the end of the Age of Sail. Moreover, twentieth-century memorials recorded by the survey, including a number from the 1980s and 1990s, show that the tradition of memorializing lost sailors remains strong in the present day.

The developed tradition of commemoration for missing sailors took several forms. When the lost sailor was memorialized with an actual grave, it was most common for them to be commemorated on the gravestones of other family members. In such cases, the name of the lost was usually added to an existing gravestone. The Newman family stone at Copp's Hill in Boston typifies this form of absent commemoration.[8] The gravestone was originally erected for Captain Robert Newman, who died in 1806. Captain Newman's name, date of death, and age are recorded near the top of the stone, followed by a long epitaph that takes up most of the front side. Added to the very bottom of the stone is a two-line listing for another Captain Robert Newman, who died at sea in 1816. The age at death, as well as the name, suggests that he was the son of the grave's original occupant. In addition, the gravestone records the death of another son, William, who died at Martinique in 1817. In this case, however, there was no more room on the front of the stone, so William's commemoration was inscribed on the back. The dates of death and the use of space on the Newman stone and many similar examples indicate that adding the names of lost mariners to existing family gravestones was the most common way of honoring absent mariners. Such commemoration was almost always done on the gravestones of immediate family members rather than on those of members of the extended family.

In other cases, it appears that no permanent memorial was erected for the sailor until a family member died and was buried, at which time the sailor's name and details of death were included on the new gravestone.

This practice is evident from stones that have a person listed first whose body is by all indications present in the grave, but whose date of death is later than that of an absent mariner who is listed after him. One of the earliest absent-body commemoration graves exemplifies this type.

> Here lyes buried ye Body
> of Mr EDWARD RICHARDS
> died FEBRUARY ye 11th
> 1747/8 Aged 70 Years.
>
> In Memory of
> Mr JOSEPH RICHARDS
> Son to Mr EDWARD &
> Mrs MARY RICHARDS who
> died at PORT MAHONE
> JANUARY ye 18th 1742
> Aged 24 Years.[9]

The distance from Boston, and the death phrase "in memory of" signal that in this case Joseph's body is not present. Furthermore, the fact that Joseph died six years before Mr. Richards shows that the family waited to erect a permanent memorial to their lost son until after the death of his father.

Some memorials of this type feature much shorter lapses in time before the creation of a permanent memorial than does the Richards gravestone. In several cases, other family members died within a year of the sailor's loss and permanent commemoration took place relatively quickly. Newport, Rhode Island, sailor Nathaniel Langley, for example, who died at sea in April 1823, is memorialized on the gravestone of his father, Captain John Langley, who passed away in September 1824.[10] The fact that father is listed before son leaves little doubt that Nathaniel was not given a permanent marker until after his father's death. Merchant captain William Forster died and was buried in Old Calabar in August 1832, just over a month before his mother passed away in the family home of Liverpool. On the family gravestone, mother is listed first, followed by her son.[11] Father and two other sons followed within the span of a decade. A change in font shows that the stone was probably erected for mother and son in the early 1830s, with the others being added later.

On the other hand, several memorials show that commemoration sometimes did not occur until decades later. The Bridgeo stone from Marblehead, Massachusetts, lists Mary Bridgeo, widow of George, first.[12] Her death occurred in 1887, so the gravestone must have been erected after that date. Listed after Mary is an entry for her husband George, who had been lost at sea forty-one years earlier. A similar stone from Portland, Maine, was erected following the death of Abigail Crosby in 1810, but also records her husband Watson Crosby, who was lost at sea in 1775.[13] In cases such as these, the family either erected a temporary memorial to commemorate the lost mariners, or the incident remained a part of family memory until permanent commemoration following the death of the seamen's widows years later. Either way, the salient point is that the memory of the lost remained powerful enough for the family to create a permanent form of commemoration, sometimes decades after the event.

In addition to commemoration on the gravestones of family members, numerous empty graves devoted solely to lost mariners were recorded. The graves discussed in this chapter so far are cenotaphs of a sort, in that they commemorate sailors whose bodies rest elsewhere. The term *cenotaph*, however, generally refers to a tomb or monument where no body is present, and in this sense, these memorials are not true cenotaphs because the graves do contain the bodies of other family members.[14] The grave of Captain Amos Sheffield, located in the Old Town Cemetery in Stonington, Connecticut, is the earliest true cenotaph recorded by the survey.

> This stone is erected
> in memory of
> Capt Amos Sheffield
> who died at Demerara
> Dec. 25 1799
> in the 34 year
> of his age.
>
> *O every Sympathizing heart drop*
> *with me a Silent tear for he that*
> *went returnes no more.*[15]

Captain Sheffield's grave is located close to those of several other Sheffields, almost certainly relatives. Despite having other gravestones at hand to which Captain Sheffield's commemoration could have been added, his family chose to honor him with his own grave (figure 5.3). However, the

Figure 5.3. The earliest empty grave recorded during the survey. Old Town Cemetery, Stonington, CT. Photo by author.

fact that he died in South America, along with the epitaph, make it likely that Captain Sheffield's body is not buried in Stonington.

Empty graves were more common in the United States than in England. This may be because space was more at a premium in English cemeteries, and the cost of purchasing a grave and gravestone solely for a missing person was too great for most English maritime families. However, there is reason to believe that some English graves were originally dedicated solely to missing mariners, but later became family plots as other family members died and their bodies were interred at the grave site. A gravestone in St. James' Cemetery, Liverpool, provides an example of this phenomenon.

> In MEMORY of
> Captn W^M PROWSE,
> who was lost on his Passage from St Domingo
> in the year 1823, Aged 25 Years.
> *Deeply Regretted by his Widow,*
> *And Respected by his Friends.*
> ALSO OF
> W^M Williams, *Shipwright*, died 5th March
> 1840, Aged 58 Years.
> ALSO OF
> THOMAS WILLIAMS died January
> 5th 1848, Aged 45 Years.
> ALSO OF
> MARY KIRKBY, who died January
> 19th 1865, Aged 76 Years.
> *For 50 years a faithful and respected*
> *servant in the family of M*^{RS} *ATKINSON,*
> *SEAFORTH.*
> Also of SUSANNAH HAWKINS,
> Relict of the above Captn Prowse,
> who died April 11th 1870, Aged 73 Years.[16]

The time difference of seventeen years between Captain Prowse and the next person listed suggests that the gravestone was originally erected following his death and the others' names were added later. The fact that all five persons commemorated are listed in chronological order according to date of death also suggests that the gravestone was added to over the years. Blank areas on other gravestones in St. James' Cemetery show that gravestones were erected with space for names to be added later. Such examples invariably feature one or two people listed near the top, while the rest of the stone was left blank. Space was set aside for additional names that for one reason or another were never added. While more common in England, the practice of dedicating a grave for an absent mariner and later interring other family members there was also sometimes practiced in the United States. The gravestone of Captain Joseph Weeks, who died returning from the West Indies in 1797, was later added to as other members of his family passed away.[17] First to be added was his son Daniel, who like his father was lost at sea, this time in 1815. Lois, widow of Joseph and mother of Daniel, was the last to be added. She died in 1829, and hers is the only body that actually occupies the grave. In 1803, the family of Newport, Rhode Island, mariner Joseph Barker erected a gravestone to him after he died aboard ship and "was buried in the Ocean" while returning from Jamaica.[18] A quarter century later, his widow Hannah was buried in the grave and her name added to the marker upon her death in 1828.

A few cenotaphs for multiple lost sailors from the same family were also recorded. One gravestone in Portland, Maine, tells the story of three sons of the Cobb family, all of whom went to sea and never returned (figure 5.4). The first, William, died at sea in 1805, his brother Daniel died at

Figure 5.4. Three seafaring sons of the Cobb family are commemorated with this cenotaph. All three died in separate incidents. Eastern Cemetery, Portland, ME. Photo by author.

St. Bartholomew's in 1810, and the third, Smith Woodward, was lost at sea in 1815.[19] Another example from Portland records the loss of two sons of the Morss family, while a third from Newport, Rhode Island, describes the deaths of a father and son, the former in Africa and the latter in Hawaii.[20]

Along with gravestones, monuments were also commonly used in the nineteenth century to mark family burial plots. As with gravestones, it was common for lost sailors to be added to such family monuments. In such cases, the graves of family members were usually grouped around the monument; sometimes these graves were marked with individual headstones as well. At the Deane family burial plot in the Western Cemetery in Portland, Maine, the graves of numerous Deanes are grouped around a monument that preserves the family record of mortality.[21] Although most of the monument commemorates family members who are buried close by, one side is devoted to two brothers, one of whom was lost at sea in the 1830s and the other who died at sea in the 1860s. Many more examples of this type of commemoration were recorded in the United States.[22] Only a single example of this type was discovered in England, the Newlands family monument in Liverpool, suggesting that the practice may not have been as widespread there.

In a similar manner to the empty graves described above, some monuments were dedicated solely to lost sailors. A tragic example of this type is the Denison monument at Evergreen Cemetery in Stonington, Connecticut, which commemorates four brothers, all of whom died in separate incidents.[23] Each of the monument's four sides tells one brother's story. The first, Ezra, sailed aboard an American privateer during the War of 1812. In December 1812, Ezra went aboard a captured English vessel as part of a prize crew. The following night, a great gale arose, and the vessel and its crew were never heard from again. Four years later, a similar fate befell Ezra's brother Amos, who was swept from the deck of a schooner and lost at sea. Two other brothers died in distant foreign ports: Charles in Surinam in 1817 and Edward in Batavia in 1818. While not on as large a scale as the Denison monument, similar monuments were erected by other families to record the loss of their seafarers at sea and in foreign lands.[24]

Another common form of family memorialization for lost sailors was the dedication of mural plaques inside churches. Many of these survive in excellent condition because they have been protected from the elements. Plaques are common in churches with a strong maritime focus, such as

Portsea St. Mary's in Portsmouth, England, St. Mylor near Falmouth, England, and the Seamen's Bethel in New Bedford, Massachusetts. Like external monuments, mural plaques were dedicated both to individuals and to multiple lost seafarers.

In addition to remembrance on family monuments, the missing were commemorated on collective memorials. The earliest one recorded by the survey is the gravestone at Portsea St. Mary's, Portsmouth, dedicated to the loss of HMS *Royal George* near Portsmouth in 1782.[25] This gravestone originally marked the final resting place of thirty-five victims of the tragedy who were buried in a mass grave in St. Mary's churchyard.[26] The stone was later moved from the grave site to prevent deterioration, and is now located inside the church. Although in this case the bodies of some victims were buried in the grave, the gravestone also commemorated the hundreds of others whose bodies were never recovered.

> A testimony of
> sympathy
> for the unfortunates
> who perished by the sinking
> at Spithead of the
> HMS Royal George
> August 29th 1782
> erected by one who
> was a stranger both to officers
> and the ship's company

The same holds true for other collective memorials recorded during the survey. A tablet on an outside wall of All Saints Church in Wyke Regis records the fateful story of the *Alexander*, which wrecked near Portland in a storm in 1815.[27] The tale of the *Alexander* is particularly tragic because the ship was returning from a voyage to India, and had made it to within a day's sail of its destination port of London when a storm drove the vessel ashore, killing everyone aboard except for five men. As with the *Royal George*, some bodies were recovered and buried at All Saints, and the plaque lists others that were retrieved and buried at various other points along the bay. Many bodies, however, were lost forever. The monument makes a point of listing the names of all of those reclaimed from the sea and their places of final burial. On the other side of the ocean, the residents of New London, Connecticut, erected an obelisk for the victims

Figure 5.5. Marblehead Charitable Seamen's Society monument, Old Burial Hill, Marblehead, MA. Photo by author.

of the steamer *Atlantic*, which wrecked near that port in 1846.[28] Like the *Alexander* memorial, the creators of the *Atlantic* monument felt it important to record the names of those who were recovered and buried in their cemetery. In this case, the city even voted in favor of allocating public funds to pay for the funerals of victims of the tragedy.[29] The monument also makes it clear, however, that many others who died were never found, and that these are also being remembered.

With the growth of seamen's aid societies in the nineteenth century, these groups also began erecting monuments to honor lost members. A good example of this type is the obelisk erected in 1848 by the Marblehead Charitable Seamen's Society "in memory of its deceased members on shore and at sea."[30] Prominently situated with a view of the harbor and the open Atlantic beyond, the four sides of the obelisk provide details about the fate of Marblehead seamen (figure 5.5). One face is dedicated to those lost in the great gale of September 1846, another lists members lost at sea in other incidents, and a third records the names of those who died on shore. Whether commissioned by families, communities, sailors, or aid societies, the purpose of all of these memorials is the same: to provide a focus for remembrance for the countless sailors who lost their lives at sea or in distant corners of the world.

Why did commemorating the missing become such a concern within Anglo-American maritime culture near the end of the eighteenth century? Why go to the trouble of erecting memorials for men who would never return? Especially in the cases, and there are many, when an actual grave and marker were purchased for a body that would never occupy the space? Why did families, communities, and shipmates feel it necessary to do this, and why did this phenomenon suddenly experience a boom near the end of the eighteenth century? The reason lies in a shift in attitude toward the dead that took hold on both sides of the Atlantic at that time.

Romantic Ideals and Individualism

The practice of commemorating the missing has deep historical roots. Among Anglo-American mariners, however, memorials for the missing blossomed in the late 1700s. The creation of memorials to honor those who never returned formed part of a broader shift in attitudes toward the dead that took place in both England and the United States during the eighteenth century. At that time, there was a growing belief that the memory of each individual was important. The Romantic movement, which began in the mid-eighteenth century, stressed ideals such as individualism and emotional love, both of which increased the importance of the physical body. These principles became prevalent in many aspects of Anglo-American culture, including memorialization practices. In memorialization, the increase in individualism was expressed as a greater emotional attachment among family members, along with the desire to have a relationship with loved ones after their deaths.

Many scholars have noted the growth of individualism in memorialization practices in the eighteenth century.[31] While the idea of increasing individualism is widely accepted among many scholars today, some remain cautious. Ralph A. Houlbrooke maintains that interpreting evidence for individualism in eighteenth-century funerary practices is problematic for two reasons.[32] First, the term *individualism* has numerous meanings and is used in different ways by different scholars. Second, the evidence for individualism is open to more than one interpretation. In particular, Houlbrooke disagrees with Lawrence Stone's interpretation of the increasing importance of the family.[33] According to Houlbrooke, Stone's interpretation is based on eighteenth-century wills that show that a greater proportion of wealth was distributed to the family than in previous centuries. Houlbrooke's study of medieval wills, however, supports a different interpretation. Prior to the Reformation, will makers distributed their wealth in two ways. First, money was left to the family, just as it would be in later centuries. Medieval wills, however, also left money to the church to pay for prayers and funeral masses for the deceased's soul. After the Reformation, Protestant doctrine, which held that the fate of the soul was determined at death, removed such provisions. Since it was no longer necessary to leave money for the provision of one's soul, will makers after the Reformation began leaving this money to their families. Rather than showing an increase in sentiment toward the family during the eighteenth century, Houlbrooke maintains, such money was simply a byproduct of the Protestant Reformation. Houlbrooke also points out that grief at the loss of a loved one did not begin in the eighteenth century, but was present in earlier times as well.

Houlbrooke's reevaluation of the data from wills seems valid. Nevertheless, as Houlbrooke acknowledges, there was growing respect for the memory of the deceased and an increase in care of the physical body beginning in the late seventeenth century.[34] This increasing concern manifested in two ways. First, coffins came into widespread use in the second half of the seventeenth century. Prior to that time, most bodies were buried in shrouds, which soon resulted in deterioration of the corpse. Coffins offered better protection of the body, allowing it to remain intact longer. The increase in the erection of monuments, which began in the eighteenth century, also shows increasing concern with the individual. It is these shifts that form the crux of the argument for an increase in the importance of individuals in the eighteenth century. Houlbrooke is correct that the family was important, and people felt grief at the death of loved ones, before that time. During the eighteenth century, however, people began manifesting a greater concern with both the deceased's memory and the actual physical remains.

This shift in attitude is documented in studies of English and American mortuary practices. For the British Isles, Tarlow provides the best archaeological interpretation for the increase in individualism in the eighteenth century.[35] In her study of memorialization trends in Orkney, Tarlow noted a large increase in the number of gravestones in the late eighteenth century, which she terms the "gravestone boom." A similar trend exists throughout the British Isles, although the increase occurred at different times in different locations.[36] Tarlow links the great increase in memorials to the idea of "affective individualism" put forth by Stone.[37] Affective individualism, in keeping with the principles of Romanticism, emphasized emotion and love toward one's family. In earlier centuries, most people in England did not receive a permanent grave, nor were most graves permanently marked.[38] As churchyards filled up, remains would be moved to charnel houses to make room for new interments. In the late eighteenth century, however, Romantic notions made the practice of moving bodies unacceptable. The new attitude held that every person deserved a grave of his or her own that should remain undisturbed for all time. In memorialization, the Romantic spirit is shown by emotional wording such as "beloved," and also by an increase in the number of husbands and wives who were buried in the same grave. In addition, the provision of permanent graves made it possible for people to have a continuing relationship with loved ones after their deaths. People could go to churchyards or cemeteries to visit the actual spot where their loved one was buried. Occasions such as the anniversary of death were popular times for visits to grave sites.[39] This practice became common in England in the nineteenth century and held sway in America as well.

In New England, memorialization practices also showed an increasing concern with commemorating both the memory and the body during the eighteenth century. David E. Stannard states that New England Puritans originally buried their dead with little or no ceremony, in accordance with their prevailing belief in the simplicity of burials.[40] The earliest Puritan burials in New England were either not marked at all or were marked only with simple fieldstones. These would typically be inscribed only with the initials and date of death. As in England, the earliest New England graves do not appear to have been designed to last in perpetuity, as very few graves from the earliest period of settlement remain. By the late seventeenth century, however, Puritan attitudes toward memorialization were changing. Funerals became more elaborate, and the Puritans began marking their graves with permanent headstones. Throughout the eighteenth century, the changing designs on New England Puritan gravestones reveal much about the increase in concern for both the deceased's memory and his or her actual physical body.

In their classic studies of changing symbolism in New England cemeteries, Deetz and Dethlefsen interpreted the adoption of the cherub motif in the mid-eighteenth century as an emblem of immortality. In contrast to the earlier death's heads, which had symbolized mortality, cherubs demonstrate a shift in emphasis to the soul's flight to heaven after death. Deetz also noted a change in the introductory phrases associated with cherub stones.[41] Whereas earlier inscriptions usually began with "here lies," the inscriptions on stones featuring cherubs typically began "here lies buried the body." To Deetz, the specific reference to the physical body emphasized the separation of corpse and soul that occurred after death. What was once one person had now become two parts, the body lying in the ground and the soul winging its way to heaven. The mention of the body in the introductory phrase also indicates the growing concern with the disposition of the physical body in mid-eighteenth-century America.

By the 1780s, the urn and willow motif replaced the cherub as the dominant symbol on New England gravestones. The urn and willow emphasizes the memory of the deceased rather than the actual physical remains.[42] Introductory phrases such as "sacred to the memory of" illustrate the same concern. However, concern with the fate of the body was still evident in late-eighteenth-century gravestones by the continued use of introductory phrases mentioning the body, which are found on many urn and willow stones. In addition, the gravestones of the late-eighteenth and early-nineteenth centuries tend to stress individual accomplishments. These changes occurred in the United States at the same time as the increase in individualism in the British Isles. On both sides of the Atlantic, the trend indicates the beginning of the belief that each individual should have his or her own marked grave that should remain undisturbed for all time.

Just as noted by Tarlow for Britain, the increase in individual graves in New England facilitated use of the grave site as a focal point for visitation. This signals a shift in the relationship with the dead. No longer were the dead simply left in the ground. Instead, families and friends viewed the grave site as a place to visit and continue a relationship with the departed. In the United States, this trend, which began in the second quarter of the nineteenth century, is best exemplified by Rural Cemeteries and their successors the Landscape-Lawn and Memorial Park cemeteries.[43] These types of cemeteries were intended to be far more than places to bury the dead. They were landscaped like parks, and were consciously designed to provide both peaceful places for the deceased to sleep as well as aesthetically pleasing and tranquil settings for the living to visit. Kristin Ann Haas argues that the new rural cemeteries "transformed burial markers in America from reminders of the fact of death to remembrances of the past."[44] In reality, this transformation was under way by the turn of the nineteenth century, as shown by the individual graves of that period marked with urn and willow symbols. Instead of transforming American attitudes toward death, the rural cemeteries reflected the Romantic notions prevalent when they were created. As noted by Linden-Ward, rural cemeteries "echoed cultural trends and tastes shared by many Americans," which included Romantic ideals such as the serenity of nature and providing a space to visit deceased loved ones.[45] What Haas saw in the rural cemeteries is a developed form of remembrance incorporating Romantic ideals, not the origins of such ideals. The work of scholars such as Dethlefsen and Deetz makes it clear that the need to commemorate the memory of individuals and a concern for the fate of the physical body were already in place by the late eighteenth century. This shift in attitudes toward death in the United States corresponds to, and takes a form broadly similar to, the shift in attitudes toward death noted in the British Isles. In Great Britain, as in the United States, large parklike cemeteries were the dominant burial ground form in the nineteenth century, while smaller urban churchyards largely went out of use. In Britain, however, the popularity of cremation in the twentieth century resulted in the creation of Gardens of Remembrance within many older urban churchyards.[46] As the name implies, this form of commemoration, like the parklike cemeteries in both Britain and the United States, is geared toward providing a place for remembrance and visitation.

In both Britain and the United States, then, by the end of the eighteenth century, prevailing sentiment regarded each person as worthy of remembrance and also held that each person's body deserved to be buried in a grave that would remain undisturbed until the Resurrection. This attitude led to the creation of cemetery forms that prevailed on both sides of the Atlantic from the nineteenth century to the present day. The great increase in memorials dedicated to absent mariners began at the same time as the increase in concern for individualism in Britain and America. It is in light of this new attitude toward death that the memorials for the missing should be understood.

The Problem of the Absent Body

The need to have a body to bury has been a fundamental aspect of the Anglo-American outlook on death since the eighteenth century. As discussed above, the concern with the fate of the body seems to have been a product of the rise of individualism in the eighteenth century. By the end of that century, the idea that each person deserved a proper grave that should remain undisturbed for all time took hold in both England and the United States. As part of this concern with physical remains, the English and Americans (along with many other cultures) show a great desire to recover the bodies of those killed in accidents or war. This ideal permeates English and American maritime culture as well. Anglo-American maritime folklore, for example, contains numerous practices designed to locate drowned bodies so that they may be recovered. These practices often involve the use of some object that is thought to possess a special power for locating bodies beneath the surface. While a number of objects—ranging from wooden clubs, straw, and paper—are believed to possess this power, the most common item found in European custom is a loaf of bread loaded with quicksilver (mercury). Bassett describes how this process worked, citing an account of the recovery of a body near Hull, England.

> After diligent search had been made in the river for the child, to no purpose, a twopenny loaf, with a quantity of quicksilver put into it, was set floating from the place where the child, it was supposed, had fallen in, which steered its course down the river upward of half a mile, before a great number of spectators, when, the body happening to lie on the contrary side of the river, the loaf suddenly tacked about, and swam across the river, and gradually sank near the child, when both the child and the loaf were brought up with grabbers ready for the purpose.[47]

Exactly how bread infused with quicksilver worked to locate bodies was apparently a matter of some debate. Bassett quotes one explanation that claimed a simple reason: that a loaf loaded with mercury would act just like a body and therefore be carried by the water to the same place.[48] This matches well with the description quoted above, where the bread seems, *contra* to the beliefs of the observer, to be merely drifting along on the current. The act of suddenly crossing the river, which apparently so impressed the observer, could in fact be due to a place where the channel switched from one side of the stream to another.

In addition to objects believed to act as special agents for finding bodies, loud noises were believed to bring a body to the surface. Thunder, for example, was widely believed to have this effect. Humans have not always waited for Mother Nature to supply a loud booming sound, however. Artificial blasts created by cannon fire or the ringing of bells were believed to work just as well.[49]

Whether there was any truth to any of these beliefs is debatable, but they were certainly widespread in both England and the United States. For instance, the efficaciousness of bread infused with quicksilver penetrated as far up the Mississippi River as Samuel Clemens' hometown of Hannibal, Missouri. Writing as Mark Twain, Clemens later incorporated cannon fire and quicksilver-laden bread into *The Adventures of Tom Sawyer* and *The Adventures of Huckleberry Finn*. In the latter story, the irascible Huck, who is in hiding from the townsfolk after staging his own death, snags one of the loaves and eats it. Vestiges of such beliefs remain today. I have heard the belief regarding loud noises in use among fishermen on the Pungo River, North Carolina, as recently as March 2006. In this case, a fisherman mentioned that he hoped that we would soon have a good thunderstorm, in order to bring up the body of a man who had recently been lost in Pamlico Sound. The number of such beliefs, along with their widespread geographical and temporal range, indicates the great need that humans have to recover those who have been lost beneath the water.

Regardless of whether such practices proved effective or not, maritime communities lost many members whose bodies were never recovered from the sea, or who died and were buried far from home. In keeping with the ideas of individual commemoration that became a part of Anglo-American mortuary practice in the eighteenth century, however, members of maritime communities felt the need to memorialize those whose bodies were absent. The solution to this problem was to erect memorials even in cases where the body of the person being remembered was not available for burial.

Like the graves discussed by Tarlow and Deetz, memorials for missing sailors provided a focus for a continuing relationship with the dead. One way to do this was to include the lost sailor's name on a family gravestone or monument. As discussed above, this was the most common form of memorial for the missing. Including the name of the absent mariner made that memorial a place for visiting not only those buried at the site, but for the missing person as well. It is as if the inclusion of the name of the missing symbolically linked the grave site to the place where the mariner's body actually rested, which in the case of those lost or buried at sea remained forever unknown. This idea is shown most clearly by those gravestones and monuments dedicated solely to absent mariners. Each one is a true cenotaph, marking a piece of ground for a person whose body will never physically occupy the space. Despite the fact that the body would never be recovered and buried in the grave, maritime families felt it necessary for their loved ones to have a space of their own. In part, this reflects prevailing attitudes regarding personal space for graves. It also speaks, however, to the power of memory and to the pain that must have been felt by those families who never received a body to bury.

While families tended to memorialize their lost mariners with graves or monuments at the family plot, the memorials erected by shipmates to honor absent comrades indicate a similar but slightly different concern. Such monuments tend to perpetuate the memory of the person rather than providing a space for visitation. They also stress duty to king or country rather than emotional love, as shown by the common use of words such as "esteem" and "respect." In addition, the location of these memorials indicates more of a communal than familial form of memorialization. For example, wall plaques in churches provide a focus for communal remembrance. This is particularly true of maritime churches such as St. Mylor, Cornwall, and the New Bedford Seamen's Bethel. Churches such as these were popular places for mariners and their families to gather. Sailors returning from or preparing to embark on voyages might visit the church to offer thanks for a safe homecoming or ask for a safe return. When their men were at sea, maritime wives visited churches to pray for their husbands' safety. Seeing the plaques dedicated to the lost would remind both sailors and maritime families how fragile the seaman's lease on life really was. They would also perpetuate the memory of lost members of the community and provide a place for other members to grieve with them.

The Importance of Place

Memorials for the missing have another significant feature. Many specify places—the last known port from which a lost mariner sailed, the name of the port in which a sailor died and was buried, or the ocean where the person was lost. Some of the latter even feature latitude and longitude coordinates. Providing such information on the memorial forges a symbolic link between the location of the memorial and the place where the deceased's body lies. A piece of ground dedicated to the missing, which could be visited, served as a proxy location for the place where the body actually rested and probably helped the family cope with the fact that their loved one's body was gone forever. But place-names also fulfilled an important role for the group as a whole.

They probably functioned as a sort of mnemonic device. Michael Rowlands has examined the ways in which images can serve as mnemonic devices to remember the order of things.[50] As schoolchildren, many of us learned to memorize the names of all five U.S. Great Lakes through the simple mnemonic device "HOMES." In this device, each letter of the word represents the first letter of one lake's name (thus Huron, Ontario, Michigan, Erie, and Superior). Place-names on memorials are also mnemonic devices, but instead of serving to help memorize a list of names, what they do is invoke images of places from the group's collective memory. Seeing "died at Demerara," for example, would have meant something different to members of the maritime folk group than to nonmembers. For sailors who had visited the place, seeing the name on a monument would have evoked firsthand memories of experiences there. Even if they had not been to the place, sailors might have known shipmates or met other mariners who had, and therefore would have heard tales about the place. Family members and other non-seafaring members of maritime communities would likewise have heard stories of distant locales. This lore would have included stories of the tragedies and types of death that occurred there. Viewing the name on a gravestone would evoke memories from the group's collective lore. It might bring to mind stories of the oppressive heat and deadly yellow fever of Jamaica or Demerara, the harsh conditions of the slave markets of Calabar, or the vast loneliness of the Indian Ocean surrounding Desolation Island.

But this does more than just bring forth an image—it also evokes the feelings and emotions associated with the place. The ways in which sensory stimuli invoke emotions are well known. Blow out a candle, and the smell takes us back to childhood birthday parties. Auditory stimuli are particularly evocative; all of us have certain songs that, when we hear them, transport us back to places in our memories. However, such stimuli do more than simply bring forth recollections of past events. They also evoke the feelings and emotions associated with the event. This, I believe, is exactly what place-names on memorials do. Seeing the names of places where fellow group members died evoked emotions such as grief, sadness, pity, sympathy, despair, and anger.

The shared understanding of places and the feelings associated with them was one way by which memorials united members of the maritime folk group. The base of knowledge shared by members of maritime communities served as a reference point for interpreting the emotions expressed in maritime memorials. Upon seeing a memorial, a member of the group would, both consciously and subconsciously, draw upon his or her maritime cultural memory to interpret the meanings expressed in the memorial. Because of their esoteric group knowledge, other members of the maritime community would understand the feelings being expressed in maritime memorials in a different way than nonmembers. The memorials encoded special meanings for group members. For this reason, the names of places where tragedy occurred set members of maritime communities apart from outsiders. Understanding the information contained in the memorials served as a sign of group affiliation. Therefore, the listing of places on memorials both drew upon shared group traditions and at the same time helped to perpetuate them.

The Hollowness of the Empty Grave

Seamen and maritime families created memorials to honor absent sailors and assuage their own grief, but such memorials were never completely satisfying. A cenotaph provided a focus for grieving, but could never take the place of the physical body. The knowledge that their loved one's physical remains were lost would forever darken the hearts of families back home. Melville, a keen observer of human nature, understood this and expressed it clearly in the Seamen's Bethel chapter in *Moby Dick*. Describing the crying widows dressed in black, Melville wrote, "Oh! ye whose dead lie buried beneath the green grass; who standing among flowers can say—here, *here* lies my beloved; ye know not the desolation that broods in bosoms like these."⁵¹ With these lines, Melville both highlighted the importance of memorializing absent mariners and showed that the empty grave or marble cenotaph could never take the place of the real body. That Melville was expressing a popular sentiment in maritime communities is borne out by memorials. Perhaps nowhere is the longing for a body expressed more heartrendingly than on a gravestone from St. Budeaux churchyard in Plymouth, England. This gravestone commemorates a Royal Navy sailor, Samuel Henry Jeffery, who died at Malta in 1862. The stone ends with the epitaph, "Could I but see the spot/ The place where he is laid/ And drop a tear upon that spot/ It would ease me of my pain."⁵² This epitaph mournfully expresses Mrs. Jeffery's grief at not being able to visit the place where her son is laid to rest. Similar expressions are recorded on memorials that commemorate sailors lost or buried at sea. "There is sorrow on the sea," states the cenotaph for Captain Peter Cromwell, who died aboard his ship after being injured in a fall during a gale off Cape Horn.⁵³ The Cobb memorial, discussed above, includes the epitaph:

> Far distant from their native land
> They perished in the yawning deep
> Without a friend to stretch the hand
> And none their early fate to weep⁵⁴

Numerous epitaphs provide a glimpse of the anguish felt for those whose bodies rest in the sea. Nantucket sailor Sylvanus Smith had "no friendly hand to wipe the tear" as he lay dying from yellow fever aboard ship.⁵⁵ In Portland, Maine, the grave of Mary Stonehouse records that she was "drowned from the Portland Packet July 12, 1807" at the age of sixty-two.⁵⁶ While Stonehouse's body was recovered and buried, Portland was no stranger to its citizens being lost at sea, as the epitaph on her gravestone clearly indicates.

> From the cold bosom of the wave,
> Where others found a wat'ry grave,
> This lifeless corpse was borne! And here,
> The friends of virtue drop the tear
> That mourn the much lamented dead,
> But ah! What bitter tears are shed,
> For fathers, mothers, babes, who sleep
> In the dark mansions of the deep!

This phrasing celebrates the recovery of Stonehouse's body and laments all those who are never found. The "dark mansions of the deep" have claimed all too many sailors over the centuries, leaving families with no clear focus for mourning.

A large part of the problem lay in the uncertainty regarding the body's ultimate disposition. Latitude and longitude recorded in a ship's log gave an approximate location, but not the exact spot. Burial at sea presented the same problem. Once the body slipped beneath the waves, those aboard ship had no way of knowing the exact spot where it had gone to rest on the seafloor. For those buried in faraway places, families took solace in knowing that their loved one had a grave, but still lamented that it was far away and thus they had little or no opportunity to visit. It was little comfort to Mrs. Jeffery that her son had a grave; she longed to see "the place where he is laid." Those whose loved ones rested in some unknown spot in the depths suffered even more. Regarding Western attitudes toward death, including those of the English and Americans, the absent body is one of the worst situations that can happen, because it prevents the survivors—family and friends back home—from being able to mourn properly, move through the grieving process, and move forward with their lives.

A good deal of work has been done on the nature of the grieving process. In her classic 1969 work *On Death and Dying*, Elisabeth Kübler-Ross was one of the first to put forth a model of the phases that dying patients go through. Her five-stage model, which includes denial and isolation, anger, bargaining, depression, and acceptance, has influenced many later scholars. Kübler-Ross and other grief-process pioneers were themselves influenced by anthropological works dealing with changes in life stages, notably Van Gennep's *Rites of Passage* and the work of J. G. Frazer.[57] Although Kübler-Ross' five-stage model has been criticized for being too linear and inflexible, Allan Kellehear, writing in the introduction to the fortieth-anniversary edition of this classic work, argues that much criticism is misguided.[58] Kübler-Ross, according to Kellehear, never meant that these were the only processes that the dying go through or that all people progressed through them in a unilinear sequence.

Following Kübler-Ross, other scholars have developed models for the grieving process. Some view grieving as a series of stages, while others prefer to see grieving as a series of tasks that the survivor must perform in order to heal.[59] While stage- and task-based models share many similarities and are both useful concepts, it should always be kept in mind that they are in fact models. Every person grieves differently, and not all people pass through the same stages or need to accomplish all tasks. Indeed, Margaret Stroebe and Henk Schut have shown that the grieving process is not as linear as stage- or task-oriented systems imply.[60] Instead, mourners tend to oscillate back and forth between grieving and healing, rather than moving progressively through a series of steps.

Despite differences over the nature of models for grieving, scholars are in broad agreement that the grieving process fulfills several critical functions. Two of these are incorporated into most models and are of key importance to this study: the need to acknowledge and accept that the person has suffered a loss, and the necessity of re-creating a new identity and restructuring one's life in the post-loss world. John Bowlby, for example, included the concepts of acknowledging that death has occurred and the mourners' need to create a new life for themselves in his stage-based model.[61] "Acknowledging and understanding the loss" occurs in the first phase of Therese A. Rando's three-process model, while "moving adaptively into the new life" takes place in the third.[62] This final process includes such things as forming a new identity and finding appropriate ways to keep the deceased's memory alive (the creation of memorials among them). Rando stresses that the new relationship with the departed must acknowledge that the person is gone. Colin Murray Parkes and Robert S. Weiss, in their classic explication of a task-oriented system, incorporated similar ideas. These scholars formulated a three-task model, which includes the concepts of recognition of loss (in Task I), acceptance (as part of Task II), and development of a new identity (the key requirement of Task III).[63] Thus, concepts of acknowledgement and restructuring permeate Parkes and Weiss' model. Recently, J. William Worden has put forth a similar but more detailed task-based model based on four tasks. Accepting that a death has in fact occurred forms a key component of Task I, while the final two tasks include adjusting to a new environment and getting on with one's life.[64] Several models deal explicitly with the way that survivors re-create their lives. Aimed specifically at helping parents who have lost children, Dennis Klass describes the need to create a new relationship with the deceased that focuses on their changed status. The process never truly ends; according to Klass, "the end of grief is not severing the bond with a dead child, but integrating the child into the parent's life in a different way than when the child was alive."[65] Also focusing on the survivors, Thomas Attig sees grief as a necessary part of the process by which survivors relearn their world.⁶⁶ Every person's life includes core components, of which family are usually the cornerstones. When a family member dies, the survivors do not merely have to acknowledge the loss; rather, they must learn a way to live in the new world that they now inhabit. This is complicated by the fact that physical surroundings have not changed. Familiar objects and places evoke memories of the deceased, causing pain. Survivors must find a way to live in this world that looks familiar but has been forever changed by the loss of a loved one who will not return. Models of the grieving process vary, but scholarship has clearly demonstrated that acknowledgment and restructuring form critical components of the grieving process.

It is clear that, at least in Western cultures, key components of bereavement include acknowledging and accepting that a loss has occurred, and then finding a way to build a new life. This does not mean completely letting go of the deceased. Indeed, a continuing relationship with the dead can be a major part of the survivor's life. It does mean, however, that the survivor must construct a new relationship with the deceased that acknowledges that the person is, in fact, deceased, and therefore physically gone forever.

Therein lies the second great problem with those lost at sea: uncertainty as to their actual fate. Not knowing if their loved one was alive or dead prevented those back home from accepting loss and building a new identity. How could one adopt the term "widow" and dress and act accordingly, for example, without knowing whether one was, in fact, a widow? What if a sailor's wife did this, only to have her husband sail into port, years late but alive? Accounts from the Age of Sail make it clear that uncertainty over the fate of those who went to sea was one of the most difficult things for their families to deal with. John Béchervaise described how this sense of uncertainty affected his family. The gale that sent *Queen* and several other vessels onto the rocks near Falmouth lasted for nine days, and "during the whole of this time, my family were in the utmost distress: for previous to the gale, I had written to say, that I should leave Falmouth next day, so that they all the time supposed me at sea or lost."⁶⁷ Edward Coxere arrived home after one voyage to find his wife tending their newborn baby: "She, being surprised, could hardly speak to me, for she knew not before whether I was dead or alive."⁶⁸ Samuel Kelly met up with his brother, who was also a sailor, in London in 1786. The two enjoyed each other's company wandering about the city, but his brother soon succumbed to the lure of the sea and took ship for China. "After which," wrote Kelly, "I never heard what became of him correctly, therefore I imagine he soon after paid the debt of nature."[69] The possibility that their sailor would never return must have tortured the minds of many whose husbands, fathers, sons, and brothers vanished over the horizon. Like the lost themselves, the families back home existed in a liminal state, trapped forever between one world and the next. In time, many would come to at least partially accept that their loved one was gone forever, and would begin to reorder their lives. Part of this process sometimes included the creation of memorials. There was always a sense of ambiguity with commemorating the missing, however, which memorials for the missing clearly communicate.

After he was lost at sea in 1839, the widow of Lieutenant Charles Webbe, RN, erected a marble tablet to his memory in St. Mylor church (figure 5.6). The use of the phrase "supposed to have perished" gives a glimpse of Mrs. Webbe's feelings.[70] Despite what reason told her, she seemed to hold out a fragment of hope that her husband was not dead, and that someday his vessel might come sailing back into Falmouth harbor. Others show similar feelings. A pair of memorials on either side of the Atlantic express the pain felt by those who never received word of their loved one's fate. The earlier of the two is located in Newport's Common Burying Ground and is dedicated to Captain John Dennis,

> who sailed from this place
> Aug. 22 1756
> in the 42d year of his age
> was never fince heard of, doubtlefs
> made his exit in the watery element[71]

The grave of Wilfred Gilberry, whose story was told at the beginning of this book, features very similar wording.

> left Callao 30th May 1865, in command of
> the ship "Andacallo" bound for Valparaiso
> and has never since been heard of.[72]

"Has never since been heard of" is not a statement of finality. Rather, it retains a sliver of hope that someday their loved one will be found, if not still sailing at sea then perhaps discovered by visitors to some remote island. Such things were known to happen, and the sailor who returns home long after having been presumed lost has been an enduring motif in maritime lore for centuries. In one of the earliest sea stories in history, the Egyptian "Tale of the Shipwrecked Sailor," which dates to the late third millennium B.C., the lone survivor of an expedition lost in the Red Sea returns after being marooned on an island for four months.[73] Stories of such unfortunates were popular during the Age of Sail as well. Robinson Crusoe, title character of what is probably the world's best-known castaway story, spent almost thirty years stranded on an island off the coast of South America before returning home. While it is widely believed that Daniel Defoe based Crusoe on the real-life Scottish mariner Alexander Selkirk, it is probable that he was influenced by the many castaway stories that circulated in popular culture at the time.[74] Either way, Defoe's story became so popular that it went through six editions before the end of 1719, the year in which it was first published.[75] The popularity of castaway tales shows how important this motif was to the public imagination and makes

Figure 5.6. Marble plaque for Lt. Charles Webbe, which hints at his widow's grief over his loss. St. Mylor, Falmouth, Cornwall, U.K. Photo by author.

it easy to see why families retained hope that their lost sailor might someday return. While the dramatic return of a lost sailor provided the happy ending to many a story, reality was far different. For every lost mariner who returned, thousands never did.

The memorials make it clear that the ambiguous nature of being lost at sea must have been heart-wrenching to the families involved. After a time, they erected memorials to their loved ones, knowing that they were almost certainly dead, and yet holding out some hope that they might still be found alive. Such memorials could never quite fulfill the need for closure or allow those left behind to create a new life.

Contesting Imperialism and Capitalism

The study of power relations has become one of the chief concerns of historical archaeology over the past several decades. Numerous studies have examined the ways by which indigenous peoples and minorities protest Western imperialism and capitalism.[76] Maritime memorials provide testaments to this struggle. Ships have been the principal means by which Western nations spread military and economic power around the globe, and thus sailors can be viewed as active agents of Western domination. As previously discussed, official memorials erected by the state typically celebrate ideals such as victory, nationalism, and patriotism. Trafalgar Square, the USS *Constitution*, and similar memorials can be seen as monuments to the success of British and American colonialism and capitalism. But there is another side to this story. The spread of Western power and commerce around the globe over the past five hundred years cost thousands of seafarers their lives. Global seafaring brought wealth to some, but many members of the maritime folk group paid for it with their lives. The bodies of countless sailors were lost or buried in the deep. Others lay interred in distant corners of the globe, where most families could never visit. Creating memorials to these lost men provided a place for family remembrance and likely served another function as well. Many of the memorials for the missing are situated in prominent places where they would be viewed by many people. Examples of such locations include mural plaques next to doorways in churches and cenotaphs placed at the intersections of major pathways in cemeteries. The placement of these memorials does not seem to be accidental. Rather, they invite fellow seafarers and the public at large to participate in the process of remembering those who will never return. As such, these memorials functioned to remind the public that ideals such as imperialism, colonialism, and patriotism are not merely abstract concepts but carry real-world consequences.

The memorials for the missing served as one way in which the families left behind could remind society of their anguish. The widow of George Williams, for example, erected a cenotaph to her husband, who died off the coast of Australia in 1860. Williams' cenotaph is located alongside one of the major paths in New London's Cedar Grove Cemetery (figure 5.7). The touching epitaph "his grave was in the deep" reminds passersby that Mr. Williams never came home.[77] The outdoor monuments erected by

Figure 5.7. Gravestone for George Williams, which states that "his grave was in the deep" off the coast of Australia. Cedar Grove Cemetery, New London, CT. Photo by author.

ships' crews seem purposely designed to fulfill the same function. They tend to be prominently situated where they can be viewed by all members of the community. In the mid-nineteenth century, for example, Royal Navy crews erected a series of obelisks along the seawall in Portsmouth. In this busy location, the monuments still attract attention today. Each lists the names of deceased sailors and the means by which they died, reminding the public of the toll that naval power exacted on seamen. Similarly, crew monuments in cemeteries, such as the monuments in the Royal Navy Cemetery at Haslar and Kingston Road Cemetery, Portsmouth, tend to be located close to the intersections of major walkways, so that those strolling through the cemeteries see them easily. These memorials can be viewed as a form of resistance against the success stories displayed on national memorials. While state-level monuments proclaim the success of maritime enterprises that spread colonialism and capitalism around the globe, the unheralded cenotaphs for thousands of missing seamen speak of the horrific cost of these endeavors to human lives.

Conclusions: Ships That Don't Come In

Ships that don't come in—a metaphor for missed opportunities, unrequited love. What is to us a metaphor was reality for countless maritime families in the Age of Sail. Those whose loved ones were buried or lost at sea or interred in foreign graveyards longed to see the place of burial. Lacking the ability to do so, they created memorials to absent sailors in an attempt to symbolically link the memorial spot with the location of their loved one's body. Like burials at sea, however, memorials for the missing proved ultimately unsatisfying. While they provided a symbolic link to the missing and a focus for commemoration, empty graves could never take the place of physical remains. Just as the sea provided no permanent barrier preventing the return of the dead, the ambiguous nature of being lost or buried far from home prevented maritime families from completely accepting the loss and moving on with their lives. Both the missing sailor and the family back home remained trapped in a liminal state.

Untold widows, parents, siblings, and friends went to their graves wondering what fate befell their loved ones. Some probably spent the rest of their lives being tugged back and forth between hope and despair, at times optimistic that word of the missing would arrive, at other times accepting that it would not. Countless maritime families have gone through this over the millennia. This heart-wrenching tug of war must rank among the most dreadful aspects in all of humanity's tragic history on the sea. The magnitude of loss was such that it forced many maritime families to take measures for comfort: to embrace religious revival movements that took place in both Great Britain and the United States in the eighteenth and nineteenth centuries.

6

"Rocks and Storms I'll Fear No More"

THE ANCHOR AND THE CROSS

Portland peninsula juts from England's southern coast, roughly midway between Plymouth and Portsmouth. Steep, rocky, and windswept, its prominence made the peninsula useful as a navigational landmark for vessels passing along the Channel coast. Unfortunately, the very feature that made the peninsula an effective landmark—the fact that it projected some eight miles into the Channel—also made it a dangerous obstacle to vessels transiting the area, especially in poor weather. To make matters worse, Portland Race, a strong current just offshore, makes the seas around Portland even more treacherous. Over the centuries, hundreds of vessels have wrecked on Portland's rocky coast. Although disparaged as "an appendix of Dorset left to the mercy of the philistine Royal Navy," Portland mariners were also involved in coastal and international trade, as well as fishing.[1] Memorials in the churchyard of Portland St. George, located atop the cliffs that form the western side of the peninsula, reflect the area's seafaring heritage and the tragedies that have taken place there. If you take the time to hack through the heavily overgrown western side of the churchyard, you can find numerous gravemarkers commemorating maritime tragedies. Among these is that of John Bower, who died in 1912 at only thirty-eight years of age. Bower's neglected stone—overgrown but still in good condition due to the fact that it is made of durable Portland stone—contains the epitaph "Rocks and Storms I'll Fear No More."[2] This simple phrase, one line from a maritime-themed hymn celebrating the victory of eternal life over death, exemplifies a major development that began in maritime memorialization in the late-eighteenth century. Before that time, only a few maritime memorials featured any form of religious symbolism or inscriptions. The frequency of memorials with religious themes began to increase around the turn of the nineteenth century, and soared dramatically in the second quarter of that century. The percentage remained significant until the end of the Age of Sail.

The rise of religion on maritime memorials seems to contradict our commonly accepted view of sailors. Seamen had a reputation—largely deserved—for wild ways. This included a dislike of religion, which is reflected in maritime lore in superstitions such as a taboo against having clergy members aboard ship. Although somewhat stereotypical, it is nevertheless largely true that seafaring and religion did not mix. Contrary to the historical record, however, the material-culture evidence provided by memorials shows that beginning in the nineteenth century, religion became a key theme in English and American maritime memorialization. This chapter explores the nature of the nineteenth-century maritime religious boom and places it within its historical context. Like memorials for the missing, faith was another way by which maritime culture attempted to cope with the deadly nature of seafaring life.

Sailors and Religion

Both their contemporaries and modern scholars agree that seafarers in the Age of Sail were not generally religious. Landsmen tended to view sailors as wild heathens, a view that was given weight by the way sailors often acted when on shore. By the early eighteenth century, religious leaders such as Boston's Cotton Mather exhorted ship captains to do more to make religion a part of shipboard life:

> It is a matter of the saddest complaint and wonder, That there should be no more Serious Piety, in the Seafaring Tribe. . . . Old Ambrose called the Sea, The School of Vertue. It afflicts all vertuous Men, that the Mariners of our Dayes do no more make it so. . . . The Company aboard with you is Your Family. Family-Worship is Expected from all that would not forfeit the Name of Christianity. For such a Society to Live without any Social Acknowledgment of a God would be a Practical Atheism . . . [3]

Attempts were made to introduce religion into the wooden world, and modern historians are divided over the success of these endeavors. During the Commonwealth period in England, for example, Puritans attempted to make the navy more religious. The 1652 edition of the Articles of War, which governed conduct aboard English naval vessels, ordered that captains perform regular services. This was the first time that such an order had been issued.[4] As noted in chapter 4, the 1662 edition of the *Book of Common Prayer* was the first edition to contain specific instructions for the burial of the dead at sea and forms of prayer to be used aboard ship. Despite these measures, however, there is little evidence that religious fervor took hold in the mid-seventeenth-century English navy. While a number of officers were religious and made an attempt to inculcate these views among their crews, such measures met with little success and most sailors remained irreligious.[5]

Marcus Rediker provides a detailed analysis of the role of religion aboard ship in the first half of the seventeenth century. Rediker argues that while most sailors were not religious, a number of religious sailors did exist and were generally tolerated aboard ship as long as they did not try to impose their views upon their shipmates. Even those who were avowedly religious, however, also relied on superstition and ritual. According to Rediker, "the uncontrollable vicissitudes of nature, the extreme vulnerability of seamen, and the frequency of death at sea gave a special power to superstition, omens, personal rituals, and belief in luck."[6] Religious and irreligious mariners alike followed a belief system that included "Christian and pre-Christian beliefs, referents, and orientations" and that drew upon material from the Bible, classical mythology, and personal experience narratives that seamen swapped among one another.[7]

Rediker identifies three main reasons why religious sentiment was not strong at sea. First, distance from land-based social institutions, such as the church, caused sailors to lose touch with religion. A second factor was the nature of the maritime work experience. When a sailor entered the shipboard community, he underwent an initiation process to become a member of the group. This process involved putting aside previous beliefs and adopting group values. Since irreligion was a prevailing value among mariners, most newcomers became irreligious as well. Finally, Rediker notes that the working class, from which most common sailors came, had a tradition of skepticism. By the eighteenth century, religious sentiment had declined among working-class people. Thus, many sailors came from a background that was already cynical toward the clergy.[8]

British sailors seem to have been no more religious by the nineteenth century. The Reverend Edward Mangin, who served briefly in the Royal Navy in 1812, described the difficulties faced by a chaplain aboard a naval vessel. Admiralty regulations specified certain official duties for chaplains, but Mangin complained that these amounted to an attempt "to do some things which are improper, and some which are impossible."[9] Chaplains were supposed to assist with handling quarrels between sailors and see that just punishment was meted out. According to Mangin, however, any attempt to do so would draw the wrath of the captain and officers, who saw this as an infringement on their responsibilities. A similar problem occurred when dealing with the sick. Regulations stated that chaplains should visit the sick, but naval surgeons frowned on this, as they were afraid that the presence of the chaplain in the sick bay would cause ill sailors to give up hope. Chaplains were also supposed to help teach midshipmen mathematics. In Mangin's view, this was a task best left to sea officers who understood navigation rather than clergy who did not. Finally, the chaplain performed no necessary task in the day-to-day operation of the ship, and in fact had to take care to avoid getting in the way. Attempts to bring religious devotion to the operation of a vessel could result in a backlash. In Mangin's words,

> As for the Chaplain's constant efforts to rebuke the seamen, etc. for profane swearing, and intemperate language of every kind, the injunction sounds plausible: but when the after-guard is called, and the people are lazy in turning up; or at the coming on of a gale, when the order is given to strike top-gallant masts, and this is clumsily done; the Chaplain had better spare both his lungs and his ears and retreat, as fast as he can, to his own deck, or to the ward-room.[10]

Because of the atmosphere aboard ship, Mangin concluded that "nothing can possibly be more unsuitably or more awkwardly situated than a clergyman in a ship of war," and left the Royal Navy after serving less than four months.[11] His experience was probably not unique.

To make matters worse for those who wished to bring faith aboard ship, sailors have a long-standing superstition against having religious officials aboard. Members of the clergy are considered unlucky and were not welcome aboard ship during the Age of Sail. Maritime folklorist Horace Beck explains this belief by noting that sailors typically have a suspicion toward having anything aboard that would anger the sea.[12] Christian priests and ministers qualify because they would offend the gods that sailors have associated with the oceans since pre-Christian times. For all of these reasons, the deck was stacked against those who wanted to bring religion to mariners.

Religion in Maritime Memorials

The memorials show expressions of religious sentiment beginning in the late-eighteenth century. Although few in number at first, a boom in religious expression occurred in the nineteenth century. The following sections describe the forms that this phenomenon took, discuss the role played by various maritime groups in expressing religious sentiment, and illustrate some of the functions that religion played in maritime memorialization.

Prior to the late-eighteenth century, symbolism on maritime memorials broadly reflected the mortuary symbolism of society as a whole. Death's heads were common on maritime gravestones in the first half of the eighteenth century, while the urn and willow motif became more common in the second half of that century. This is in keeping with the changes in symbolism noted by scholars for both England and the United States. Likewise, inscriptions on maritime memorials featured little religious sentiment until the late eighteenth century.

Maritime memorials with religious epitaphs began to appear in the late-eighteenth century, but only a few maritime memorials with religious sentiment were recorded from that time. The earliest religious maritime memorial recorded by the survey is the gravestone of John Cox, from the Eastern Cemetery in Portland, Maine, which dates to 1785.[13] Like many gravestones of the period, Cox's stone features an urn and willow design. The connection of religious sentiment and maritime views, however, is expressed in the epitaph. Cox, who died at only twenty years of age, was commemorated by his parents with the epitaph:

> Boreas winds & various Seas
> Have tofs'd me to & fro,
> In Spite of both, by God's decree,
> I harbour here below:
> Where I do now at Anchor ride
> With many of my fleet,
> Yet once again I shall Set Sail
> My Admiral Christ to meet

The same epitaph is present on the gravestone of Captain Robert Newman of Boston, who died in 1806.[14] The idea of being anchored safely awaiting the resurrection was also recorded on an early religious gravestone from Old Burial Hill in Marblehead. The gravestone of Frances Doliber, who died in 1806 at age forty-seven, includes the epitaph:

> Storms & tempests now are over,
> Foes no more disturb my breast,
> In the realms of peace & glory,
> Anchor'd safe my soul to rest.[15]

Doliber's epitaph juxtaposes maritime worldview with religious comfort: the "realms of peace and glory" provide succor from life's "storms and tempests." The gravestone of Henry Roby in Boston's Copp's Hill burial ground represents another example of the way that religious sentiment and maritime metaphors were intertwined to express faith in resurrection in early-nineteenth-century America. Roby, who died in 1807, was memorialized with the epitaph:

> Supported by that hope which as an anchor
> to the soul, is sure and steadfast, he desired to
> depart, and to be with the Lord Jesus Christ.[16]

This epitaph is an adaptation of Hebrews 6:19, which asserts the belief that those who believe in Christ will have eternal life: "we have this as a sure and steadfast anchor of the soul, a hope that enters into the inner shrine behind the curtain."[17] The connection of Christ with the anchor was a theme in Christianity from its earliest times. Early Christians used the symbol of the anchor as a secret sign of belief in the days of Roman persecution. As will be discussed below, the anchor served as the cornerstone of the boom in religious sentiment that occurred in maritime memorials in the mid-nineteenth century. These examples from late-eighteenth and early-nineteenth-century America foreshadow later developments. At the turn of the nineteenth century, however, the connection between the anchor, Christ, and mariners was only expressed on a few maritime memorials. Moreover, all were concentrated in Puritan areas, which may account for the higher degree of religiosity.

By the same token, other forms of maritime religious sentiment were expressed in the late-eighteenth and early-nineteenth centuries, but they were few and far between. Captain Addison Richardson of Salem composed his own epitaph, which both reflects his experiences of a lifetime at sea (Addison died in 1811 at age seventy-two) and expresses his faith in another life to follow.

> Having weathered life's wintry storm & its fevr'd pestilential summers, the victor death by one mighty effort, has at length dislodged the tenant, & the frame is crumbling into dust, food for worms. But he maintained a firm belief that the great Architect will one day restore the fabric anew with imperishable materials; & put the tenant in full possession never more to be separated; beyond the reach of sin & sorrow; beyond the jurisdiction of DEATH: which finally shall be vanquished & swallowed up in victory. God shall be all in all.[18]

A similar theme was echoed on the tombstone of Addison's contemporary Captain Edward Russell (d. 1815), across town in Salem's Old Burying Point.

> Now safe arrives the heavenly mariner:
> The battering storm the hurricane of life
> All die away in one eternal calm.
> With joy divine full glowing in his breast,
> He gains the port of everlasting rest.[19]

Note that both of these epitaphs allude to storms, which as discussed in chapter 2 had a great impact on the maritime group psyche. A key component of the maritime religious revival was the concept of heaven as a safe port from the storms of life, whether literal or metaphorical. Like the equation of Christ with the anchor, this idea became a major theme in maritime memorials in the mid-nineteenth century, and will be discussed in greater detail below. However, in the 1810s, when Addison and Russell were laid to rest, such sentiments were rare on maritime gravestones.

Rare as it was in America, the early American maritime memorials, with their religious sentiment, stand in sharp contrast to contemporary English ones. John Powell's gravestone in Holy Trinity, Hull, serves as a good example of the lack of religious sentiment on late-eighteenth- and early-nineteenth-century English maritime gravestones. Powell's epitaph, which states "from sea and rocks/from storm and tide/I safely here at anchor ride," makes explicit the idea of anchoring safely at the end of life's voyage.[20] While the idea of resting at anchor is the same maritime metaphor expressed on the American stones, in contrast to the American memorials, there is no explicit connection with religion. In fact, only three late-eighteenth- through early-nineteenth-century maritime memorials with religious sentiment were recorded in England. Even on these, religious sentiment does not seem to form as much of a centerpiece as it did on the American ones. The memorial plaque for Edward Bayntum Yescombe in St. Mylor Church, Cornwall, offers a typical example.

> Sacred
> to the Memory of
> EDWARD BAYNTUM YESCOMBE Esq.
> late Commander of
> the King George Lisbon Packet,
> who was alike distinguished for
> His Manners as a Gentleman
> His Conduct as an Officer
> and
> His Benevolence as a Christian
> A Man of strict Integrity
> worthy of Imitation
> in his public Capacity
> and in his domestic Life
> honored and beloved
> He lost his Life
> in bravely defending his ship
> against the Enemy
> He died August the 12th 1803 Aged 38[21]

Yescombe's widow, who erected the tablet, chose to emphasize his worldly qualities and brave defense of his vessel, while devoting only one line to "his benevolence as a Christian." Similarly, the widow of Royal Navy Captain Sir Thomas Byard expressed her belief "in the firm hope of a blessed resurrection" on the marble plaque devoted to her husband, who died at sea in 1798.[22] Only one line was devoted to Mrs. Byard's hope for life eternal, while the majority of the message on the plaque describes her husband's qualities as a sailor and captain.

> To perpetuate the Memory of Sir Thos. Byard Kt.
> late of Mount Tamer, in this Parifh.
> Who to the Service of his King and Country
> devoted the greateft Part of his Life,
> This Marble is erected by the Grateful Affection
> of his furviving Family
> It is not for them to record thofe Actions
> which gained their beloved Friend fo much Honour
> They are chronicled in the naval Annals of his Time
> and engraven in the Hearts of all thofe
> who had the good Fortune to ferve under
> his aufpicious Command

The last passage, which begins "it is not for them to record," represents a stock epitaph in circulation at the time. Almost the same wording was employed on the memorial plaque for Admiral Marriott Arbuthnot in Wyke Regis.[23] The memorials for Yescombe and Byard clearly show that service, duty, and honor were considered more fitting sentiments to express on the tablets of naval officers. The only other English maritime memorial from the early-nineteenth century that expresses religious sentiment follows a similar pattern. The tablet erected by the owners of the ship *Alexander*, which wrecked near Portland in 1815, includes:

> May angels guide your
> [unreadable] the blest regions of eternal day
> Where no rude blasts provoke the billowy roar
> Where virtues kindred meet to part no more.[24]

Even here, however, most of the tablet is devoted to the circumstances of the vessel's loss and the names of those whose bodies were recovered. It appears, then, that religious sentiment was not strong in late-eighteenth- and early-nineteenth-century English and American maritime memorials. In England, it was practically nonexistent, while in the United States, religious sentiment was the exception rather than the rule.

A sharp increase in the number of maritime memorials with religious sentiment occurred in the nineteenth century in both England and the United States. This phenomenon took several forms. First and foremost was the use of the anchor as a symbol for Christ. By the mid-nineteenth century, the anchor became the single most dominant symbol on British and American maritime memorials, and remained so until the twentieth century. At the same time, the connection of the anchor with Jesus Christ became the most common form of expressing religious sentiment on maritime memorials.

Mariners quite naturally adopted the anchor symbol for two main reasons. On the most basic level, anchors symbolized sailors. From uniforms to tattoos, anchors marked a man as a mariner. The second reason that maritime culture adopted the anchor was that sailors understood its symbolism of hope. Just as the identification of Christ as an anchor signified hope in the Christian liturgy, so too did the anchor quite literally symbolize hope to mariners. A ship's anchors were, in a very real sense, often the last hope before being forced onto a rocky shore. Casting out the anchors was often the last desperate act performed by a ship's crew before being wrecked. Seventeenth-century English sailor Edward Coxere provides an excellent example of the anchor as a last resort, when his ship was attempting to cross through the Straits of Gibraltar. Encountering storms that reduced visibility to only a few yards, Coxere and his shipmates suddenly found themselves perilously close to a lee shore.

> We suddenly saw the land on the weather bow, a sad sight with the sea raging on the rocks at one side and it falling so violently on us on the other side, which was such a dismal sight to us as is hard to be expressed the manner of it, so violently did the sea press us towards the shore, insomuch that we were forced to let run our yards and sails down and cut away our mainmast and hove yards and sails overboard and put overboard one anchor. We finding the sea heaving us still to the shore, we put over another anchor and, finding the wind and sea still press us to the shore and but little more drift, we cut overboard our foremast and put over another anchor, which was the last we had to trust to. Then we found the ship to ride fast.[25]

In this instance, disaster was averted by the combination of three anchors and the toppled masts. In many other instances, however, crews were not so lucky. Unlike Christ, whose hope was viewed as "sure and certain," real anchors offered only the promise of succor, a promise that was not always delivered.

Anchors on gravestones were not always expressions of faith; many signified occupational identity rather than religious sentiment. Others were polysemous, serving both to signify maritime identity and to express religious sentiment. The juxtaposition of anchors with religious symbols and biblical quotations makes the interpretation of the anchor as a religious motif undeniable. The Gilman Low monument from Boston contains a carved anchor above the inscription (figure 6.1):

<blockquote>
GILMAN S. LOW
BORN MAR 13 1810
DIED AUG 16 1863

CHRIST OUR HOPE
WHICH HOPE WE HAVE AS AN
ANCHOR OF THE SOUL BOTH SURE
AND STEADFAST[26]
</blockquote>

Figure 6.1. Detail of monument for Gilman Low, showing anchor and biblical verse (Hebrews 6:19). Forest Hills Cemetery, Boston, MA. Photo by author.

Numerous variations on the theme of Christ as an anchor were recorded. Anchors wrapped around crosses (figure 6.2), held by angels (figure 6.3), or used to form other Christian motifs (figures 6.4 and 6.5) provide powerful visual symbolism of the maritime-religion juxtaposition. All of these memorials, which couple sacred and maritime symbols and text, leave no doubt that they are intended to be religious in nature.

Although anchors represent the most prominent symbol of the nineteenth-century maritime religious boom, other forms of religious expression were also recorded. Christian symbols such as the cross, the "IHS" symbol, and the finger pointing heavenward also occur on maritime memorials. In addition, religious phrases and epitaphs occur frequently on maritime gravestones from the nineteenth century on. Religious inscriptions take the form of Bible verses, lines from hymns, and stanzas from

Figure 6.2. Anchor and chain wrapped around cross. Highland Road Cemetery, Portsmouth, Hampshire, U.K. Photo by author.

Figure 6.3. Angel holding anchor on crew monument for HMS *Severn*. Portsea St. Mary's, Portsmouth, Hampshire, U.K. Photo by author.

Figure 6.4. Anchor incorporated into "IHS" Christian symbol. Falmouth Cemetery, Cornwall, U.K. Photo by author.

Figure 6.5. Another version of the "IHS" anchor, this time on a Celtic cross. Photo by author.

poetry. The common theme linking all of them is the connection between religious sentiment and maritime life.

The Maritime Religious Boom in Context

The maritime religious boom was part of a larger religious movement that took place in both British and American societies. The ideas and symbols found on maritime memorials were directly related to religious trends that took place in both nations beginning in the late-eighteenth century. In the United States, this resurgence of religious sentiment was known as the Second Great Awakening, and featured two main characteristics, both of which have a bearing on this study.[27] First, the theology of the Second Great Awakening emphasized salvation through Jesus Christ. Previously, Protestant theology had advocated the Calvinist doctrine of predestination. This belief held that the fate of everyone's soul was divinely preordained, and that there was nothing that one could do to alter it. If one was numbered among the elect chosen to go to heaven, that would happen;

if not, one would go to hell. Individual acts or beliefs had no bearing on the fate of the soul. These ideas began to crumble during the First Great Awakening, which took place in the mid-eighteenth century, but were not completely eliminated until the Second Great Awakening.[28] The theology exemplified by the Second Great Awakening rejected predestination in favor of the Arminian belief in personal salvation. Under this view, nothing was predetermined. A person's beliefs and actions would influence the fate of his or her soul after death. Following from this, the religion of the Second Great Awakening held that heaven could be gained through personal belief in Jesus Christ.

The second major facet of the Second Great Awakening followed naturally from this changed perception of salvation. Since souls could now be saved, a strong evangelical movement arose to fulfill that purpose. Revivals, large meetings that lasted for days or even weeks at a time, became a major part of the Second Great Awakening. Thousands of sinners were brought to Jesus at these events. In addition to salvation, evangelicalism also featured a strong social-reform component. This was an outgrowth of eighteenth-century Enlightenment philosophy, which emphasized a concern for downtrodden members of society. In the nineteenth century, Protestant reformers combined this philosophy with the idea that "every man was his brother's keeper."[29] Reformers sought to help the poor, slaves, the mentally handicapped, prisoners, and other disadvantaged people. To do this, evangelicals organized reform societies, temperance unions, Bible distribution societies, and other groups that spread reform—and with it the gospel—to those whom they believed were in need of both aid and salvation.

While the Second Great Awakening was an American phenomenon, the ideals that it promulgated were by no means restricted to North America. Looking beyond the shores of the New World, it is easy to see that the Second Great Awakening was part of a larger worldwide missionary evangelical movement. In Britain, similar reform movements with a strong evangelical religious base were also taking place by the turn of the nineteenth century. Indeed, the American evangelical movement was influenced most strongly by the Evangelical Revival of Britain, which was itself part of a pan-European revival that spread across the continent in the first half of the eighteenth century.[30] Carwardine has justly referred to the "transatlantic character of the First Great Awakening" to describe the influence that Great Britain had on American religion in the mid-eighteenth century.[31] This influence was not only one way, however; notable American revivalists of the Second Great Awakening, including Charles Grandison Finney, preached extensively throughout Britain. Unlike in the United States, however, the American penchant for revivals—in terms of large gatherings such as camp meetings—never gained hold as much in Great Britain (although they did occur), largely because revivals were frowned upon by the established Church.[32] Despite this difference, nineteenth-century British religion shared in common with American revivalism the concern with individual salvation. It is this core belief that matters for the purposes of this study, as salvation through Jesus Christ formed the cornerstone belief of the maritime religious revival in nineteenth-century Britain and the United States.

The Bethel Movement

The maritime folk group, as a subgroup within British and American societies, was neither unaware nor unaffected by events taking place around it. Three reform movements, in fact, directly targeted maritime culture: the Bethel movement, the temperance crusade, and the campaign against corporal punishment aboard ship. While all three were tied to the religious ideals of the time, it is only the Bethel movement, a concerted effort by a determined group of reformers to spread the gospel among mariners, that need concern us here. Kverndal provides detailed studies of the development of seamen's missions.[33] The earliest effort to bring religion to sailors consisted of the distribution of Bibles and religious tracts. These media reached a much wider audience than missionaries were able to do in person. Many sailors considered it unlucky to have a religious leader aboard ship, so it was difficult for ministers to go to sea. Written materials, however, met with no such objection. In fact, religious writings provided sailors with something to read, or have read to them, during tedious sea voyages. According to Kverndal, the distribution of religious literature to sailors first began to bear fruit in the Royal Navy during the Napoleonic Wars. During this time, British sailors who read the tracts spread the holy word throughout the Royal Navy and to other parts of the world. Also, the wars allowed English missionaries to preach to captured foreign seamen. With the coming of peace, these sailors spread religion among the merchant and naval fleets of their nations.

With the distribution of religious literature well under way by the early-nineteenth century, efforts to minister directly to sailors soon followed. The first mariner's church opened in London in 1818.[34] Appropriately, it was located on the former Royal Navy warship *Speedy*. Other maritime churches were soon established, but efforts to preach to sailors initially met with poor results. This was largely because sermons attacked seamen for drinking, gambling, swearing, and other vices. Sailors, always an independent, stubborn group, did not respond well to attacks on the few pleasures that they enjoyed. The missionaries learned, therefore, that they would have to be positive rather than negative if they wanted to convert mariners. To this end, missionaries began providing services that sailors needed. Seamen's Friend societies, for example, helped sailors find employment and assisted them with legal matters. Sailors' Homes provided mariners with affordable, comfortable housing during time in port, while Sailors' Rests gave elderly seamen a place to live after retirement. All of these institutions brought sailors to the church, where missionaries could then work to convert them. Thus, missions to seamen in the nineteenth century utilized the same pattern that missionaries often employ among cultures in third-world countries today. Modern missionaries offer services, such as food and health care, as enticements to attract people whom they wish to convert. From the point of view of the missionaries, of course, such actions exemplify the biblical command to demonstrate their faith through good works.

At times, the practices of reformers caused friction with sailors who understood what the reformers were up to. Nathaniel Ames, who served in both the U.S. Navy and the merchant marine, believed that his fellow seamen understood the true motives of the reformers: "why will not these self-constituted reformers of morals reflect, if only for one moment, that if sailors are 'babes in grace' they are by no means babes in common sense? [Sailors] are by no means so easily gulled as the fabricators of this pious magazine may think."[35] Ames' scathing indictment demonstrates that not all sailors welcomed reform movements. It also presents an apparent paradox. If sentiment against religion was still strong among nineteenth-century sailors, as it had been with their shipmates for centuries, how can we explain the boom in religious-themed maritime memorials that took place during that time? A closer look at the evidence reveals the maritime religious boom to have been a phenomenon linked largely to a specific segment of the maritime folk group.

Explaining the Increase in Religious Sentiment

If sailors were irreligious, how do we explain the clear increase in maritime memorials with religious themes that began in the mid-nineteenth century and continued until the end of the Age of Sail? Did a majority of sailors suddenly "get religion" at this time? Upon closer inspection, the evidence indicates otherwise. Analysis shows that most maritime memorials with religious themes were not erected by sailors. Rather, religious sentiment was expressed most often by other members of the maritime folk group, primarily wives, parents, and siblings of sailors.

Despite the fact that the clear majority of religious maritime memorials express the sentiment of seafarers' wives and families, nearly one-fifth were created by sailors themselves. It is likely that these represent the impact of the Bethel movement on seafaring culture. Two pieces of evidence support this interpretation. First, the increase in religious sentiment among mariners began in the 1840s, several decades after the birth of the Bethel movement. It is possible that religious sentiment penetrated seafaring slowly, so that its impact was not seen in memorials until several decades after the movement began. Second, many of the memorials that include religious sentiments of sailors came from places of worship. For example, six were recorded in the Seamen's Bethel in New Bedford, Massachusetts. Three others came from inside the church of Portsea St. Mary's in Portsmouth. All of these were erected by ship's companies to commemorate lost shipmates. It is important to note, however, that even in these places of worship, sailors erected memorials to lost comrades that did not contain any religious imagery or inscriptions. Their only connection with religion is the fact that they were placed in churches. Thus, although the memorials show that sailors participated in the mid-nineteenth-century religious boom, they may not have felt religious sentiment to the same degree as other members of maritime communities.

Religious maritime memorials are most valuable for their revelation of the ways that the maritime folk group used religion. While society around them was experiencing a religious revival, it is difficult to say how deeply this penetrated maritime culture. In all probability, non-seafaring group members such as wives, parents, and siblings likely had more religious faith, while those who spent their lives on the waves remained less religious, as sailors had always been. This accounts for the fact that non-seafaring group members erected more religious-themed maritime memorials than did sailors. However, all members of the group, both sailors and shore-based people alike, recognized several important ways that religion could help with the struggles that maritime life entailed. The maritime folk group chose from the religious reawakening around it ideas and images that resonated and used them to express a uniquely maritime view of the world.

The imagery, text, and themes of religious memorials of the nineteenth-century maritime religious boom were taken directly from the repertoire of ideas and symbols of the religious reawakening occurring in British and American society at that time. Epitaphs that feature Christ as the pilot or heaven as a safe haven at the end of one's life highlight the idea of salvation. Similarly, symbols such as the anchor express the hope that one has achieved salvation. The themes expressed on nineteenth-century maritime memorials, in fact, are also found on gravestones of non-mariners from the same period.

Nevertheless, it would be wrong to see the nineteenth-century maritime religious boom only in terms of these larger societal trends. It is true that maritime society participated in the pattern of its parent cultures, expressing the idea of salvation using some of the same phrases and symbols. This does not mean, however, that there is no greater meaning to be found on nineteenth-century maritime memorials. Rather, the meaning to maritime society lay specifically within the phrases and symbols chosen for inclusion on maritime memorials. Rather than just mimicking the religious sentiment taking place around them, maritime culture practiced agency, picking and choosing which elements of the religious revitalization movement to emphasize on their memorials. The group chose text and symbols that held a deeper meaning to them as a group specifically because they expressed maritime symbolism.

By way of comparison, it is useful to consider the religious symbols typically found in nineteenth-century Christianity. The idea of Christ as a shepherd, taking care of his flock, was a common Christian religious emblem.[36] This motif, however, is never found on maritime gravestones. Rather than Christ as a shepherd, which had meaning to landsmen but not to sailors, the maritime folk group preferred Christ as the anchor or as a fisherman. Gravestone symbolism followed the same pattern. The most common nineteenth-century Christian symbols were the finger pointing heavenward, clasped hands, Bibles, anchors, laurel wreaths, and flags.[37] The finger pointing heavenward has the double meaning that Christ is the way to salvation and that the person buried in the grave has gone to heaven. The clasped-hands symbol also has a double meaning, in this case signifying farewell to earthly concerns and welcoming of the soul into heaven. The Bible emphasizes the individual nature of salvation, while laurel wreaths and flags denote victory over death. The final common Second Great Awakening symbol, the anchor, is the one that concerns us most here. Anchors symbolize hope, as well as the idea that that hope—and therefore salvation—lies directly in Christ, who in the Bible is expressly given the symbolism of the anchor.

While all of these symbols are commonly found on nineteenth-century gravestones, only the anchor commonly appears on maritime gravestones. The other symbols do occur, but their numbers are dwarfed by the number of maritime gravestones featuring anchors. The reason for this is that mariners could directly relate to the anchor as a symbol of hope. Likewise, maritime culture chose inscriptions that were also explicitly maritime themed. Bible verses chosen for inclusion on maritime memorials were those that expressed the idea of finding a safe port or returning from the sea. This provides the key to interpreting the meaning that the nineteenth-century religious boom held for maritime culture. The images used—overwhelmingly the anchor—and the verses emphasizing finding a safe haven demonstrate that to maritime culture the religious revival of the time was another way of attempting to cope with the deadly nature of maritime life. As I have already discussed, the group values that maritime culture developed can be viewed as a response to the deadly environment of seafaring, especially the threat of nature and accidents. Likewise, the burial at sea ceremony and memorials for the missing were attempts to properly place the dead and to create a focus to mourn those who never returned. Both of these attempts ultimately proved unsatisfying. Those buried in the sea or in distant corners of the world, or lost beneath the depths, were always a source of heartbreak to their families, and no cenotaph could assuage that grief. In response, some turned to the religious revival movement taking place around them in the nineteenth century to find another way to cope with this eternal problem of maritime life. Rather than blindly following the winds of the times, however, maritime families used religion to highlight specific themes that were meaningful to them in their quest to soften the pain caused by the loss of so many sailors. The ways that they did so, and the meanings that they reveal about the maritime folk group, are explored in the following section.

Functions of Religion in Maritime Memorials

Sailors and other members of seafaring communities turned to religion as a source of comfort against hardship and loss. Religious imagery and inscriptions expressed the belief that God would take care of loved ones who were lost at sea, died at sea, or buried on the far side of the world. Religion also provided hope that sailors would anchor safely in the port of heaven following their final voyage. Finally, maritime wives and families used religious sentiment to express the faith that they would meet their lost sailors again following the Resurrection.

Hope in the Face of Tragedy

A number of memorials express faith that God will take care of sailors who succumbed to the dangers of the sea. The obelisk erected for Walter C. Ewer, discussed at the beginning of the previous chapter, provides a good example. A finger pointing heavenward adorns the top of the obelisk, showing where Walter's spirit has gone. Around this, the phrase "the sea his body, heaven his spirit holds" emphasizes the same idea.

Numerous other examples of the same theme exist among the memorials recorded by the survey. In Stonington, Connecticut, the headstone of Captain William Beck, who died at sea in 1846, includes the epitaph, "If Life's wide Ocean smile or roar, Still guide them to the Heavenly shore."[38] The gravestone of James Stephenson from Hull describes his loss in the sinking of the fishing smack *Olive Branch* in February 1889. The gravestone includes a depiction of the smack with a broken mast, symbolizing a life cut short. In addition, the epitaph "come unto Me, all ye that are weary, and I will give you rest" (Matthew 11:28) expresses the hope of Stephenson's parents that their son made it safely to heaven.[39] The verse "Blessed are the dead who die in the Lord" (Revelation 14:13) was also used to express the hope of salvation for those lost at sea. Both of these phrases were common on nineteenth-century gravestones, but were deemed particularly appropriate for those who died in tragic circumstances. The latter epitaph appears on the gravestone of Captain Charles Vail of New London, Connecticut, who was lost at sea in 1874.[40] The same verse was recorded twice in England. The first appears on the gravestone of William Edward Bolitho of Plymouth.[41] Bolitho drowned in Malta harbor in 1864 and was buried in a churchyard on that island, never returning to his family in Devon. Similarly, the family of James Smallridge Jeffery chose the verse to commemorate their son, who died in a shipwreck on the coast of Northumberland in 1857.[42] Whether or not any of these sailors were religious is unknown, but their families certainly hoped that the Lord would take care of them.

Perhaps the memorial that best exemplifies the themes discussed here is the stained-glass window in St. Mylor church, Cornwall, dedicated by the widow of John Downey, commander of the packet *Briseis*, which was lost in the North Atlantic in 1838 (figure 6.6).[43] The description of Captain Downey's loss is written at the bottom of a panel depicting the biblical story of Christ and his disciples on the Sea of Galilee (Luke 14:22–33) (figure 6.7). In the story, Jesus walked across the water to his disciples, who were in a boat upon the sea. At first, the disciples feared they were seeing a ghost, but soon were reassured that it was indeed their savior. Jesus then called to Peter to walk across the water to him. Peter did so, but became frightened by the wind and waves and began to sink. Peter called out for help, whereupon Jesus reached out and saved him, saying, "O man of little faith, why did you doubt?" The moral of the story is that salvation comes through faith in Christ. The juxtaposition of the story of Downey's loss with this particular scene expresses the widow's faith that Jesus also reached out to her husband in his hour of need. The panel on the right shows the story of the flood, with Noah's ark floating safely upon the waters. In the foreground, the arms of a drowning person reach beseechingly from the depths (figure 6.8). The inclusion of this scene provides a glimpse into what Downey's widow believed her husband's last moments in this world were like. Unlike the unbelievers who were drowned and lost forever, she had faith that Christ would rescue her husband's soul from the waters, as the Lord had promised for Noah and his family.

In Holy Trinity Church, Hull, a stained-glass window commissioned by another maritime wife expresses a similar theme. Sarah Leetham dedicated the stained-glass window to her husband, a ship owner and master, two sons who were sailors, and a third son who died as a young child.[44] The window consists of four panels, each of which depicts a scene from the Bible. From left to right, the window shows the story of the flood (Genesis 6–9), Moses being rescued from the Nile (Exodus 2:3–9), Jesus and his disciples on the Sea of Galilee (Luke 14:21–33), and God bringing sailors safely into port (Psalm 107). Inscriptions under each panel tell the stories of the deaths of her four loved ones. The far left, accompanied by the scene of the flood, describes the death of her husband at Nervi,

Figure 6.6. Stained-glass window commemorating Captain John Downey, RN, who drowned when the packet *Briseis* foundered in 1838. St. Mylor, Cornwall, U.K. Photo by author.

Italy, in 1875. To the right of this is the story of her son John, who was "accidentally drowned at Ipsamboul, on the Nile," in 1879. This inscription accompanies the story of Moses being rescued from the Nile, which includes the verse "I drew him out of the waters." This scene symbolizes Sarah Leetham's faith that her son, like Moses, was indeed "saved" from the Nile. Like the widow Downey, Mrs. Leetham envisioned her loved one's soul being taken up to heaven rather than perishing in the water. The next panel to the right, which shows Jesus saving his disciples on the

Figure 6.7. Detail of the lower left panel of the Downey memorial, showing Christ and his disciples on the Sea of Galilee. Photo by author.

Sea of Galilee, is accompanied by the description of the death of Walter Leetham at Kensington in 1880. Although nothing in the description indicates that Walter's death was related to the sea, the use of the image of Christ rescuing those upon the waters indicates that Mrs. Leetham considered the maritime imagery appropriate for commemorating her son. Finally, the last panel depicts a scene of mariners safely entering port, and includes the verse "so He bringeth them unto the desired haven" (Psalm 107:30). This scene is above the description of William Henry Leetham, who died in 1850 at only three years of age. Obviously, William was too young to have been a sailor. In this case, the imagery of anchoring safely in the haven probably stands for all four Leetham men, expressing Mrs. Leetham's belief that all her men found a safe harbor for eternal rest. As

Figure 6.8. Detail of the lower center panel of Downey's memorial, showing the story of Noah's ark. A drowning person's arms reach beseechingly from the waves. Photo by author.

will be discussed below, the image of anchoring safe in God's harbor at the end of life's voyage was a common theme in the religious maritime memorials of the nineteenth century.

As with those lost at sea, religion could provide a comfort to the families of sailors who died and were buried in foreign lands. Such a theme appears on a memorial brass in Bristol Cathedral that was erected by the widow of Captain John Sanderson, RN.

TO THE MEMORY OF
MY BELOVED HUSBAND
JOHN SANDERSON,
A CAPTAIN IN THE ROYAL NAVY,
WHO DIED WHILE ON ACTIVE
SERVICE, IN COMMAND OF
HER MAJESTY'S SHIP "ARCHER"
OFF THE CONGO RIVER, SOUTH-
AFRICA, JUNE 27TH 1859, AND
WAS BURIED AT LOANGO.

"BLESSED ARE THE
PURE IN HEART, FOR
THEY SHALL SEE GOD."

"WHAT I DO, THOU KNOW-
EST NOT NOW, BUT
THOU SHALT KNOW
HEREAFTER"[45]

The first part of the inscription asserts the widow's conviction that Sanderson was doing his duty when death overtook him. As discussed in chapter 3, attention to duty was a core value of maritime life. Performing one's duty was an essential part of ensuring the safe operation of a vessel, so it is easy to see why Mrs. Sanderson would think it important to note this point. The rest of the inscription, however, makes it clear that the knowledge that her husband was performing his duty served as little comfort to her. In addition to expressing her faith that her husband will be with God, the final part of the epitaph speaks of Mrs. Sanderson's struggle to accept the fact that her husband would never return. The final lines represent an attempt to cope with the fact that her husband will never return by viewing his death as divine will, which cannot be known to her now but will be understood in the fullness of time.

Faith also served as a comfort to those faced with the sudden death of a loved one that was a fundamental part of life in maritime communities. Sculcoates Lane Cemetery in Hull contains a gravestone for seaman Robert Smith, who "died suddenly" in 1872 at age twenty-seven from unstated causes.[46] The epitaph "Life how short! Eternity how long" emphasizes the brevity of a sailor's life. The stone includes a carving of a cross, anchor, and heart, symbolizing Christianity's three theological virtues of faith, hope, and love (figure 6.9). This symbolism expresses the Smith family's belief that even though their son was taken suddenly, his soul was saved. The gravestone of Thomas Atwill of Plymouth represents another whose life was suddenly cut short by an accident.[47] The epitaph asserts his widow's belief that "in heaven we hope to meet again." The phrase "in the midst of life we are in death," which forms part of the Anglican burial service, likewise expresses the fact that death can come suddenly at any time. It was recorded on two memorials in England. The first, a gravestone in Portland St. George, Dorset, was erected by their siblings to honor three seafaring brothers who met untimely ends.[48] The first two brothers, Captain Thomas Elliott Read and John Read, perished in the sinking of the steamship *Theban* in January 1870. Less than a year later, a third brother, Joseph Read, died in the wreck of the steamship *Cambria*. While the gravestone also commemorates the mother and a sister, both of whom are probably present in the grave, the placement of the epitaph "in the midst of life we are in death" refers specifically to the three lost sailors. Thus, it was probably chosen by the Read family to illustrate the pain suffered by the sudden tragic deaths of their brothers. Far to the northeast in Hull, another

Figure 6.9. Detail of gravestone of Robert Smith, showing the Christian virtues of faith (cross), hope (anchor), and love (heart). Sculcoates Lane Cemetery, Hull, U.K. Photo by author.

seafaring family chose the same verse to express their distress at the sudden death of seaman Richard Garrick, who was lost at sea in 1889 at age seventeen.[49]

A Safe Port at the End of Life's Voyage

In a profession where so many did not return, the ending of a mariner's life peacefully at home at a full age was a subject for rejoicing. A number of memorials give thanks to God for deliverance from the dangers of the sea and joy that the sailor is now safely anchored. As discussed above, this theme was present in some of the earliest religious maritime memorials in America. As part of the nineteenth-century religious boom, the theme blossomed in both Great Britain and the United States. For example, the gravestone of John Moore, RN, who died in 1872 at age seventy-seven, contains the epitaph "He hath delivered me from the stormy wind and tempest."[50] In nearby Falmouth, maritime wife Sophia Maunder chose a similar epitaph for her husband Henry upon his death in 1905: "The tempest may sweep o'er the wild stormy deep, he is safe where the storm comes no more."[51] Both of these gravestones specifically link the mariners' concern about storms with the comfort supplied by religious faith, and illustrate the relief and thanks shown by maritime families whose loved ones had made it through the perils that took so many other sailors from their communities.

A number of other maritime memorials also contained variations of the phrase "safe in port." Not all of these necessarily connote religious sentiment. For example, two English gravestones, for mariners Richard Lee and Josiah Heath, contain the simple epitaph "safely anchored."[52] Heath's, in fact, is carved on an anchor representation, demonstrating that the anchor does not stand only for maritime identity, but is also a metaphor for the conclusion of life's voyage. Similarly, the gravestone of English seaman William Hopper includes the epitaph "Safe home in port."[53] From the same churchyard, the gravestone of another English mariner, Robert Wallace, contains the same epitaph, along with a carved anchor symbol.[54] A similar epitaph, "safe in port," was recorded on the gravestone of Captain Alvan Fengar in New London, Connecticut, while the gravestone of another American mariner, Captain Daniel Humphrey of New Bedford, Massachusetts, included the similar phrase "safe in harbor."[55] Although all of these examples express the idea of being safely anchored at the end of life's voyage, none is explicitly religious.

Variations on the same theme, however, contain wording that shows that the safe harbor is indeed heaven. In the church of Portsea St. Mary's, the memorial brass for Basil Hall (whose description of a burial at sea was quoted in chapter 4) and his son, both captains in the Royal Navy, serves as a good example of the use of the haven as a metaphor for heaven.

> To the Glory of GOD
> and in loving memory of
> BASIL HALL, Captain Royal Navy,
> Born 31st December 1788.
> Laid to rest in the ground near this Church in September 1844.
> Also in loving memory of
> BASIL SIDMOUTH DaROS HALL, Captain Royal Navy,
> Son of the above, Born 8th August 1833,
> Died at Mayrair in Germany 11th July 1871.
>
> "Then are they glad because they are at rest;
> and so He bringeth them unto the
> haven where they would be."[56]

The epitaph, which is from Psalm 107, confirms that in this case the haven refers to heaven. The first line of the memorial also expresses religious sentiment. It is likely that the gravestone of John France from Hull, which contains the epitaph "safe in the haven" is meant to express the same religious idea as the Hall memorial brass.[57] In France's case, the inclusion of an anchor reinforces the idea of being safely at rest in harbor.

The image of heaven as a safe harbor at the end of life's stormy voyages was not unique to maritime communities. It formed part of the general religious sentiment of the nineteenth century, and appears in many hymns from the period. Three memorials, two from England and one from the United States, include an epitaph from a hymn that became a favorite among mariners. The gravestone of English sailor John Bower in Portland St. George, which was quoted at the beginning of this chapter, commemorates him with the epitaph "Rocks and storms I'll fear no more."[58] Bower's gravestone also includes an "IHS" motif, further indication of religious sentiment. In New London, Connecticut, Captain John Ewen's epitaph provides a more complete version than Bower's:

> Rocks and storms I'll fear no more
> While on that eternal shore
> Drop the anchor furl the sail
> I am safe within the vail.[59]

Ewen's epitaph is the chorus from the hymn "Safe Within the Vail," the full version of which runs as follows:

> "Land ahead!" Its fruits are waving
> O'er the hills of fadeless green;
> And the living waters laying
> Shores where heavenly forms are seen
> *Chorus*
> Rocks and storms I'll fear no more,
> When on that eternal shore:
> Drop the anchor; furl the sail:
> I am safe within the vail
> Onward bark: the cape I'm rounding:
> See the blessed wave their hands;
> Hear the harps of God resounding
> From the bright immortal bands.
> Now we're safe from all temptation,
> All the storms of life are past:
> Praise the Rock of our salvation:
> We are safe at home at last.[60]

It is easy to see why this hymn struck a chord within maritime culture. After a difficult and dangerous life on the sea, "hills of fadeless green" where one could rest free from "all the storms of life" must have held great appeal.

Different subgroups within the maritime folk group expressed the idea of safely reaching port in different ways. Memorials for pilots sometimes employed a motif that exemplified their unique job. The task of the pilot was to guide a vessel safely into or out of port. Unlike bluewater sailors who spent much of their time far out of sight of land, pilots rarely ventured far from the port at which they were based. This did not mean, however, that their job was devoid of danger. The opposite was in fact true; pilots spent much of their time herding large vessels through channels that were often narrow, shallow, and shifting. For some pilots, the motif that expressed the essence of their task was the successful passage over the bar, the area of shallow, high-energy water that marks the transition from protected waters to the open sea. Tides and currents flow swiftly across the bar, and their shallow water is often churned up into short, confused waves. The forces of wind, current, and tide make bars tricky and dangerous places for navigation. Pilots, whose jobs made them experts on local conditions and who were paid for their expertise accordingly, became intimately familiar with the bars associated with their ports. Even their local knowledge, however, did not ensure complete safety, as weather changes and shifting channels always made bars a hazardous place for navigation. Whatever the season, the bar was a dangerous place, and the pilot's contribution was to bring others safely across it. Some celebrated this idea on their memorials by including Alfred Tennyson's maritime-themed religious poem "Crossing the Bar." While the entire poem includes a mixture of maritime and religious images celebrating life's journey as a metaphorical sea voyage, the last stanza was particularly appropriate for seafarers.

> For though from out our bourn of Time and Place
> The flood may bear me far,
> I hope to see my Pilot face to face
> When I have crost the bar.[61]

Accordingly, although the entire poem was sometimes reproduced on a memorial, it was more common to incorporate part of the final stanza, which most clearly expresses the idea of transitioning to safety with God. One example comes from the gravestone of William John Lowry in Falmouth Cemetery, Cornwall, which paraphrases Tennyson: "we shall meet our pilot face to face/when we have crossed the bar."[62] Like hymns such as "Safe Within the Vail," this poem was not a piece of lore generated by the maritime folk group. Group members chose it, however, because it expressed an idea that had meaning to maritime culture.

Faith in Resurrection

Closely connected to the idea of being safely anchored at the end of life's voyage was the expression of faith in resurrection at the end of the world. This theme was sometimes used for mariners who passed away peacefully at the end of their lives. The gravestone of Charles Davidson, Master Mariner of Hull, who died in 1873 at age sixty-eight and was buried in that city, includes an anchor design and the epitaph "my flesh shall also rest in hope."⁶³ Both the anchor and the epitaph signify belief in another life ahead. The gravestone of John Scriven in Portland St. George makes the connection of the anchor and hope even more explicit. Scriven's stone includes an anchor at the top surrounded by the phrase "in sure and certain hope" (figure 6.10).⁶⁴ Scriven, who died in 1902 at the advanced age of eighty-six, was also commemorated with the epitaph "for he giveth his beloved sleep." Taken together, the elements on Scriven's stone symbolize the mariner sleeping peacefully awaiting the resurrection. Susanna Gilbert, maritime wife in Cornwall, also believed that her husband would rise again at the end of time. The epitaph she chose for her husband Richard upon his death in 1910 at age seventy-two, no doubt after many years at sea, states:

> ONCE A MARINER OF THE DEEP
> NOW LYING IN SILENT SLEEP
> WAITING THE TRUMPET SOUND⁶⁵

Like Davidson's gravestone, Gilbert's includes an anchor symbol, which both identifies him as a mariner and reinforces the idea of hope. Emma Hill, a sailor's wife from Liverpool, expressed the same idea in her epitaph dedicated to "my dear husband" Master Mariner William Hill, who died in 1891 at age seventy-one.

> THE TOILSOME VOYAGES NOW ARE PAST,
> THE WEARIED MARINER RESTS AT LAST,
> AND WHEN THE LAST TRUMPET'S CALL SHALL SOUND,
> MAY HE AMONG THE BLESSED BE FOUND.⁶⁶

Although expressions of faith that God would raise their loved ones at the end of time were appropriate for those who died on land and whose bodies were present in their graves, such sentiments were even more appropriate for those whose bodies were lost beneath the waves. The parents of Benjamin Ewen used religion as a comfort when their son was lost at sea in 1856.

> IN
> Memory of
> BENJAMIN B.
> Son of John & Mary Ewen
> born July 24, 1836,

was lost overboard at Sea
from the Bark Alexander
Capt. W. Bush,
on the 30 of Nov. 1856,
in Lat. 30° South, Long. 133° West
while in the act of furling
the Main top gallant sail &
never was seen more.
Our God with eyes that never sleeps
Will watch our loved one in the deep
Will jealous care where now he lies
Till the last trump shall bid him rise.[67]

In addition to epitaphs such as this, two Bible verses associated with the sea were often used to express faith that those lost there would return at the end of time. The phrase "when the sea shall give up her dead," a reference to Revelation 20:13, was recorded on memorials in England and in the United States. In all cases, it was used to commemorate those who died at sea or who were lost at sea. For example, the verse was used

Figure 6.10. Anchor and phrase "in sure and certain hope" on the gravestone of seaman John Scriven. AAMMD #32, Portland St. George, Dorset, U.K. Photo by author.

to memorialize American sailor James Graham, who died at sea in 1857. Graham's gravestone also includes the epitaph "For if we believe that Jesus died and rose again, even so them also who sleep in Jesus will God bring with him."[68] Once again, this reiterates the faith that God will resurrect the body of their loved one, no matter where that body lies. In New Bedford, the gravestone of John A. Peirce notes that "the grave holds not thy precious form," but expresses faith that "the Sea shall give up its dead."[69]

A second verse, "I shall bring my people again from the depths of the sea" (Psalm 68:22) was also commonly employed to express faith that God would resurrect those lost at sea. The family of George Mant chose this psalm to express their belief that Mant, who was lost at sea in 1880, would return at the end of time.[70] The verse also appears on the monument for HMS *Eurydice*, which wrecked upon the Isle of Wight while a young Winston Churchill looked on.[71] *Eurydice*'s elaborate memorial includes not only Psalm 68:22 but also "and the sea gave up the dead which were in it" (Revelation 20:13) and "which hope we have as an anchor of the soul" (Hebrews 6:19). The inclusion of an iron anchor recovered from the wreck further underscores the symbolism of hope.

Conclusions

Preceding chapters have illustrated how the hardships and dangers of maritime life, especially the power of nature and the problem of missing bodies, affected maritime worldview and was in turn reflected in memorials. Sudden death was a fact of life for mariners, who developed a set of group values and beliefs for dealing with it. Chapter 5 demonstrated how families used memorials as foci for remembrance and visitation when sailors died at sea or in foreign lands. However, empty graves were never a truly adequate substitute for the missing bodies of those who never returned. It is in this light that the increase in religious sentiment in maritime communities in the nineteenth century should be viewed. If rocks, storms, and missing bodies were symptoms of maritime life, then the nineteenth-century religious revival can be thought of as an attempt to use faith as a cure. Members of the maritime folk group, particularly wives and families, turned to religion as a source of comfort. In the memorials, religious sentiment expressed the belief that God would protect sailors against the dangers of the sea, the hope that mariners would anchor safely in the port of heaven at the end of life's voyage, and the faith that maritime families would meet their lost loved ones after the Resurrection. Variations of the verses "I shall bring my people again from the depths of the sea," (Psalm 68:22) and "the sea gave up the dead that were in it" (Revelation 20:13) had particular meaning for families whose sailors were lost or buried in the depths.

Although a significant number of maritime memorials from the 1800s on exhibit religious sentiment, this does not indicate that the majority of sailors suddenly "found religion" at that time. Instead, analysis reveals that many of the memorials with religious themes were erected by maritime wives, parents, or other non-seafaring members of the maritime community. Thus, a number of the religious memorials can be explained as the product of the general religious revival that took place in Great Britain and the United States in the nineteenth century. Shore-based members of the folk group, such as parents, wives, and siblings, who were more in touch with the mainstream culture around them, seem to have participated in this revival to a greater extent than bluewater sailors. Nevertheless, sailors did create about 20 percent of the religious maritime memorials, a fact that can probably be attributed to the impact of the Bethel movement.

The rise in maritime religion had the goal of defeating the dangers that framed maritime life. Rocks and storms as objects of horror were transformed into "rocks and storms I'll fear no more." This statement acknowledged that the dangers of seafaring life could never be defeated, but asserted the belief that they need not be feared because a supreme deity would provide in the end. The extent to which this hopeful sentiment was accomplished, however, probably varied based on the depth of faith of each individual.

7

Conclusions

A LIVING TRADITION

St. David's, Bermuda, September 2008

To reach Bermuda's Lost at Sea memorial, you follow a winding lane past Lord's Cricket Ground through a quiet residential neighborhood until you reach the windswept cliffs at the northeast tip of the islands. Bermuda's monument is a fitting place to end this story. Bermuda sits, isolated, between the two great maritime cultures that serve as the focus of this book: the parent, the British Isles, more than three thousand miles to the northeast, and its offspring in America only six hundred miles west. The spot where the English vessel *Sea Venture* wrecked in 1609 while carrying colonists to the fledgling Jamestown colony is visible from the memorial. Bermuda's appropriateness is more than geographical, however. Bermuda's Lost at Sea memorial provides a modern example of the memorialization traditions that English and American maritime cultures developed in order to deal with the countless tragedies that they have witnessed in the four hundred years since *Sea Venture* tore itself onto Bermuda's reefs.

How these tragedies have been remembered has been told in previous chapters. But the story does not end there. English and American maritime memorialization is a living tradition, as evidenced by Bermuda's Lost at Sea memorial. Although recent—the memorial was constructed in 2005—it incorporates traditions and motifs that date back at least as far as *Sea Venture*'s day. The centerpiece of the memorial is a bronze sculpture shaped like half of a lifeboat, with the bow pointing upward toward the sky. This form gives the appearance of a sinking boat, especially when viewed against the backdrop of the ocean (figure 7.1). The impression of a sinking boat is strengthened by jagged holes fashioned into the hull. The design and placement of the monument invokes an image of the moment of disaster, just as maritime memorials from previous centuries did. Inside the hull, additional elements strengthen the link to past memorials. A life preserver, an oar, an hourglass, and a pair of dividers are all elements that can be found on memorials from the Age of Sail. The hull features two circular holes representing eyes gazing out to sea in a perpetual vigil for the lost, while below a map of Bermuda represents a teardrop.[1] The outside of the hull also features representations of aquatic creatures such as a starfish, seashells, and a fish skeleton, symbolizing the importance of fishing in Bermuda's history.

The boat sculpture is set atop a pedestal that is surrounded by granite panels inscribed with the names of Bermudians lost at sea from the seventeenth through the twenty-first centuries. The list of names hearkens back to nineteenth-century forerunners. This is surrounded by a brick paved area in the shape of a ship's compass, with the cardinal compass points delineated by radiating lines of bricks. Outside the paved area, benches provide places for quiet contemplation.

As a whole, the memorial provides a place to commemorate the lost while at the same time displaying symbols of maritime culture. This design is no accident. The memorial was created by Bermudian sculptor Bill Ming, who had himself been a sailor. As a maritime group member, Ming understood the motifs appropriate for a memorial for the missing. "The theme of maritime life is very close to my art and ideas," Ming said in an interview, and continued that he designed the memorial as a place "where family members can reflect on the lives of their loved ones."[2] Providing a place for visitation and continued commemoration was a principal reason why memorials for the missing were created in the first place. As the modern incarnation of a tradition that began in the late-eighteenth century, Ming's sculpture provides a place to remember all those who never returned from the sea.

The modern maritime remembrance tradition has evolved from its Age of Sail forebears but still features motifs and themes from earlier times. In the Age of Sail, mariners were constantly at the mercy of the forces of nature, and numerous memorials speak of this struggle and the group values that mariners developed to deal with it. The forces of nature are

Figure 7.1. Bermuda's Lost at Sea memorial, designed by ex-seaman turned artist Bill Ming. Photo by author.

not as prominently represented on modern maritime memorials, however. Storms and shipwrecks still claim lives, but the vivid imagery of humans battling the forces of nature is no longer as prevalent as it once was. Improvements in vessel safety, weather forecasting, navigation, and lifesaving services all make rocks and storms less of a threat today than in previous centuries. While this accounts for some of the decrease in the humans versus nature theme, it is also likely due in part to the cultural shift away from dramatic representations on gravestones. Modern British and American attitudes toward death favor more low-key themes rather than the dramatic imagery that prevailed during the Romantic period.

Mariners' fear of rocks and storms has provided one of the most enduring legacies of the Age of Sail, however, as shown by the way that the humans versus nature motif runs strong in popular culture. Tales of shipwrecks and disaster at sea continue to fascinate the public to this day. Books, movies, and television shows with maritime subjects emphasize over and over again the theme of humans battling the elements. In 1976, Canadian folksinger Gordon Lightfoot captured the imaginations of both Canadians and Americans with his song "The Wreck of the *Edmund Fitzgerald*," which described the tragic loss of that vessel on Lake Superior in November 1975. This haunting ballad reached number two on the Billboard charts and remains popular on oldies radio stations today.[3] Films featuring humans struggling against the sea remain popular also. The popularity of the 1956 film adaptation of Melville's classic *Moby Dick* resulted in a large increase of tourists at the Seamen's Bethel in New Bedford. In the 2000 motion picture *The Perfect Storm*, audiences empathized with the six-man crew of the ill-fated swordboat *Andrea Gale*, alone on the ocean and facing a tremendous storm. The climactic scene of the film occurs when the fishing vessel struggles to reach the top of a towering wave, only to be swallowed up. This signifies, as on Age of Sail memorials, the importance of the moment of tragedy. Near the end, the crew of another boat finds *Andrea Gale*'s gas cans floating; these are all that have ever been found of the vessel.[4] Such material culture ephemera symbolizes confirmation that the vessel has indeed been lost. The human versus nature struggle is so ingrained that some maritime films with this theme have gone on to rank among the top money makers of all time. Probably the most famous (and perhaps most melodramatic) example is the 1997 motion picture *Titanic*, which made approximately $1.02 billion, making it the sixth highest grossing film ever.[5] *Titanic*'s message, in which the forces of nature (in the form of icebergs and the frigid sea) defeat the "unsinkable" product of human hubris, resonated with audiences because it expressed fundamental themes of human existence. Two other maritime-related movies rank among the one hundred highest grossing films of all time. *Jaws*, Steven Spielberg's classic 1975 film of a rogue great white shark terrorizing a beach resort community, nips at *Titanic*'s stern with $1.01 billion in profits when adjusted for inflation. The 1972 version of *The Poseidon Adventure* comes in at number seventy-four, having grossed an estimated $436 million.[6] On television, the growth of "reality TV" has spawned several series that chronicle humans versus the elements, including the Weather Channel's "Storm Stories" series and the Discovery Channel's "Deadliest Catch," which follows Alaskan crab fishermen at work in the deadly waters of the Bering Sea. Uncountable books on historical shipwreck events have been written, so that even a simple bibliographic search yields hundreds of titles on particular vessels destroyed by nature. Clearly, the human fascination with the eternal struggle against nature has not diminished.

Compared to earlier times, accidents feature more prominently on recent maritime memorials than storms and shipwrecks. Ships are dangerous work environments, and deaths through falling, drowning, or accidents with machinery remain common. In Plymouth, England, a section of the wall of the Plymouth Lifeboat Guild is designated as the Boatmen's Shelter. It contains plaques commemorating local fishermen who have been killed since the 1930s. Two of the plaques commemorate mariners who lost their lives due to accidents. Fisherman Chris Welburn, a man described as "Big, Brave, Bold, Bald and Sometimes Bloody Difficult!" was "Tragically Killed on The Quay" in 2000.[7] Fellow Plymouth fisherman Michael Aitken was "accidentally killed on the MFV *Scarlet Thread*," though the year is not given.[8] The data from modern maritime memorials agree well with Roberts' recent study that shows accidents as among the leading causes of death in modern British seafaring.[9]

By far the most heartrending conclusion to come from this study is the way that the maritime folk group had to deal with the huge number of missing bodies. In this sample of more than two thousand maritime memorials, over 40 percent commemorate seafarers who never returned home. About half of the bodies that make up this number lie buried in other parts of the world, but still around 20 percent, or one in five, maritime memorials commemorate sailors whose bodies were never recovered.

This is a staggering figure. Folk groups in other dangerous occupations, such as logging, also lived with the constant threat of fatality and developed many of the same values as mariners. While death was a constant part of their lives, most other groups did not have to deal with missing bodies the way that the maritime folk group did. Accidents killed many loggers each year, but the bodies were usually recoverable and could be buried. Cowboys often died out on the range, far from civilization, similar to sailors who died in distant parts of the globe. Cowboys, however, did not have to deal with the huge numbers of missing bodies that sailors did. The occupational group that comes closest to the experience of the maritime group is the military. Outside of times of war, however, the military did not typically have to deal with the large number of missing bodies. Like cowboys, group members might be buried far from home, but at least they were buried. Sailors, unique among occupations, had to deal with the problem that many of their dead were simply gone. This fact had a huge impact on group culture.

In the late-eighteenth century, changing attitudes toward the deceased led to a greater concern with preserving both the memory and the physical remains of persons after death. This change in the Anglo-American attitude toward death was marked in cemeteries by an increase in permanent graves and gravemarkers. Like the larger society of which they were a part, maritime communities wanted to have a continuing relationship with their dead as well. This was complicated, however, by the fact that so many sailors died away from home. The bodies of such men were seldom returned. Seafaring communities coped with this problem by commemorating the memory of the missing. This often took the form of adding the names of the lost to family or collective monuments. In some cases, the missing person was given an actual grave. Cenotaphs provided a focus for rituals of remembrance. Despite such efforts, the inscriptions on many memorials for absent sailors clearly reveal that cenotaphs were never a fully adequate substitute for the missing body.

The problem of missing bodies remains an endemic part of maritime life, and this theme continues to figure prominently on modern memorials. Bermuda's Lost at Sea memorial is one example, but many others can be found in ports throughout the world. Cornwall's St. Mylor church, home to so many memorials commemorating tragedies from previous centuries, also houses a recent lost-at-sea memorial. This memorial commemorates "thirty-one men women and children lost at sea in the motor vessel *Darlywyne*" in July 1966.[10] Maritime motifs such as an anchor, life preserver, buoy, sailboat, compass, ship's bell, capstan, and ship's wheel hearken back to earlier times, and the designers of the *Darlywyne* memorial need have looked no further than St. Mylor church and its churchyard to find Age of Sail examples of many of them. As I was completing this manuscript in March 2009, a North Carolina scallop fishing boat, the *Lady Mary*, sank off the coast of New Jersey. Only one of her seven-member crew survived. The bodies of four others were recovered, but two men remain missing. Newspaper accounts reveal how these men and their families feel trapped in a liminal state. Almost two months after the tragedy, the brother of one of the missing fishermen was quoted as saying, "We are just waiting to hear and holding fast to our faith. . . . We believe he was on that boat and we know that it went down. But we are holding on as long as we can."[11] Maritime families from the Age of Sail would have understood this sentiment completely.

The dangers of seafaring life led maritime communities to turn for solace to the religious revivals of the eighteenth and nineteenth centuries. Most of the religious maritime memorials were erected by the wives and families of lost sailors. The memorials that they created express the faith that God would take care of their missing loved ones and that everyone would be reunited in heaven and made whole again following the Resurrection. This increase in religion was not unique to maritime communities during the first half of the nineteenth century. Rather, maritime religious memorials reflected the upsurge in religious sentiment that took place in England and the United States during that time. The use of religious sentiment to mourn those lost or buried far away, however, represented the maritime manifestation of this religious movement. Such memorials typically employed maritime metaphors as well.

Sailors themselves did create some religious tributes, however, and this rise in religion was likely due to the impact of the Bethel movement. This reform movement sought to bring sailors closer to God while also providing practical services for them. A number of religious maritime memorials erected by sailors were associated with houses of worship. Nevertheless, many memorials erected by sailors, even in places of worship, did not express religious sentiment. If memorials are any indication, it seems that the impact of the Bethel movement on sailors was limited.

The theme of religion has continued in modern maritime memorials. Overt expressions of religious fervor have become more common in

American culture during the past several decades, and this may account for some of the modern American religious-themed maritime memorials. The similarity of wording, however, may indicate that these memorials represent a carryover of the maritime religious tradition that began in the late-eighteenth century. The gravestone of New Bedford sail maker Ernest Smith shows similarities to nineteenth-century maritime religious memorials. As befits a memorial for a sail maker, the stone includes an illustration of a vessel under sail, but also contains the full text of the poem "The Haven of His Love" by Jon Gilbert (figure 7.2).[12] The motifs of this poem, which include Christ as a pilot, guiding a vessel through the storms of life to a safe harbor, echo nineteenth-century religious maritime memorials. The same is true for Texas mariner Billy Stanley, whose 1997 gravestone contains an illustration of a river steamboat and the epitaph "God is your wheelman now."[13] Modern maritime memorials with religious themes are not limited to the United States. Though Great Britain is a more secular society, the tradition of religious maritime memorials continues there as well. The plaque for Plymouth fishermen Gary Searle and Henry Crews includes the verse "I will make you fishers of men" (Matthew 4:19).[14] Fellow fisherman Victor Rixon's epitaph, "at rest in God's eternal harbour," restates a common theme from nineteenth-century maritime memorials.[15] These memorials show that the theme of religion as a source of comfort and help with the dangers and death inherent in seafaring life remains a part of the maritime mindset. Conspicuously absent from modern memorials, however, is the theme of Christ as the anchor, which figured so prominently in the maritime religious tradition of the nineteenth century. Anchors are still commonly used as maritime occupational identifiers, but the explicit connection of the anchor as Christ is rarely made. Like the paucity of modern memorials depicting rocks and storms, this may reflect the fact that modern vessels are less at the mercy of wind and current, and thus the anchor no longer holds the symbolic association of the last hope to the extent that it once did.

The capacity for memorials to teach succeeding generations proper commemoration practices was discussed in chapter 3, and it seems likely that maritime memorials represent one vehicle by which maritime traditions have been passed down to succeeding generations of the maritime folk group. It is possible to see a great deal of continuity in maritime memorials from the Age of Sail to the present day. The Bermuda Lost at Sea memorial is a recent example of this, while the *Darlywyne* memorial

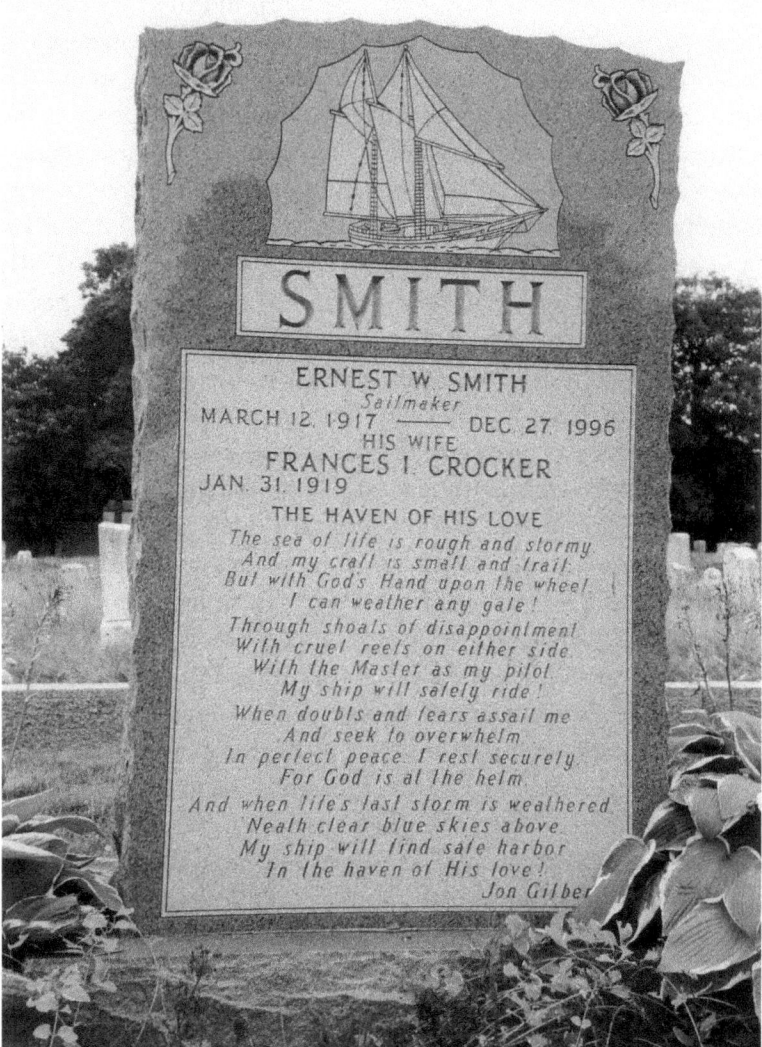

Figure 7.2. A modern religious maritime memorial: the gravestone of sail maker Ernest Smith from New Bedford's Rural Cemetery. Photo by author.

provides an example from the late 1960s. While I do not have enough twentieth-century data to postulate a direct line of continuity between Age of Sail maritime memorials and modern ones, I believe it probable that such a link exists. Creators of twentieth-century memorials likely learned proper wording by looking at examples from earlier times. By the mid-nineteenth century, wood and sails were giving way to steel and steam. Mariners from the days of sail continued to ply the seas well into the twentieth century, and sailing ships remained in active duty in some places (in the United States, the Chesapeake Bay skipjack fleet remains a sailing fleet, the last one in the country), but by the early-twentieth century, a new generation of sailors had come onto the scene. Many twentieth-century sailors never served aboard a wooden vessel, or one that was powered by wind. Nevertheless, the new generation learned many traditions from men who began their seafaring careers in wooden sailing vessels before transitioning into iron and steel steamships. This transitional phase took place in the late-nineteenth and early-twentieth centuries. During this period, mariners from the Age of Sail passed on group traditions to their successors. Twentieth-century sailors walked steel decks that vibrated to the throbbing of engines, but the maritime group maintained many of the core beliefs from earlier times. Memorialization traditions were probably passed on as well. The similarity of themes and wording on early-twentieth-century memorials makes it probable that twentieth-century sailors used memorials put up by preceding generations of sailors, among other forms of lore, as templates for proper maritime memorialization forms. The memorial for Royal Navy seaman Herbert Neighbour, killed when the submarine M1 sank in the English Channel in 1925, serves as a good example of the continuation of tradition. The memorial notes that Neighbour "rests with his comrades" in the sunken submarine.[16] His body was never recovered, but as had been the case since the late-eighteenth century, Neighbour's family felt the need to provide a focus for commemoration. Further research into early-twentieth-century maritime memorials might well yield interesting insights into continuity and change in memorialization practices, and group beliefs, as the maritime folk group transitioned to the modern world of steel-hulled, engine-powered vessels.

The story of maritime life is thus one of hardship and loss. But there is another way to look at this. The maritime folk group would never have become the high-context group that it was if it had not been engaged in such a deadly occupation. The sea took thousands, but it also provided many people their livelihood. You can see both a hatred for and a love of the sea in maritime memorials and in other lore. Samuel Kelly claimed that "I may date the beginning of the troubles of [my] life" to the day when he first went away to sea, and Edward Barlow called seafaring a "hard and miserable calling."[17] Edward Coxere spent most of his first voyage seasick, and determined "not to live that miserable sea-life," although he later returned to it for many years.[18] Sentiments such as these were common, but it is also true that those who met the challenge often looked back with nostalgia on their seafaring days. The sense of pride that sailors gained from braving a hazardous occupation comes across clearly in memorials that highlight a man's duty and service. Jacob Havens' gravestone proudly notes that he was the "last of the Whaling Captains" of Sag Harbor, New York.[19] "He loved the sea, 'twas the home of his choice," states the epitaph for Henry Howard, who was buried beneath the waves.[20] You can see this sentiment in other ways as well. The gravestones of Harry Grant and John Read state that both men were "born at sea," a fact that their families saw worthy of noting.[21] From birth to death, the sea played a major role in the lives of the maritime folk group. There *was* a romance to seafaring in the Age of Sail, and in fact, danger and romance were coupled together. "It is the excitement, danger, and money that a sea life Brings that keeps me at sea, nothing else," said American mariner Charles Benson.[22] British sailor William Robinson, writing under the pen name Jack Nastyface, looked back on his career at the end of his autobiography. Nastyface's words sum up the mixed bag that was life at sea.

> In contemplating the varied scenes of so motley a profession as that of a sailor, there is much to be thought on with pleasure, and much with a bitter anguish and disgust. To the youth possessing anything of a roving disposition it is attractive, nay, it is seducing; for it has its allurements, and when steadily pursued and with success, it ennobles the mind, and the seaman feels himself a man. There is, indeed, no profession that can vie with it.[23]

The sea was never trustworthy, but it was nonetheless the home that seafarers were forced to accept. They viewed it as a cruel, but fundamental, part of life.

Future Research Directions

This book has focused on the beliefs and values of mariners as an occupational folk group. Study of memorials, however, can provide insight into other aspects of maritime society. One obvious avenue for future research is to compare the results from this study with mariners from other ethnic, national, and religious backgrounds. This study examined memorials for English and American seafarers who were primarily Caucasian and from

Protestant religious backgrounds. European nations such as Portugal, Spain, the Netherlands, and France played important roles during the Age of Sail. Their sailors came from a variety of cultural and religious backgrounds, and I wonder how their maritime memorials compare to English and American ones. It would be interesting to see, for example, if and how Catholic seafarers melded maritime and religious ideas on memorials. Likewise, sailing ship crews included sailors from many ethnicities. It was not unusual to find Africans, Asians, and Pacific Islanders, among others, crewing English and American vessels. How these groups integrated into the maritime folk group can be explored through memorials. Since the maritime folk group is an occupational group that transcends national and ethnic boundaries, memorials created by sailors of various ethnic and religious groups should show broad similarity to English and American ones. Another way of saying this is that once a person becomes a member of the group, the group's traditions should take precedence over ethnic, national, or religious differences. However, people are members of more than one folk group at the same time, and therefore the themes expressed on the memorials represent a mediation of ideas from among the different groups to which they belong. Members of the Anglo-American maritime group, as we have seen, adopted symbolism and ideas from the nineteenth-century religious revival from their parent culture and used them to express group values and concerns. Members of other maritime subgroups likely did something similar.

Recently, Joe Flatman has highlighted Marxist perspectives, including the study of power relations, in his discussion of areas in which maritime archaeology can contribute to a broader understanding of cultural history.[24] I heartily agree with his assessment, and as discussed in chapter 5, maritime memorials can provide information about domination and resistance. Memorials exist always in a contested landscape in which different groups vie with one another to enshrine their views of history. I have only taken a few tentative steps down this avenue of research.[25] One area that holds particular promise is a deeper exploration of the actions that take place at memorial sites. The symbolism of imperialism contained in state-level maritime memorials is not lost on those who oppose such ideas, and for this reason, sites such as war memorials are sometimes chosen for protest. Since its construction in the 1850s, Trafalgar Square, for example, has often been used as a forum for social protest.[26] Anti-imperialism, along with other concerns such as worker's rights and women's rights, are just a few of the social movements that have used the square to proclaim their messages. The choice of Trafalgar Square is no doubt partly due to the fact that it provides a large open space in a prominent location within England's capital city. Nevertheless, this choice has probably also been motivated by the fact that it is in many ways the quintessential symbol of the British empire and the status quo.

State-level memorials are not the only sites where the social order is contested. When I attended the annual commemorative ceremony at the Fishermen's Memorial in Gloucester, Massachusetts, in August 2002, the event included speeches by local politicians that called on the federal government to help the region's ailing fishing industry. A forum ostensibly intended to remember the dead was thus turned into a place for expressing group concerns and the unhappiness that the group felt toward the government. Sailors using memorial sites to protest those in authority over them is nothing new. Eighteenth-century British mariner Samuel Kelly recalled visiting the monument for Sir Cloudesley Shovell in Westminster Abbey, and described the actions that took place there: "I think the Admiral is laying in a recumbent posture in white marble and may be known by his dirty face, arising from the juice of tobacco thrown at his face by British tars out of revenge. He having been the first promoter of Burgoo in the Navy, which seamen much dislike."[27] Burgoo, a boiled oatmeal dish, was despised by sailors, who found a way to enshrine their feelings at Shovell's memorial site. One has to wonder, however, if Kelly has not softened the record here somewhat: I suspect that rather than throwing, the sailors found another way to send tobacco juice to their target. Colorful glimpses such as this reveal the wealth of data on power relations that awaits future maritime scholars.

Researchers interested in what memorialization can reveal about maritime group beliefs need not limit themselves to the types of memorials utilized in this study. Maritime group culture, like all folk culture, remains dynamic. Memorialization traditions have evolved, and will continue to evolve, to suit changing ideas of proper mortuary behavior. In recent decades, three trends in particular are worth noting. Describing the burial of a shipmate at sea, Captain Samuel Samuels called the ocean "the grave that no monument can mark."[28] What was true in the nineteenth century no longer applies. Modern technology now allows vessels lost in the depths of the oceans to be located and marked. HMS *Hood*, sunk by the German battleship *Bismarck* in May 1941 with the loss of 1,413 lives, was discovered in July 2001. Shortly thereafter, the last remaining *Hood* survivor, Mr. Ted Briggs, laid a wreath on the surface above the site, which lies more than ten thousand feet beneath the North Atlantic. A bronze plaque was also placed on the seabed near the warship's bow.[29] True to tradition, the plaque lists the names of all those who died aboard. British divers who helped raise the ill-fated Russian submarine *Kursk*, which sank in the Barents Sea, killing all 118 crew members, placed a memorial plaque at the site in memory of the tragedy.[30] Such commemorations are not limited to official remembrances of famous events. Rather, they are very much a folk tradition. Recreational divers, for instance, have begun to place memorials to comrades on sites accessible by scuba equipment. I saw one example on the wreck of the bulk carrier *Continental* while doing fieldwork in Lake Michigan. This plaque reads:

>1985
>IN MEMORY
>OF A GOOD
>FRIEND AND
>DIVER
>TOM JOHNSON[31]

While submersible technology now allows previously inaccessible wreck sites to be marked, access to deepwater sites remains closed to all but the few who possess the proper technology. Other group members and the public at large still feel the need to connect to the spot of the tragedy, and since the 1970s, a new form of doing so has emerged. Spontaneous shrines, which consist of temporary collections of artifacts placed at the scenes of tragic or violent death, have become a ubiquitous part of mourning the victims of tragedy in both Great Britain and the United States. As with most folk phenomena, no one knows when the first spontaneous shrine was created, but early examples include ones placed at Graceland following the death of Elvis Presley in August 1977 and in New York after the murder of John Lennon in December 1980. In the United States, key developments in the spontaneous shrine phenomenon occurred with the opening of the Vietnam Veterans Memorial in 1982, when visitors began leaving all manner of items at the site, and with the highly publicized outpourings of mourning that occurred after the bombing of the Alfred P. Murrah Federal Building in Oklahoma City in April 1995 and the terrorist attacks of September 11, 2001. In Great Britain, watershed events for spontaneous shrine development include shrines created to honor soccer fans crushed to death at Hillsborough stadium in Sheffield in April 1989, and the massive display of public grief following the death of Princess Diana in August 1997. In both countries, these and other tragic events have burned the spontaneous shrine phenomenon into public consciousness, with the result that such shrines are now a traditional part of the public mourning process accompanying virtually any tragic death.[32]

The mass media, unfortunately, persists in referring to spontaneous shrines as "makeshift memorials," a term that implies disorder and haphazardness. In fact, they are anything but. While the eclectic collection of objects may on the surface appear to be haphazard, closer scrutiny reveals that artifacts placed at shrines are chosen because they have some cultural connection with the person or persons affected by the tragedy. Moreover, items are placed at shrines in a thoughtful, purposeful manner. These assemblages are, therefore, sites whose constituent parts and form embody cultural meanings of the group or groups affected by the tragedy. Viewed as such, spontaneous shrines, like other forms of memorials, can reveal much about the group beliefs and values of the people who create them.

Spontaneous shrines created in the aftermath of maritime tragedies, therefore, should encode the beliefs of the maritime communities that create them. Moreover, participation in the creation of spontaneous shrines is not typically limited; they tend to be public, and therefore anyone who can travel to the shrine site is allowed to place items at it. Because of this, spontaneous shrines should also include material from non-maritime group members, allowing researchers to see how the wider community views the maritime subculture. Spontaneous shrines thus have the potential for scholars to study interactions between the maritime folk group and its parent culture.

To date I know of no studies that specifically address maritime spontaneous shrines, but internet research reveals that such shrines do in fact exist. One of the earliest that I have seen reference to was for three Vietnamese fishermen out of Ventura, California, who were killed when their fishing boat sank seven miles off the California coast in April 1997. Friends and family created a spontaneous shrine near the empty slip where their boat had docked. Beer cans and cigarettes were among items placed at the shrine. In an interview with the *Los Angeles Times*, a family friend noted the cultural importance of the items left at the shrine: "Whatever they favored when they were living, [mourners] put out for them after they died."³³ This statement clearly shows the potential value that spontaneous shrines hold for understanding group beliefs.

The third recent development in memorialization has removed commemoration from the physical sites of tragedies to the virtual realm. Computer technology has resulted in a new form of memorialization in cyberspace. Online commemorations abound, not only for victims of tragedies, but also as a way for family and friends to pay tribute to loved ones. From treasured pets to favorite automobiles, websites commemorating them can be found on the internet. Following this trend, former shipmates, families, and friends who have lost loved ones in maritime tragedies have created websites to honor them. Websites provide virtual forums for many of the ideas discussed throughout this book. Because the internet is also widely accessible to a broad section of society, online memorials also provide a forum for those who wish to challenge the official version of events. One online tribute to the USS *Cole*, for example, provides photos and tributes to the seventeen sailors killed in the attack. The backdrop includes red, white, and blue patriotic motifs and quotes reiterating the value of the military. The site also includes the full text of an article claiming that then-President Bill Clinton was complicit in the terrorist attack that damaged the vessel.³⁴ Given the ever increasing use of computers in twenty-first-century life, it is all but certain that online memorialization will continue to grow for the foreseeable future. Such commemorations provide an easily accessible location for future "fieldworkers" who will be able to access the thoughts and feelings of millions of people without ever having to tromp through a cemetery.

None but a Sailor Knows

In the introduction to his seminal work on maritime folklore, Beck commented perceptively that "because man is not indigenous to the sea, neither is folklore entirely indigenous. Rather the majority of this material comes from the land and is adjusted to fit the aquatic climate."³⁵ This study of maritime memorials supports Beck's statement. Maritime memorialization practices from the Age of Sail must be viewed first as a reflection and adaptation of the mortuary rituals and attitudes toward death practiced in Anglo-American society. Yet seafarers did not simply mimic the rituals of their parent cultures. The maritime folk group creatively adapted prevailing societal customs to fit their group circumstances and worldview. It is in these adaptations—the ways in which Anglo-American mortuary traditions were "adjusted to fit the aquatic climate," as Beck puts it—that we find expressions of the values and worldview of the maritime folk group. This study of maritime memorials and death rituals has, I believe, told us much about the way that English and American maritime culture saw the world and the beliefs that they held.

No matter how extensive our research, however, we will never know all of the emotions experienced by sailors when faced with the loss of a close shipmate. Mariners from the Age of Sail knew that they formed a unique group and that outsiders would never completely understand them. This attitude is shown by a memorial plaque from the Seamen's Bethel in New Bedford, Massachusetts. The officers and crew of the ship *Abraham H. Howland* erected the plaque in honor of four shipmates who were lost at sea in 1847, and put forth their feelings on the relationship between sea and land with the following epitaph.

> None but a sailor knows how sailors feel
> When men like these are called their life to yield,
> Without a moments thought, or time to say
> Farewell; I die to live in endless day.
>
> Captain, and Officers and crew as one,
> All mourn the loss of these noble sons;
> And hope when lifes rough voyage and toil is o'er,
> To meet them all in Heaven to part no more
>
> By this let every sailor understand,
> How frail is life both on the sea and land,
> And look to God for peace and bliss divine:
> Where saints unnumbered will forever shine.[36]

While none but a sailor can know everything about how a sailor feels, maritime archaeologists are better equipped than most to learn something about their culture. As archaeologists, we have the capacity to utilize material culture, texts, and ethnographic data. This is a powerful toolkit. A methodology that combines examination of all of these forms is certain to yield many new insights into maritime life. The best part of such an approach is that it allows us to see the humanity of the maritime folk group. Understanding human behavior is, after all, the raison d'être of archaeology, whether one practices it on land or under the sea.

This book provides one way of studying maritime peoples based on examining the material culture that they left behind. I do not suggest, however, that the study of memorials is the only way or even the best way of learning about maritime culture. On the contrary, the study of memorials is merely one path for exploring seafaring life. Many others exist. In recent years, nautical archaeology has made key strides in examining maritime culture, but much work remains to be done. I hope that this book has given future scholars some ideas for ways to do so.

Notes

Chapter 1. Introduction

1. Shipping Intelligence, *Liverpool Mercury*, 9 March 1855.
2. *The Glasgow Daily Herald*, 2 January 1865. The same advertisement ran throughout December 1864 and January 1865.
3. Morrell, *A Narrative of Four Voyages*, 180.
4. Bromley, *A Woman's Wanderings*, 256.
5. Merwin, *Three Years in Chili*, 27. Nineteenth-century travelers who wrote accounts of Callao invariably commented on the shabby appearance of the town and the lack of rain.
6. *Liverpool Mercury*, 19 October 1865.
7. AAMMD #132, St. James' Cemetery, Liverpool, U.K.
8. Fatality rates were calculated using data from the Census of Fatal Occupational Injuries, Bureau of Labor Statistics, U.S. Department of Labor, http://www.bls.gov/. In 2008, the BLS added calculations of hours on the job rather than strictly number of workers employed. For this reason, data from 2008 onward has not been included, because it would not be comparable to that from earlier years.
9. Marine Accident Investigation Branch, *Analysis of UK Fishing Vessel Safety*.
10. Ibid., 1.
11. Roberts, "Occupational Mortality among British Merchant Seafarers," *Maritime Policy & Management*, 2000; "Hazardous Occupations in Great Britain," *The Lancet*, 2002; "Fatal Work-Related Accidents in UK Merchant Shipping," *Occupational Medicine*, 2008.
12. Roberts, "Fatal Work-Related Accidents in UK Merchant Shipping," 134.
13. Royal Commission on Loss of Life at Sea, *Final Report of the Royal Commission on Loss of Life at Sea*.
14. Scrutton, "Preventible Loss of Life at Sea," 3. Scrutton was a ship owner, and much of this article was devoted to refuting reformers' claims.
15. Ibid., 9.
16. Lloyd, *The British Seaman 1200–1860*, 65.

17. Ibid., 259.

18. Lewis, *A Social History of the Navy*, 419.

19. Lloyd, *The British Seaman 1200–1860*, 289.

20. Pope, *Life in Nelson's Navy*, 131. This book states that the Royal Navy lost 133,700 men to disease and desertion during the Seven Years War (1756–63), while only 1,512 were killed in action. During the Revolutionary and Napoleonic Wars, the navy lost more than 85,000 men to shipwrecks, disease, and accidents, and only 1,875 in fleet battles.

21. Procter Brothers, *The Fishermen's Own Book*, 262. This book and its predecessor, *The Fishermen's Memorial and Record Book*, provide detailed descriptions of vessel and crew losses in the Gloucester fishing fleet for each year.

22. The Massachusetts Vital Record Project, July 30, 2010, http://ma-vitalrecords.org/MA/Essex/Gloucester/History.shtml.

23. Hohman, *The American Whaleman*, 316–17.

24. Creighton, "The Private Life of Jack Tar," 15–16.

25. Calculated from data provided by the Mine Safety and Health Administration (MSHA), U.S. Department of Labor, June 10, 2010, http://msha.gov/stats/centurystats/coalstats.asp.

26. Wyman, *Hard Rock Epic*, 114–15 and additional discussion in Brown, *Hard-Rock Miners*, 81–82.

27. Hunt, *British Labour History*, 43–44.

28. Rule, "A Risky Business," 155.

29. Ibid., 162. Rule's figures come from Burt, *The British Lead Mining Industry*, 184.

30. Muckelroy, *Maritime Archaeology*, 228.

31. Westerdahl, "The Maritime Cultural Landscape," 5–6.

32. For his discussion of maritime enclaves, see Westerdahl, "Maritime Cultures and Ship Types," 267.

33. Hunter, "Maritime Culture," 262.

34. *Odyssey* 11: 120–131.

35. An excellent introduction to the folk group concept can be found in Toelken, *The Dynamics of Folklore*, 55–115. See especially his comprehensive bibliographic essay on pages 109–15. Other standard works on folk groups include: Brunvand, *The Study of American Folklore*, 48–70; Oring, *Folk Groups and Folklore Genres*, especially Oring's chapter on ethnic groups and McCarl's on occupational folklore; Noyes, "Group"; and Mitchell, "Occupational Folklore—The Outdoor Industries."

36. See Santino, "Flew the Ocean in a Plane," for a discussion of airline occupational lore.

37. Toelken, *The Dynamics of Folklore*, 56.

38. For the ways that rookie firefighters learn from experienced colleagues, see McCarl, *The District of Columbia Fire Fighter's Project*, especially pages 38–48; McCarl, "You've Come a Long Way"; and McCarl, "Occupational Folklore."

39. Toelken, *The Dynamics of Folklore*, 58.

40. Ibid.

41. Hall, *Beyond Culture*, 79.

42. Jansen, "The Esoteric-Exoteric Factor in Folklore," 207.

43. The basic study of dyads is Oring, "Dyadic Traditions."
44. Adams, *The Education of Henry Adams*, 29–30.
45. Hunter, "Maritime Culture: Notes from the Land," 262.
46. Toelken, *The Dynamics of Folklore*, 76.
47. Forbes, *Gravestones of Early New England*, 113.
48. Esdaile, *English Church Monuments*; Anderson, *Looking for History in British Churches*.
49. Tarpley, "Southern Cemeteries," 323.
50. Their most important publications are: Dethlefsen and Deetz, "Death's Heads, Cherubs, and Willow Trees"; Deetz, *In Small Things Forgotten*, 64–90; and Dethlefsen, "The Cemetery and Culture Change."
51. Dethlefsen and Deetz, "Death's Heads, Cherubs, and Willow Trees," 502.
52. Deetz, *In Small Things Forgotten*, 90. Deetz and Dethlefsen's interpretations have been questioned by some scholars. Watters, *"With Bodile Eyes,"* 5–9, for example, criticizes earlier scholars for misinterpreting the symbolism of Puritan grave markers. In Watters' view, the form of the eyes of the death's heads and cherubs represents a peculiarly Puritan view of the afterlife. The point, however, is that Watters, like those he criticizes, accepts the idea that gravestones symbolically express the beliefs of the society that produced them. Thus, while Deetz and Dethlefsen's original interpretations have been called into question, their approach remains valid.
53. So many gravestone studies have been conducted since the 1960s that the bibliography has now grown to daunting proportions. Bell, *Vestiges of Mortality and Remembrance* and Mytum, *Mortuary Monuments* provide excellent overviews of the literature.
54. Tashjian and Tashjian, *Memorials for Children of Change*, xiv.
55. Meyer, "Image and Identity," "And Who Have Seen the Wilderness," "Images of Logging."
56. Finch, "According to the Qualitie"; McGuire, "Dialogues with the Dead" and "Building Power"; Wurst, "Employees Must Be of Moral and Temperate Habits."
57. Tarlow, *Bereavement and Commemoration*, 35.
58. Henningsen, "The Life of the Sailor Afloat and Ashore," 143; Westerdahl, "Maritime Cultures," 265.
59. For prehistoric memorials from the British Isles, see Cummings and Fowler, *The Neolithic of the Irish Sea*; Cummings and Pannett, *Set in Stone*; Cummings and Whittle, *Places of Special Virtue*; Fleming, "Megaliths and Post-Modernism"; and Phillips, "Seascapes and Landscapes."
60. Clissold, "Ships and Monuments" and "More Memorials"; Phillips, "British and American Naval Tombs"; Kilminster and Mytum, "Mariners at Newport, Pembrokeshire"; Mytum, "Mariners at St. Dogmael's, Pembrokeshire"; Spinney, "Some Naval Memorials"; Summerson, "The Monuments in the Church of St. Nicholas."
61. Northan, "Man of Unity"; Renner, "The Memory of a Brave Man"; Tomlinson, "Battle Reliefs."
62. See Tarlow, "Romancing the Stones" for a succinct discussion of the arguments.
63. See Mytum, *Mortuary Monuments*, 211–17, for a discussion of gravestone preservation.

64. For survey locations, methodology, and an overview of the data, see Stewart, "Rocks and Storms I'll Fear No More" and Stewart, "Gravestones and Monuments."

65. Genealogical and historical societies, for example, often record memorials in the churches and cemeteries in their areas. These sources can be difficult to locate but provide a wealth of information for gravestone scholars. In England, the National Maritime Museum maintains an online database of maritime memorials: http://www.nmm.ac.uk/memorials/.

66. Gravestones were typically put in place within a few years of the person's death, but could be placed much later. Gravestones that commemorate more than one person were sometimes added to over time, and at other times were not put in place until after the last person had died. It is usually possible to track the chronology of a gravestone through examining such features as changes in symbolism, wording, or font. Mytum, "The Dating of Graveyard Memorials," provides the best description of this process. I did not have access to Mytum's study during the early phases of this project, but working independently, I devised a methodology for dating maritime memorials that agrees almost exactly with Mytum's conclusions. I thus believe that our chronological interpretations are accurate. When in doubt, a memorial was assigned to the latest date listed or left out of the study entirely.

Chapter 2. "Death Stands Ready at the Door": The Dangers of Maritime Life

1. Churchill, *My Early Life*, 6–7.

2. Caesar, *The Gallic War*. For a discussion of archaeological finds of pre-Roman vessels of the region, see Hocker, "Bottom-Based Shipbuilding in Northwestern Europe."

3. Churchill, *My Early Life*, 6–7. Churchill's memory is somewhat fuzzy (he was only three years and four months old at the time). *Eurydice* was actually carrying sail trainees, not soldiers.

4. Ibid., 7.

5. AAMMD #11, Royal Naval Cemetery, Haslar, Hampshire, U.K. Shipwrecked Mariners' Society, "Memorial of H.M.S. Eurydice," 280.

6. Braithwaite, *Whimzies*; quoted in Lloyd, *The British Seaman*, 73.

7. AAMMD #48, Plympton, St. Maurice, U.K.

8. AAMMD #772, St. Brannock's, Braunton, Devon, U.K.

9. AAMMD #796, St. Akeveranus Church, St. Keverne, Cornwall, U.K. Cited from the National Maritime Museum maritime memorials database, M5013.

10. AAMMD #200, Boston, MA.

11. D'Entremont, *The Lighthouses of Massachusetts*, 371–81.

12. A comprehensive survey of navigation is given in Bowditch's *The American Practical Navigator*, originally published in 1802. Good modern works include Taylor, *The Haven Finding Art*, and Williams, *From Sails to Satellites*. For Harrison's solution to the longitude problem, see Howse, *Greenwich Time*, and Sobel, *Longitude*.

13. AAMMD #55, St. Budeaux, Devonport, U.K.

14. This description of the loss of HMS *Serpent* draws on stories published in the *London Daily News, Bristol Mercury and Daily Post, Trewman's Exeter Flying Post or*

Plymouth and Cornish Advertiser, and *Hampshire Telegraph and Sussex Chronicle etc.*, between 13 and 18 November 1890.

15. Larson, *Isaac's Storm*.

16. Blake, Rappaport, and Landsea, *The Deadliest, Costliest, and Most Intense United States Tropical Cyclones*, 5.

17. Myers, *Ned Myers*, 81.

18. Ibid., 82.

19. Cassavoy and Crisman, "The War of 1812: Battle for the Great Lakes," 176.

20. Ibid.

21. Beck, *Folklore and the Sea*, 77–103; Beck, "Sea Lore," 2.

22. AAMMD #1634, Oakland Cemetery, Sag Harbor, NY.

23. AAMMD #287, Evergreen Cemetery, Stonington, CT.

24. AAMMD #285, Old Town Cemetery, Stonington, CT.

25. *Oxford English Dictionary*, 2nd ed., s.v. "billow."

26. AAMMD #83, St. Mylor, Cornwall, U.K.; AAMMD #91, Falmouth Cemetery, Cornwall, U.K.; AAMMD #178, Kingston Cemetery, Hampshire, U.K.

27. *Times* of London, 21 January 1814.

28. Béchervaise, *Thirty-Six Years*, 80.

29. Ibid., 81.

30. AAMMD #28, All Saints, Wyke Regis, U.K.

31. Green, *Jottings from a Cruise*, 154.

32. Ibid.

33. Ibid., 155.

34. Palmer, *Oxford Book of Sea Songs*, 27–29 ("Sailors for My Money"), 107–9 ("The Wreck of the *Rambler*"), 198–200 ("Loss of the *Amphitrite*"), and 208–9 ("Grace Darling").

35. AAMMD #301, Newport, RI.

36. AAMMD #111, St. James' Cemetery, Liverpool, U.K.

37. AAMMD #68, St. Mylor, Cornwall, U.K.

38. McKee, *A Gentlemanly and Honorable Profession*, 402. The author notes that about half of all accidental drowning incidents among U.S. naval officers occurred during small-boat operations.

39. Hawk: AAMMD #19, St. Thomas à Becket, Warblington, Hampshire, U.K. Bourchier: St. Mylor, Cornwall, U.K.

40. AAMMD #14, St. Mary the Virgin, South Hayling, Hampshire, U.K.

41. Dana, *Two Years Before the Mast*, 28.

42. For example, AAMMD #s 78 and 82, both from St. Mylor, Cornwall, U.K, and AAMMD #92, from Falmouth Cemetery, Cornwall, U.K.

43. AAMMD #271, Cedar Grove Cemetery, New London, CT.

44. AAMMD #78, St. Mylor, Cornwall, U.K.

45. AAMMD #817, Stranger's Cemetery, Fortuneswell, Dorset, U.K. Listed as M2217 in NMM database.

46. AAMMD #70, St. Mylor, Cornwall, U.K; AAMMD #593, St. John's, Liverpool, U.K.

47. AAMMD #164, Highland Road Cemetery, Portsmouth, Hampshire, U.K.
48. AAMMD #698, Winchester Cathedral, Hampshire, U.K.
49. AAMMD #16, St. Thomas à Becket, Warblington, Hampshire, U.K.
50. AAMMD #266, Cedar Grove Cemetery, New London, CT.
51. AAMMD #761, Old British Cemetery, Livorno, Italy; M5124, NMM database.
52. AAMMD #31, Portland St. George, Dorset, U.K.
53. AAMMD #25, All Saints, Wyke Regis, Dorset, U.K.
54. The earliest depiction of ships involved in battle comes from the Gebel el-Arak knife from Egypt, which dates to the Late Gerzean period (c. 3200–3100 B.C.). See Bénédite, "Le couteau De Gebel-el-'Arak." A good photograph of the knife can be seen in Bass, *A History of Seafaring Based on Underwater Archaeology*, 26, fig. 5.
55. Lewis, *A Social History of the Navy*, 421, 442.
56. McKee, *A Gentlemanly and Honorable Profession*, 402.
57. AAMMD #710, St. Andrew with St. Luke, Stoke Damerel, Devon, U.K; M4264, NMM database.
58. Lavery, *Nelson's Navy*, 11.
59. AAMMD #316, Rural Cemetery, New Bedford, MA.
60. AAMMD #93, Falmouth Cemetery, Cornwall, U.K.
61. AAMMD #351, St. James' Cemetery, Liverpool, U.K.
62. AAMMD #284, Old Town Cemetery, Stonington, CT.
63. Mytum, *Mortuary Monuments and Burial Grounds*, 154.
64. Hand, "California Miners' Folklore: Below Ground," 140. Hand's other studies of miners are "Folklore of Utah's Silver Mining Camps" and "California Miners' Folklore: Above Ground."
65. Meyer, "Image and Identity in Oregon's Pioneer Cemeteries"; "Images of Logging"; "And Who Have Seen the Wilderness."
66. Meyer, "And Who Have Seen the Wilderness," 201.
67. Meyer, "Images of Logging," 71.
68. AAMMD #227, Old Burial Hill, Marblehead, MA.
69. AAMMD #144, Sculcoates Lane Cemetery, Hull, Yorkshire, U.K.
70. AAMMD #280, Old Town Cemetery, Stonington, CT.
71. AAMMD #43, Plympton St. Mary's, Plymouth, U.K.
72. AAMMD #8, Royal Naval Cemetery, Haslar, Hampshire, U.K.
73. Goldstein, "Faith and Fate," 90.
74. Rediker, *Between the Devil and the Deep Blue Sea*, 185–86.
75. Myers, *Ned Myers*, 86.
76. Dana, *Two Years Before the Mast*, 26.
77. Olmsted, *Incidents of a Whaling Voyage*, 319.
78. AAMMD #17, St. Thomas à Becket, Warblington, U.K.
79. AAMMD #19, St. Thomas à Becket, Warblington, U.K.
80. AAMMD #413, Evergreen Cemetery, Portland, ME. My thanks to Dr. James C. Bradford for photographing this memorial.
81. Melville, *Moby Dick*, 582.
82. Béchervaise, *Thirty-Six Years*, 82.

83. Palmer, *Oxford Book of Sea Songs*, 274–75.
84. AAMMD #140, Sculcoates Lane Cemetery, Hull, U.K.
85. AAMMD #147, Hull Holy Trinity, U.K. Fortunately, the gravestones used for pavement were placed facing up.
86. AAMMD #215, Old Burying Point, Salem, MA.
87. AAMMD #220, Broad Street Cemetery, Salem, MA.
88. Nicol, *The Life and Adventures*, 211.
89. Smith, *A Sea Grammar*. Cited from Lloyd, *The British Seaman 1200–1860*, 62–63.
90. Lloyd, *The British Seaman 1200–1860*, 64–65.
91. Ibid., 68.
92. Gardner, *Above and Under Hatches*, 173.
93. Ibid., 171.
94. Ibid., 173.
95. Lloyd, *The British Seaman 1200–1860*, 249.
96. AAMMD #81, St. Mylor, Cornwall, U.K.
97. AAMMD #4, Royal Navy Cemetery, Haslar, U.K.
98. AAMMD #9, Royal Navy Cemetery, Haslar, U.K.
99. AAMMD #179, Kingston Road Cemetery, Portsmouth, U.K.
100. AAMMD #310, Rural Cemetery, New Bedford, MA.
101. Snyder, "Innocents in a Worldly World."
102. Malinowski, *Magic, Science and Religion and Other Essays*, 31. Quoted from Mullen, *I Heard the Old Fishermen Say*, 10.
103. Gmelch, "Baseball Magic."
104. Poggie and Gersuny, "Risk and Ritual."
105. Poggie, Pollnac, and Gersuny, "Risk as a Basis for Taboos."
106. Mullen, *I Heard the Old Fishermen Say*, xxx.
107. Ibid., 35. See Mullen, "Belief and the American Folk," 128–29, for a self-criticism of this work, in which Mullen regrets overly romanticizing the fishermen's belief in magic. Despite this, Mullen's basic point that the Texas fishermen's lore emphasizes danger remains valid.
108. AAMMD #57, St. Budeaux, Devonport, U.K.
109. For good vs. bad deaths, see the classic studies by Ariès, *Western Attitudes Toward Death* and *The Hour of Our Death*. Mytum's "Death and Remembrance" contrasts the deaths of emigrants, who expected to die and be buried in the colonies, with those of travelers who did not. The latter can be viewed as victims of bad death. See also Mytum, *Mortuary Monuments and Burial Grounds*, 158–59.

Chapter 3. Values for a Dangerous World

1. AAMMD #259, Cedar Grove Cemetery, New London, CT.
2. Military: Mytum, *Mortuary Monuments*, 151; stagecoach drivers and railroad firemen: Meyer, "Image and Identity in Oregon's Pioneer Cemeteries," 204.
3. Botkin and Harlow, *A Treasury of Railroad Folklore*, 47.
4. Cederlund, *Vasa I*, 53.

5. AAMMD #138, St. James' Cemetery, Liverpool, U.K.
6. AAMMD #164, Highland Road Cemetery, Portsmouth, U.K.
7. Coxere, *Adventures By Sea*, 7–8.
8. Cremer, *Ramblin' Jack*, 49.
9. Barlow, *Barlow's Journal*, 416.
10. AAMMD #74, St. Mylor, Cornwall, U.K.
11. AAMMD #72, St. Mylor, Cornwall, U.K.
12. AAMMD #224, Old Burial Hill, Marblehead, MA.
13. AAMMD #367, Old Burial Hill, Marblehead, MA.
14. AAMMD #123, St. James' Cemetery, Liverpool, U.K.
15. AAMMD #60, St. Budeaux, Devonport, U.K.
16. AAMMD #115, St. James' Cemetery, Liverpool, U.K.
17. AAMMD #63, St. Andrew's, Plymouth, Devon, U.K.
18. Northan, "Man of Unity." Allen's memorial continues to be a focus of the performance of British–American solidarity. When I visited the site in summer 2002, a church employee told me that people gathered at the spot on September 11, 2001, to show support for the United States during the terrorist attacks taking place on that day.
19. AAMMD #290, Evergreen Cemetery, Stonington, CT.
20. AAMMD #4, Royal Navy Cemetery Haslar, Hampshire, U.K.
21. Brooks, *The Kru Mariner*.
22. AAMMD #406, Seaman's Bethel, New Bedford, MA.
23. AAMMD #24, All Saints, Wyke Regis, Dorset, U.K.
24. AAMMD #57, St. Budeaux, Devonport, U.K.
25. AAMMD #10, Royal Navy Cemetery, Haslar, U.K.
26. AAMMD #43, Plympton St. Mary, Devon, U.K.
27. AAMMD #175, Kingston Road Cemetery, Portsmouth, U.K.
28. AAMMD #7, Royal Navy Cemetery, Haslar, U.K.
29. AAMMD #262, Cedar Grove Cemetery, New London, CT.
30. AAMMD #324, Rural Cemetery, New Bedford, MA.
31. Nelson, "The Naval Battle of Medinet Habu"; Raban, "The Medinet Habu Ships: Another Interpretation"; Wachsmann, "The Ships of the Sea Peoples"; Wachsmann, "The Ships of the Sea Peoples: Additional Notes"; Wachsmann, *Seagoing Ships*, 166.
32. Murray and Petsas, "Octavian's Campsite Memorial," 56.
33. Mayo, *War Memorials*, 181.
34. Ibid., 182–83.
35. Ibid., 130–31.
36. Mytum, *Mortuary Monuments*, 150.
37. *Times* of London, 24 October 2005.
38. Hallas, "The Search for John Paul Jones."
39. Ibid., 36–37.
40. King, *Memorials of the Great War*; Mytum, *Mortuary Monuments*, 99–100, 151.
41. Borg, *War Memorials*, 87–88.
42. Dana, *Two Years Before the Mast*, 42.
43. Votive models represent a unique form of maritime commemoration that

sometimes served a memorialization function as well. See Harley, *Church Ships*, for an introduction to this form of maritime material culture.

44. Parker, "A Maritime Cultural Landscape," 338–40.
45. Kelly, *Samuel Kelly*, 267.
46. Nordhoff, *Whaling and Fishing*, 271–72. "Tom Bowling" is the title character of a sea song; it seems likely that Nordhoff forgot the actual name on the marker and substituted a fictional one instead.
47. AAMMD #78, St. Mylor, Cornwall, U.K.
48. AAMMD #82, St. Mylor, Cornwall, U.K.
49. AAMMD #92, Falmouth Cemetery, Cornwall, U.K.
50. AAMMD #89, St. Mylor, Cornwall, U.K. The HMS *Ganges* association maintains the memorial to this day. Their website is http://www.hmsgangesassoc.org.
51. Mullen, *I Heard the Old Fishermen Say*, 3–22 and 155–58.
52. Bancroft, "Folklore of the Central City District"; Hand, "California Miners' Folklore: Above Ground" and "California Miner's Folklore: Below Ground."
53. Bancroft, "Folklore of the Central City District," 324–25.
54. Santino, "Flew the Ocean in a Plane" and "The Outlaw Emotions."
55. Santino, "Characteristics of Occupational Narratives," 202–4.
56. Gargulinski, "Stand Clear of the Closing Doors!" 38.
57. Korson, *Coal Dust on the Fiddle*, 213–14.
58. Danker, "Trucking Songs." *Journal of Country Music* 6 (1978): 78–89.
59. Hand, "Folklore from Utah's Silver Mining Camps," 153.
60. Smith: AAMMD #273; Skinner: AAMMD #270. Both in Cedar Grove Cemetery, New London, CT.
61. Olmsted, *Incidents of a Whaling Voyage*, 36.
62. Kottak, *Anthropology*, 42.
63. Nicol, *The Life and Adventures*, 94–95.
64. Newhall, *The Adventures of Jack*, 26.
65. See Ferguson, *Empire*, 251–59, for a thought-provoking discussion of the ways that the British popular press perpetuated the ideals of imperialism.
66. Burg, "Women and Children First," 9.
67. Rediker, *Between the Devil and the Deep Blue Sea*, 46.
68. Nicol, *The Life and Adventures*, 37.
69. Ibid., 67, 69.
70. Rodger, *The Wooden World*, 161.
71. Creighton, "The Private Life of Jack Tar," 99–101.
72. Bolster, *Black Jacks*, 216.
73. Ibid., 5.
74. Spavens, *The Narrative of William Spavens*, 144.
75. Ibid.
76. Bolster, *Black Jacks*, 77–81.
77. Béchervaise, *Thirty-Six Years*, 83.
78. Bathurst, *The Wreckers*, 305–6.
79. Ibid., xxi–xxii.

Chapter 4. "The Natural Sepulchre of a Sailor": Burial at Sea as Ritual Performance

1. Anderson, *Journals of Sir Thomas Allin*, 7.
2. See Stewart, "Burial at Sea: Separating and Placing the Dead During the Age of Sail," for an earlier version of this chapter. Stewart, "Burial at Sea," provides a global historical overview of burial in water.
3. Henningsen, "Somandens Vade Og Torre Grav."
4. Mack and Connell, *Naval Ceremonies*, 175–180.
5. Bassett, *Legends and Superstitions*, 321–26; Beck, *Folklore and the Sea*, 283–84; LeGuin, "Sea Life," 121–22.
6. Perry, *Fair Winds and Foul*, 70–71.
7. Anderson, *Looking for History*, 240.
8. Rodger, *The Safeguard of the Sea*, 312.
9. Smith, *Sea Grammar*, 61.
10. Barlow, *Barlow's Journal*, 133.
11. Ibid., 276.
12. Noble, *Sam Noble*, 189–91.
13. Horrox, "Purgatory, Prayer, and Plague," 99.
14. Hall, *Voyages and Travels*, 294.
15. Bassett, *Legends and Superstitions*, 135–38; Beck, *Folklore and the Sea*, 283.
16. Hall, *Voyages and Travels*, 294.
17. Bassett, *Legends and Superstitions*, 136–37.
18. Ibid., 136.
19. Beck, *Folklore and the Sea*, 283.
20. Contrary to the popular contemporary legend, Nelson's body was preserved in "spirits of wine" rather than rum during the voyage home: Brunvand, *The Choking Doberman*, 114–18, and *Too Good To Be True*, 197–98.
21. AAMMD #729, Holy Trinity Church, Salcombe, Devon, U.K. M3774, NMM database.
22. AAMMD #1603, Oakland Cemetery, Sag Harbor, NY. Cited from Vail, *Grave Stone Inscriptions from Oakland Cemetery*, 22.
23. AAMMD #62, St. Budeaux, Devonport, Devon, U.K.
24. AAMMD #1526, Prospect Hill Cemetery, Nantucket, MA. Cited from Nantucket Historical Association Research Library & Archives online cemetery database, March 11, 2009, http://www.nha.org/library/cemeteries/index.html.
25. AAMMD #1465, Crossways Cemetery, Martha's Vineyard, MA, July 21, 2002, http:///www.vineyard.net/vineyard/history/cemetery/cp0611.htm.
26. AAMMD #126, St. James' Cemetery, Liverpool, U.K.
27. AAMMD #78, St. Mylor, Cornwall, U.K.
28. AAMMD #1497, Old North Cemetery, Nantucket, MA. Cited from Nantucket Historical Association Research Library & Archives online cemetery database, March 11, 2009, http://www.nha.org/library/cemeteries/index.html.
29. Gardner, *Above and Under Hatches*, 36.

30. Vincent, *Nelson*, 582.
31. Coleridge, *The Rime of the Ancient Mariner*.
32. Turner, *The Ritual Process*, 95.
33. Doerflinger, *Shantymen and Shantyboys*, 181–82.
34. Beck, *Folklore and the Sea*, 396.
35. Barber, *Vampires, Burial, and Death*, 180.
36. Richardson, "Death's Door," 96–97.
37. Parker Pearson, *The Archaeology of Death and Burial*, 124–25.
38. Gardner, *Above and Under Hatches*, 199.
39. Hills, "Saving a Sailor's Life," 217.
40. Gardner, *Above and Under Hatches*, 199.
41. Beck, *Folklore and the Sea*, 207–8.
42. Brunvand, *The Vanishing Hitchhiker*, 24–40.
43. Ibid., 20–22.
44. Van Gennep, *The Rites of Passage*.
45. Van Gennep, *The Rites of Passage*, 160–161; Bendann, *Death Customs*, 45; Taylor, *Death and the Afterlife*, 45.
46. Finucane, *Appearances of the Dead*, 18, 43–44.
47. Bassett, *Legends and Superstitions*, 285–96; Beck, *Folklore and the Sea*, 280–283.
48. Douglas, *Purity and Danger*.
49. Richardson, *Death, Dissection, and the Destitute*, 17.
50. Melville, *White-Jacket*, 316.
51. Ibid.
52. Leach, "Time and False Noses."
53. Gittings, "Sacred and Secular," 169–170.
54. Gardner, *Above and Under Hatches*, 144.
55. Tarlow, *Bereavement and Commemoration*, 133–36.
56. Noble, *Sam Noble*, 191.
57. Perry, *Fair Winds and Foul*, 70.
58. McCullough, *John Adams*, 186.
59. Richardson, "Death's Door," 95.
60. Ibid., 94–95.
61. Hall, *Voyages and Travels*, 295.
62. Bradley, "Burial Custom," 68–69.
63. Barber, *Vampires*, 158–160.
64. Bradley, "Burial Custom," 68.
65. Melville, *White-Jacket*, 317–19.
66. Litten, *The English Way of Death*, 166–67.
67. Mack and Connell, *Naval Ceremonies*, 112, 175.
68. Young, "The Adelaide Steamship," *Times* of London, 2 April 1853. Samuels, *From the Forecastle to the Cabin*, 121, describes draping the body with a flag aboard another American civilian ship.
69. Litten, *The English Way of Death*.
70. Richardson, "Death's Door," 94.

71. Hall, *Voyages and Travels*, 295; Melville, *White Jacket*, 316. On the warship described by Melville, the body was placed between two cannon.

72. Richardson, "Death's Door," 93.

73. Gardner, *Above and Under Hatches*, 107.

74. Richardson, "Death's Door," 96–97.

75. The chaplain was made an official member of the complement of English naval vessels in the mid-seventeenth century, and U.S. naval regulations also called for the appointment of chaplains from the time of the creation of the U.S. Navy in 1798. However, not all ships in the Royal Navy or U.S. Navy actually had chaplains. It was more common to find them on larger vessels than on smaller ones. Most merchant vessels did not carry chaplains. See McKee, *A Gentlemanly and Honorable Profession*, 31.

76. *Book of Common Prayer*, 1662 edition.

77. Ibid.

78. *Times* of London, 2 April 1853.

79. Leggett, *Tales and Sketches*, 89.

80. Hall, *Voyages and Travels*, 297.

81. Samuels, *From the Forecastle to the Cabin*, 121.

82. Beck, *Folklore and the Sea*, 285.

83. Dana, *Two Years Before the Mast*, 30. In this case, however, the man had been lost overboard and the body was not recovered.

84. Lloyd, *The British Seaman*, 252.

85. Bassett, *Legends and Superstitions*, 94; Beck, *Folklore and the Sea*, 281.

86. Beck, *Folklore and the Sea*, 288–89.

87. Richardson, "Death's Door"; *Death, Dissection, and the Destitute*, 17–29.

88. Davies, *The Haunted*, 57–59.

89. Grider, "Haunted Houses," 152–56.

90. Ross, "Anchors."

91. Lindenlauf, "The Sea as a Place of No Return," 416.

92. Noble, *Sam Noble*, 222.

93. Dana, *Two Years Before the Mast*, 33.

94. AAMMD #1666, Oakdale Cemetery, Wilmington, NC.

95. Richardson, "Death's Door"; *Death, Dissection, and the Destitute*, 17–29.

Chapter 5. "Was Never Since Heard Of": Remembering the Missing

1. AAMMD #308, Rural Cemetery, New Bedford, MA.

2. Jones, *A History of the Vikings*, 257–58.

3. Ibid., 267.

4. AAMMD #192, Copp's Hill, Boston, MA.

5. AAMMD #196, Copp's Hill, Boston, MA.

6. AAMMD #298, Common Burying Ground, Newport, RI.

7. AAMMD #17, St. Thomas à Becket, Warblington, Hampshire, U.K.

8. AAMMD #198, Copp's Hill, Boston, MA.

9. AAMMD #196, Copp's Hill, Boston, MA.

10. AAMMD #296, Common Burying Ground, Newport, RI.

11. AAMMD #119, St. James' Cemetery, Liverpool, U.K.

12. AAMMD #228, Old Burial Hill, Marblehead, MA.

13. AAMMD #250, Eastern Cemetery, Portland, ME.

14. The Oxford English Dictionary, 2nd edition, defines cenotaph as "an empty tomb; a sepulchral monument erected in honour of a deceased person whose body is elsewhere." This definition does not address tombs that include both burials and commemorations for absent deceased, but the connotation is that the tomb contains no bodies.

15. AAMMD #281, Old Town Cemetery, Stonington, CT.

16. AAMMD #113, St. James' Cemetery, Liverpool, U.K.

17. AAMMD #245, Eastern Cemetery, Portland, ME.

18. AAMMD #294, Common Burying Ground, Newport, RI.

19. AAMMD #249, Eastern Cemetery, Portland, ME.

20. AAMMD #243, Eastern Cemetery, Portland, ME; AAMMD #297, Common Burying Ground, Newport, RI.

21. AAMMD #241, Western Cemetery, Portland, ME.

22. Examples include ones from Mount Auburn (AAMMD #206) and Forest Hills (AAMMD #s 208, 210) cemeteries in Boston, New London, CT (AAMMD #s 273, 279), and New Bedford, MA (AAMMD #s 318, 323).

23. AAMMD #287, Evergreen Cemetery, Stonington, CT.

24. AAMMD #s 266 and 270 (Cedar Grove Cemetery, New London, CT), 306 and 308 (Rural Cemetery, New Bedford, MA), and 164 (Highland Road Cemetery, Portsmouth, U.K).

25. AAMMD #171, Portsea St. Mary's, Portsmouth, Hampshire, U.K.

26. Brewer and White, *Tales of St. Mary's*, 8–9.

27. AAMMD #28, All Saints, Wyke Regis, Dorset, U.K.

28. AAMMD #261, Cedar Grove Cemetery, New London, CT.

29. New London *Morning News*, 30 November 1846.

30. AAMMD #229, Old Burial Hill, Marblehead, MA.

31. See, for example, Ariès, *Western Attitudes Toward Death*; Gittings, *Death, Burial, and the Individual*; and Parker Pearson, *The Archaeology of Death and Burial*.

32. Houlbrooke, *Death, Religion, and the Family*, 2–3, 380–81.

33. Stone, *The Family, Sex, and Marriage*.

34. Houlbrooke, "The Age of Decency," 197.

35. Tarlow, "Romancing the Stones" and *Bereavement and Commemoration*, 112–32.

36. Parker Pearson, *The Archaeology of Death and Burial*, 48.

37. Stone, *The Family, Sex, and Marriage*.

38. Horrox, "Purgatory, Prayer, and Plague," 104–5; Tarlow, *Bereavement and Commemoration*, 124.

39. Mytum, *Mortuary Monuments*, 41–42.

40. Stannard, *The Puritan Way of Death*, 108–17.

41. Deetz, *In Small Things Forgotten*, 71–72.

42. Dethlefsen and Deetz, "Death's Heads," 507; Deetz, *In Small Things Forgotten*, 71–72.

43. Mytum, *Mortuary Monuments*, 50–51; 89.

44. Haas, *Carried to the Wall*, 71.

45. Linden-Ward, "Strange But Genteel Pleasure Grounds," 295.

46. Mytum, *Mortuary Monuments*, 90–92.

47. Bassett, *Legends and Superstitions*, 472.

48. Ibid., 473.

49. Ibid., 472–73.

50. Rowlands, "The Role of Memory."

51. Melville, *Moby Dick*, 37.

52. AAMMD #56, St. Budeaux, Devonport, U.K.

53. AAMMD #1463, Crossways Cemetery, Martha's Vineyard, MA, July 21, 2002, http://history.vineyard.net/cemetery/cp0719.htm.

54. AAMMD #249, Eastern Cemetery, Portland, ME.

55. AAMMD #1503, Newtown Cemetery, Nantucket, MA. Cited from Nantucket Historical Association cemetery database, March 11, 2009, http://12.46.127.86/dbtw-wpd/CemeteriesQuery.htm.

56. AAMMD #252, Eastern Cemetery, Portland, ME.

57. Kellehear, "Introduction," xi.

58. Ibid., ix.

59. Jeffreys, *Helping Grieving People*, 54–62, provides an excellent review of grief-process theories.

60. Stroebe and Schut, "The Dual Process Model," 215–16.

61. Bowlby, *Attachment and Loss*.

62. Rando, *Grieving*, 235–240.

63. Parkes and Weiss, *Recovery from Bereavement*, 155–61.

64. Worden, *Grief Counseling*, 27–37.

65. Klass, "The Deceased Child," 214.

66. Attig, *How We Grieve*. See especially pages 99–127, which covers how people cope with the pain caused by familiar surroundings and objects.

67. Béchervaise, *Thirty-Six Years*, 83.

68. Coxere, *Adventures by Sea*, 76.

69. Kelly, *Samuel Kelly*, 132.

70. AAMMD #69, St. Mylor, Cornwall, U.K.

71. AAMMD #298, Common Burying Ground, Newport, RI.

72. AAMMD #132, St. James' Cemetery, Liverpool, U.K.

73. Tappan, *The World's Story*, 41–46.

74. Defoe, *Robinson Crusoe*, ix. Novak, *Realism, Myth, and History*, 23–46, discusses the various factors that influenced Defoe, among them castaway tales, shipwreck stories, and accounts of people living in isolation.

75. Defoe, *Robinson Crusoe*, 238.

76. Three noteworthy studies are Johnson, *An Archaeology of Capitalism*; Leone and Potter, *Historical Archaeologies of Capitalism*; and Orser, *A Historical Archaeology of the Modern World*.

77. AAMMD #263, Cedar Grove Cemetery, New London, CT.

Chapter 6. "Rocks and Storms I'll Fear No More": The Anchor and the Cross

1. Jenkins, *England's Thousand Best Churches*, 159.
2. AAMMD #42, Portland St. George, Dorset, U.K.
3. Quoted from Kverndal, *Seamen's Missions*, 612.
4. Capp, *Cromwell's Navy*, 307.
5. Ibid.; Davies, *Gentlemen and Tarpaulins*, 116.
6. Rediker, *Between the Devil and the Deep Blue Sea*, 186.
7. Ibid., 184.
8. Ibid., 173–75.
9. Mangin, "Some Account of the Writer's Situation," 8–9.
10. Ibid., 9.
11. Thursfield, *Five Naval Journals*, 1.
12. Beck, *Folklore and the Sea*, 310–11.
13. AAMMD #248, Eastern Cemetery, Portland, ME.
14. AAMMD #198, Copp's Hill, Boston, MA.
15. AAMMD #226, Old Burial Hill, Marblehead, MA.
16. AAMMD #186, Copp's Hill, Boston, MA.
17. Hebrews 6:19, Revised Standard Version.
18. AAMMD #220, Broad Street Cemetery, Salem, MA.
19. AAMMD #215, Old Burying Point, Salem, MA.
20. AAMMD #147, Hull Holy Trinity, U.K.
21. AAMMD #74, St. Mylor, Cornwall, U.K.
22. AAMMD #62, St. Budeaux, Devonport, U.K.
23. AAMMD #22, All Saints, Wyke Regis, Dorset, U.K.
24. AAMMD #28, All Saints, Wyke Regis, Dorset, U.K.
25. Coxere, *Adventures by Sea*, 55–56.
26. AAMMD #207, Forest Hills Cemetery, Boston, MA.
27. Hatch, *Democratization*, and McLoughlin, *Revivals*, provide good introductions to the Second Great Awakening.
28. McLoughlin, *Revivals*, 113–14.
29. Langley, *Social Reform*, 44.
30. Noll, *Rise of Evangelicalism*, 18; Ward, *The Protestant Evangelical Awakening*.
31. Carwardine, *Transatlantic Revivalism*, xiii.
32. Ibid., xiv.
33. Kverndal, *Seamen's Missions* and *The Way of the Sea*.
34. Ibid., xx.
35. Langley, *Social Reform*, 57.
36. Drewer, "Fisherman and Fish Pond," 535.
37. Wurst, "Moral and Temperate Habits," 131–34.
38. AAMMD #286, Evergreen Cemetery, Stonington, CT.
39. AAMMD #140, Sculcoates Lane Cemetery, Hull, U.K.
40. AAMMD #275, Cedar Grove Cemetery, New London, CT.

41. AAMMD #54, St. Budeaux, Devonport, U.K.
42. AAMMD #48, Plympton St. Maurice, Devon, U.K.
43. AAMMD #75, St. Mylor, Cornwall, U.K.
44. AAMMD #152, Holy Trinity Church, Hull, Yorkshire, U.K.
45. AAMMD #105, Bristol Cathedral, Bristol, U.K.
46. AAMMD #144, Sculcoates Lane Cemetery, Hull, Yorkshire, U.K.
47. AAMMD #57, St. Budeaux, Devonport, U.K.
48. AAMMD #35, Portland St. George, Dorset, U.K.
49. AAMMD #142, Sculcoates Lane Cemetery, Hull, Yorkshire, U.K.
50. AAMMD #83, St. Mylor, Cornwall, U.K.
51. AAMMD #91, Falmouth Cemetery, Cornwall, U.K.
52. AAMMD #50, St. Budeaux, Devonport, U.K, and AAMMD #177, Kingston Road Cemetery, Portsmouth, U.K.
53. AAMMD #37, Portland St. George, Dorset, U.K.
54. AAMMD #40, Portland St. George, Dorset, U.K.
55. AAMMD #268, Cedar Grove Cemetery, New London, CT; AAMMD #321, Rural Cemetery, New Bedford, MA.
56. AAMMD #166, Portsea St. Mary's, Portsmouth, U.K.
57. AAMMD #141, Sculcoates Lane Cemetery, Hull, Yorkshire, U.K.
58. AAMMD #42, Portland St. George, Dorset, U.K.
59. AAMMD #272, Cedar Grove Cemetery, New London, CT.
60. Fillmore Brothers, *New Christian Hymn and Tune Book*, 298.
61. Tennyson, "Crossing the Bar." According to Ricks, *Tennyson*, 665–66, Tennyson wrote the poem while crossing the Solent, several months after recovering from a serious illness. Tennyson explained the Pilot as "that Divine and Unseen Who is always guiding us."
62. AAMMD #96, Falmouth Cemetery, Cornwall, U.K.
63. AAMMD #145, Sculcoates Lane Cemetery, Hull, Yorkshire, U.K.
64. AAMMD #32, Portland St. George, Dorset, U.K.
65. AAMMD #87, St. Mylor, Cornwall, U.K.
66. AAMMD #117, St. James' Cemetery, Liverpool, U.K.
67. AAMMD #271, Cedar Grove Cemetery, New London, CT.
68. AAMMD #291, Evergreen Cemetery, Stonington, CT.
69. AAMMD #316, Rural Cemetery, New Bedford, MA.
70. AAMMD #20, St. Thomas à Becket, Warblington, Hampshire, U.K.
71. AAMMD #11, Royal Navy Cemetery, Haslar, U.K.

Chapter 7. Conclusions: A Living Tradition

1. *Bermuda Sun*, 23 September 2005.
2. *Bermuda Sun*, 30 April 2004.
3. Gordon Lightfoot, October 17, 2003, http://gordonlightfoot.com/Lyrics/WreckOfTheEdmundFitzgerald.html.

4. Junger, *The Perfect Storm*.

5. *Titanic* is the second-highest grossing film ever, with $1.8 billion in box-office receipts worldwide. When adjusted for inflation, however, *Gone with the Wind* breezes into the top spot, and *Titanic* sinks to number six. Box Office Mojo, September 5, 2010, http://boxofficemojo.com/alltime/adjusted.htm.

6. Ibid. High-ranking non-maritime films that explore the humans vs. nature theme include *Jurassic Park* and its sequel *The Lost World: Jurassic Park* (#s 18 and 94, with $685 million and $396 million, respectively) and *Twister* (#76, with $434 million).

7. AAMMD #346, Plymouth, U.K.

8. AAMMD #331, Plymouth, U.K.

9. Roberts, "Fatal Work-Related Accidents," 130.

10. AAMMD #73, St. Mylor, Cornwall, U.K.

11. "Fisherman's Ashes Will be Returned to Pamlico County," New Bern *Sun Journal*, 19 May 2009.

12. AAMMD #387, Rural Cemetery, New Bedford, MA.

13. AAMMD #1490, Palacios, TX.

14. AAMMD #334, Plymouth, U.K.

15. AAMMD #343, Plymouth, U.K.

16. AAMMD #829, Turville, Buckinghamshire, U.K.

17. Kelly, *Samuel Kelly*, 132; Barlow, *Barlow's Journal*, 112.

18. Coxere, *Adventures by Sea*, 6.

19. AAMMD #1661, Oakland Cemetery, Sag Harbor, NY.

20. AAMMD #1666, Oakdale Cemetery, Wilmington, NC.

21. Grant: AAMMD #1656, Oakland Cemetery, Sag Harbor, NY. Read: AAMMD #34, Portland St. George, Dorset, U.K.

22. Creighton, "The Private Life of Jack Tar," 215.

23. Robinson, *Jack Nastyface*, 134–35.

24. Flatman, "Cultural Biographies."

25. See Stewart, "Naval Monuments and Memorials," for a more in-depth study of this issue.

26. See Mace, *Trafalgar Square*.

27. Kelly, *Samuel Kelly*, 267.

28. Samuels, *From the Forecastle to the Cabin*, 121.

29. Plymouth *Evening Herald*, 27 July 2001.

30. *Sunday Mercury*, 14 October 2001.

31. AAMMD #1461, Two Rivers, WI.

32. Grider, "Spontaneous Shrines," provides the best overview of this phenomenon. My discussion of spontaneous shrines is based on the characteristics that she develops in this article.

33. *Los Angeles Times*, 27 April 1997.

34. Tim Jacobs, December 14, 2006, http://www.timjacobs.com/uss_cole.htm.

35. Beck, *Folklore and the Sea*, xiii–xiv.

36. AAMMD #407, Seamen's Bethel, New Bedford, MA.

Bibliography

Adams, Henry. *The Education of Henry Adams.* Edited with an introduction and notes by Ira B. Nadel. New York: Oxford University Press, 1999.
Anderson, Mary Désirée. *Looking for History in British Churches.* London: J. Murray, 1951.
Anderson, R. C., ed. *The Journals of Sir Thomas Allin 1660–1678.* Vol. II, *Publications of the Navy Records Society LXXX.* London: Navy Records Society, 1940.
Ariès, Philippe. *Western Attitudes toward Death: From the Middle Ages to the Present.* Baltimore: Johns Hopkins University Press, 1974.
———. *The Hour of Our Death.* New York: Knopf, 1981.
Attig, Thomas. *How We Grieve: Relearning the World.* New York: Oxford University Press, 1996.
Bancroft, Caroline. "Folklore of the Central City District, Colorado." *California Folklore Quarterly* (1945): 315–42.
Barber, Paul. *Vampires, Burial, and Death: Folklore and Reality.* New Haven and London: Yale University Press, 1988.
Barlow, Edward. *Barlow's Journal of His Life at Sea in King's Ships, East & West Indiamen & Other Merchantmen from 1659 to 1703.* London: Hurst & Blackett Ltd., 1934.
Bass, George F., ed. *A History of Seafaring Based on Underwater Archaeology.* London and New York: Thames and Hudson, 1972.
Bassett, Fletcher S. *Legends and Superstitions of the Sea and of Sailors in All Lands and at All Times.* Detroit: Singing Free Press, 1971.
Bathurst, Bella. *The Wreckers: A Story of Killing Seas and Plundered Shipwrecks, from the Eighteenth Century to the Present Day.* Boston: Houghton Mifflin, 2005.
Béchervaise, John. *Thirty-Six Years of a Seafaring Life, by an Old Quartermaster.* Portsea: W. Woodward, 1839.
Beck, Horace P. "Sea Lore." *Northwest Folklore* 2, no. 2 (1967): 1–13.
———. *Folklore and the Sea.* Middletown, CT: Published for the Marine Historical Association Mystic Seaport by Wesleyan University Press, 1972.
Bell, Edward L. *Vestiges of Mortality & Remembrance.* Metuchen, NJ, and London: The Scarecrow Press, Inc., 1994.

Bendann, Effie. *Death Customs: An Analytical Study of Burial Rites.* Detroit: Gale Research Co., 1974.

Bénédite, G. "Le Couteau De Gebel-El-'Arak." *Monuments et memoires publies par l'Academie des Inscriptions et Belles Lettres, Fondation Eugene Piot* 22 (1916): 1–34.

Blake, Eric S., Edward N. Rappaport, and Christopher W. Landsea. *The Deadliest, Costliest, and Most Intense United States Tropical Cyclones from 1851 to 2006 (and Other Frequently Requested Hurricane Facts).* NOAA Technical Memorandum NWS TPC-5. Miami: NOAA, National Weather Service, National Hurricane Center, 2007.

Bolster, W. Jeffrey. *Black Jacks: African American Seamen in the Age of Sail.* Cambridge, MA: Harvard University Press, 1997.

Borg, A. *War Memorials: From Antiquity to the Present.* London: Leo Cooper, 1991.

Botkin, Benjamin Albert, and Alvin F. Harlow, eds. *A Treasury of Railroad Folklore.* New York: Crown Publishers, 1953.

Bowditch, Nathaniel. *The American Practical Navigator: An Epitome of Navigation.* Bicentennial Edition. Bethesda, MD: National Imagery and Mapping Agency, 2002.

Bowlby, John. *Attachment and Loss.* London: Hogarth, 1969.

Bradley, G. P. "Burial Custom Formerly Observed in the Naval Service." *Journal of American Folk-Lore* 7 (1894): 67–68.

Braithwaite, R. *Whimzies, or, a New Cast of Characters.* London: Printed by F.K., 1631.

Brewer, Ron, and Trevor White. *Tales of St. Mary's: The Sinking of the H.M.S. Royal George.* Portsmouth: Portsea St. Mary's, nd.

Bromley, Clara Fitzroy. *A Woman's Wanderings in the Western World : A Series of Letters Addressed to Sir Fitzroy Kelly, M. P.* London: Saunders, Otley, and Company, 1861.

Brooks, Jr., George E. *The Kru Mariner in the Nineteenth Century: A Historical Compendium.* Newark, DE: Liberian Studies Association in America, Inc., 1972.

Brown, Ronald C. *Hard-Rock Miners: The Intermountain West, 1860–1920.* College Station, TX: Texas A&M University Press, 1979.

Brunvand, Jan Harold. *The Vanishing Hitchhiker: American Urban Legends and Their Meanings.* New York: Norton, 1981.

———. *The Choking Doberman and Other "New" Urban Legends.* New York: W. W. Norton, 1984.

———. *The Study of American Folklore: An Introduction.* 4th ed. New York: Norton, 1998.

———. *Too Good to Be True: The Colossal Book of Urban Legends.* New York: W. W. Norton, 1999.

Burg, B. R. "'Women and Children First': Popular Mythology and Disaster at Sea, 1840–1860." *Journal of American Culture* 20, no. 4 (1997): 1–9.

Burt, Roger. *The British Lead Mining Industry.* Trewolsta, Cornwall: Dyllansow Truran, 1984.

Caesar, Julius. *The Gallic War.* Translation by H. J. Edwards. Loeb Classical Library. Cambridge, MA: Harvard University Press, 1952.

Capp, Bernard. *Cromwell's Navy: The Fleet and the English Revolution 1648–1660.* Oxford: Clarendon Press, 1989.

Carwardine, Richard. *Transatlantic Revivalism: Popular Evangelicalism in Britain and America, 1790–1865.* Westport, CT: Greenwood Publishing Group, Inc., 1978.

Cederlund, Carl Olof. *Vasa I: The Archaeology of a Swedish Warship of 1628*. Edited by Frederick M. Hocker. Stockholm: National Maritime Museums of Sweden, 2006.

Church of England. *The Book of Common Prayer, and Administration of the Sacraments, and other Rites and Ceremonies of the Church, According to the Use of the Church of England, Together with the Psalter or Psalms of David, Pointed as they are to be Sung or Said in Churches*. London: John Bill and Christopher Barker, 1662.

Churchill, Winston. *My Early Life: A Roving Commission*. New York: Charles Scribner's Sons, 1930.

Clissold, Peter. "Ships and Monuments in Churches in the Solent Area." *Mariner's Mirror* 58 (1972): 205–15.

———. "More Memorials in the Solent Area." *Mariner's Mirror* 67 (1981): 367–70.

Coleridge, Samuel Taylor. *The Annotated Ancient Mariner. The Rime of the Ancient Mariner*. Introduction by Martin Gardner. New York: Bramhall House, 1965.

Coxere, Edward, and Edward Meyerstein. *Adventures by Sea of Edward Coxere, a Relation of the Several Adventures by Sea with the Dangers, Difficulties and Hardships Met for Several Years*. New York and London: Oxford University Press, 1946.

Creighton, Margaret Scott. "The Private Life of Jack Tar: Sailors at Sea in the Nineteenth Century." Master's thesis, Boston University, 1985.

Cremer, John. *Ramblin' Jack: The Journal of Captain John Cremer 1700–1774*. London: J. Cape, 1936.

Cummings, Vicki, and Chris Fowler, eds. *The Neolithic of the Irish Sea: Materiality and Traditions of Practice*. Oxford: Oxbow Books, 2004.

Cummings, Vicki, and Alasdair Whittle, eds. *Places of Special Virtue: Megaliths in the Neolithic Landscapes of Wales*. Cardiff Studies in Archaeology. Oxford: Oxbow Books, 2004.

Cummings, Vicki, and Amelia Pannett, eds. *Set in Stone: New Approaches to Neolithic Monuments in Scotland*. Oxford: Oxbow Books, 2005.

Cummings, Vicki, and Robert Johnston, eds. *Prehistoric Journeys*. Oxford: Oxbow Books, 2007.

Dana, Richard Henry. *Two Years before the Mast: A Personal Narrative of Life at Sea*. London: Folio Society, 1986.

Danker, F. "Trucking Songs." *Journal of Country Music* 6 (1978): 78–89.

Davies, J. D. *Gentlemen and Tarpaulins: The Officers and Men of the Restoration Navy*. Oxford and New York: Clarendon Press and Oxford University Press, 1991.

Davies, Owen. *The Haunted: A Social History of Ghosts*. New York: Palgrave Macmillan, 2007.

Deetz, James. *In Small Things Forgotten: The Archaeology of Early American Life*. Garden City, NY: Anchor Press/Doubleday, 1977.

Defoe, Daniel. *Robinson Crusoe. An Authoritative Text, Backgrounds and Sources, Criticism*. Edited by Michael Shinagel. New York: Norton, 1975.

D'Entremont, Jeremy. *The Lighthouses of Massachusetts*. Beverly, MA: Commonwealth Editions, 2007.

Dethlefsen, Edwin. "The Cemetery and Culture Change: Archaeological Focus and Ethnographic Perspective." In *Modern Material Culture: The Archaeology of Us*, edited by Richard Gould and Michael Schiffer, 137–59. New York: Academic Press, 1981.

Dethlefsen, Edwin, and James Deetz. "Death's Heads, Cherubs, and Willow Trees: Experimental Archaeology in Colonial Cemeteries." *American Antiquity* 31 (1966): 502–10.

Doerflinger, William Main. *Shantymen and Shantyboys: Songs of the Sailor and Lumberman*. New York: Macmillan, 1951.

Douglas, Mary. *Purity and Danger: An Analysis of Concepts of Pollution and Taboo*. Boston: Ark Paperbacks, 1966.

Drewer, Lois. "Fisherman and Fish Pond: From the Sea of Sin to the Living Waters." *The Art Bulletin* 63, no. 4 (1981): 533–46.

Esdaile, Katharine Ada McDowall. *English Church Monuments, 1510 to 1840*. London and Malvern Wells, Worcestershire: B. T. Batsford Ltd., 1946.

Ferguson, Niall. *Empire: The Rise and Demise of the British World Order and the Lessons for Global Power*. New York: Basic Books, 2003.

Fillmore Brothers. *New Christian Hymn and Tune Book*. Cincinnati, OH: Fillmore Brothers, 1882.

Finch, J. "'According to the Qualitie and Degree of the Person Deceased': Funeral Monuments and Construction of Social Identities 1400–1750." *Scottish Archaeological Review* 8 (1991): 105–14.

Finucane, R. C. *Appearances of the Dead: A Cultural History of Ghosts*. London: Junction Books, 1982.

Flatman, Joe. "Cultural Biographies, Cognitive Landscapes and Dirty Old Bits of Boat: 'Theory' in Maritime Archaeology." *IJNA* 32 (2003): 143–57.

Fleming, Andrew. "Megaliths and Post-Modernism: The Case of Wales." *Antiquity* 79 (2005): 921–32.

Forbes, Harriette Merrifield. *Gravestones of Early New England, and the Men Who Made Them, 1653–1800*. New York: Da Capo Press, 1967.

Fraser, Flora. "If You Seek His Monument." In *The Nelson Companion*, edited by Colin White, 129–51. Annapolis, MD: Naval Institute Press, 1995.

Garces-Foley, Kathleen, ed. *Death and Religion in a Changing World*. Amonk, NY: M. E. Sharpe, 2006.

Gardner, James Anthony. *Above and Under Hatches. Being Naval Recollections in Shreds and Patches with Strange Reflections*. Edited by Christopher Lloyd. London: The Batchworth Press, 1955.

Gargulinski, Ryn. "Stand Clear of the Closing Doors!: Occupational Folklore of New York City Subway Workers." *Voices: The Journal of New York Folklore* 27 (2001): 28–31.

Gittings, Clare. *Death, Burial and the Individual in Early Modern England*. London: Croom Helm, 1984.

———. "Sacred and Secular: 1558–1660." In *Death in England: An Illustrated History*, edited by Peter C Jupp and Clare Gittings, 147–73. New Brunswick, NJ: Rutgers University Press, 1999.

Glassie, Henry. *Material Culture*. Bloomington: Indiana University Press, 1999.

Gmelch, George. "Baseball Magic." *Human Nature* 1, no. 8 (1978): 32–40.

Goldstein, Diane E., Sylvia Ann Grider, and Jeannie Banks Thomas. *Haunting Experiences: Ghosts in Contemporary Folklore*. Logan, UT: Utah State University Press, 2007.

Goldstein, Kenneth S. "Faith and Fate in Sea Disaster Ballads of Newfoundland Fisher-

men." In *By Land and by Sea: Studies in the Folklore of Work and Leisure Honoring Horace P. Beck on His Sixty-Fifth Birthday*, edited by Roger D. Abrahams, Kenneth S. Goldstein and Wayland D. Hand, 84–94. Hatboro, PA: Legacy Books, 1985.
Green, Alfred J. *Jottings from a Cruise*. Seattle, WA: The Kelly Printing Company, Inc., 1944.
Grider, Sylvia Ann. "Spontaneous Shrines and Public Memorialization." In *Death and Religion in a Changing World*, edited by Kathleen Garces-Foley, 246–64. Armonk, NY: M. E. Sharpe, 2006.
———. "Haunted Houses." In *Haunting Experiences: Ghosts in Contemporary Folklore*, edited by Diane E. Goldstein, Sylvia Ann Grider and Jeannie Banks Thomas, 143–70. Logan, UT: Utah State University Press, 2007.
Haas, Kristin Ann. *Carried to the Wall: American Memory and the Vietnam Veterans Memorial*. Berkeley: University of California Press, 1998.
Hall, Basil. *Voyages and Travels of Captain Basil Hall, R. N.* London, Edinburgh, and New York: Thomas Nelson and Sons, 1895.
Hall, Edward T. *Beyond Culture*. Garden City, NY: Anchor Press, 1976.
Hallas, James H. "The Search for John Paul Jones." *American History* 32, no. 3 (1997): 28–39.
Hand, Wayland D. "Folklore from Utah's Silver Mining Camps." *Journal of American Folklore* 54, no. 213/214 (1941): 132–61.
———. "California Miners' Folklore: Above Ground." *California Folklore Quarterly* 1, no. 1 (1942): 24–46.
———. "California Miners' Folklore: Below Ground." *California Folklore Quarterly* 1, no. 2 (1942): 127–53.
Harley, Basil. *Church Ships: A Handbook of Votive and Commemorative Models*. Norwich, UK: The Canterbury Press, 1994.
Hatch, Nathan. *The Democratization of American Christianity*. New Haven: Yale University Press, 1989.
Henningsen, Henning. "The Life of the Sailor Afloat and Ashore: Sources and Systems of Classification." In *Ships and Shipyards, Sailors and Fishermen: Introduction to Maritime Ethnology*, edited by Olof Hasslöf, Henning Henningsen and Arne Emil Christensen, Jr., 123–50. Copenhagen: Copenhagen University Press, 1972.
———. "Somandens Vade Og Torre Grav." *Sjufartshistorisk Arbok* (1990): 25–56.
Hills, P. "Saving a Sailor's Life." *Mariner's Mirror* 72 (1986): 217.
Hocker, Frederick M. "Bottom-Based Shipbuilding in Northwestern Europe." In *The Philosophy of Shipbuilding: Conceptual Approaches to the Study of Wooden Ships*, edited by Frederick M. Hocker and Cheryl A. Ward, 65–93. College Station, TX: Texas A&M University Press, 2004.
Hohman, Elmo Paul. *The American Whaleman: A Study of Life and Labor in the Whaling Industry*. New York: Longmans Green and Co., 1928.
Horrox, Rosemary. "Purgatory, Prayer and Plague: 1150–1380." In *Death in England: An Illustrated History*, edited by Peter C Jupp and Clare Gittings, 90–118. New Brunswick, NJ: Rutgers University Press, 1999.
Houlbrooke, Ralph A. *Death, Religion, and the Family in England, 1480–1750*. Oxford and New York: Clarendon Press and Oxford University Press, 1998.

———. "The Age of Decency: 1660–1760." In *Death in England: An Illustrated History*, edited by Peter C Jupp and Clare Gittings, 174–201. New Brunswick, NJ: Rutgers University Press, 1999.

Howse, Derek. *Greenwich Time and the Longitude*. London: Phillip Wilson, 1997.

Hunt, E. H. *British Labour History 1815–1914*. London: Weidenfield & Nicolson, 1981.

Hunter, J. R. "'Maritime Culture': Notes from the Land." *IJNA* 23, no. 4 (1994): 261–64.

Jansen, William Hugh. "The Esoteric-Exoteric Factor in Folklore." *Fabula* 2 (1959): 205–11.

Jeffreys, J. Shep. *Helping Grieving People When Tears Are Not Enough: A Handbook for Care Providers*. New York: Brunner-Routledge, 2005.

Jenkins, Simon. *England's Thousand Best Churches*. London: Penguin Books, 1999.

Johnson, Matthew. *An Archaeology of Capitalism*. Cambridge, MA: Blackwell Publishers, 1996.

Jones, Gwyn. *A History of the Vikings*. Revised edition ed. Oxford and New York: Oxford University Press, 1984.

Junger, Sebastian. *The Perfect Storm*. New York: HarperTorch, 1997.

Kellehear, Allan. "Introduction." In *On Death and Dying: What the Dying Have to Teach Doctors, Nurses, Clergy, and Their Own Families* by Elisabeth Kübler-Ross, vii–xviii. London and New York: Routledge, 2009.

Kelly, Samuel, and Crosbie Garstin. *Samuel Kelly: An Eighteenth Century Seaman, Whose Days Have Been Few and Evil, to Which Is Added Remarks, Etc., on Places He Visited During His Pilgrimage in This Wilderness*. New York: Frederick A. Stokes Company, 1925.

Kilminster, G., and Harold Mytum. "Mariners at Newport, Pembrokeshire: The Evidence from Gravestones." *Maritime Wales* 11 (1987): 7–27.

King, Alex. *Memorials of the Great War in Britain: The Symbolism and Politics of Remembrance*. Oxford and New York: Berg, 1998.

Klass, Dennis. "The Deceased Child in the Psychic and Social Worlds of Bereaved Parents During the Resolution of Grief." In *Continuing Bonds: New Understandings of Grief*, edited by Dennis Klass, Phyllis R. Silverman and Steven L. Nickman, 199–215. Washington, D.C.: Taylor & Francis, 1996.

Klass, Dennis, Phyllis R. Silverman, and Steven L. Nickman, eds. *Continuing Bonds: New Understandings of Grief*. Washington, D.C.: Taylor & Francis, 1996.

Korson, George. *Coal Dust on the Fiddle: Songs and Stories of the Bituminous Industry*. Philadelphia: University of Pennsylvania Press, 1943.

Kottak, Conrad P. *Anthropology: The Exploration of Human Diversity*. Thirteenth Edition ed. New York: Mc-Graw Hill Higher Education, 2009.

Kubler-Ross, Elisabeth. *On Death and Dying: What the Dying Have to Teach Doctors, Nurses, Clergy, and Their Own Families*. 40th Anniversary ed. London and New York: Routledge, 2009.

Kverndal, Roald. *Seamen's Missions: Their Origin and Early Growth. A Contribution to the History of the Church Maritime*. Pasadena, CA: William Carey Library, 1986.

———. *The Way of the Sea: The Changing Shape of Mission in the Seafaring World*. Pasadena, CA: William Carey Library Publishers, 2008.

Langley, Harold D. *Social Reform in the United States Navy, 1798–1862*. Urbana: University of Illinois Press, 1967.

Larson, Erik, and Isaac Monroe Cline. *Isaac's Storm: A Man, a Time, and the Deadliest Hurricane in History*. 1st ed. New York: Crown Publishers, 1999.

Lavery, Brian. *Nelson's Navy: The Ships, Men, and Organisation, 1793–1815*. Annapolis, MD: Naval Institute Press, 1989.

Leach, Edmund. "Time and False Noses." In *The Essential Edmund Leach. Volume I: Anthropology and Society*, edited by Stephen Hugh-Jones and James Laidlaw, 182–86. New Haven and London: Yale University Press, 2000.

Leggett, W. *Tales and Sketches by a Country Schoolmaster*. New York: Printed by J. & J. Harper, 1829.

LeGuin, C. A. "Sea Life in Seventeenth-Century England." *The American Neptune* 27 (1967): 111–34.

Leone, Mark P, and Parker B Potter Jr., eds. *Historical Archaeologies of Capitalism*. Edited by Jr. Orser, Charles E, *Contributions to Global Historical Archaeology*. New York: Kluwer Academic/Plenum Publishers, 1999.

Lewis, Michael Arthur. *A Social History of the Navy, 1793–1815*. London: Allen & Unwin, 1960.

Lindenlauf, Astrid. "The Sea as a Place of No Return in Ancient Greece." *World Archaeology* 35, no. 3 (2003): 416–33.

Linden-Ward, Blanche. "Strange but Genteel Pleasure Grounds: Tourist and Leisure Uses of Nineteenth-Century Rural Cemeteries." In *Cemeteries and Gravemarkers: Voices of American Culture*, edited by Richard E. Meyer, 293–328. Logan, UT: Utah State University Press, 1992.

Linenthal, Edward Tabor. *Sacred Ground: Americans and Their Battlefields*. Urbana: University of Illinois Press, 1991.

Litten, Julian. *The English Way of Death: The Common Funeral since 1450*. London: R. Hale, 1991.

Lloyd, Christopher. *The British Seaman 1200–1860: A Social Survey*. London: Collins, 1968.

Mace, Rodney. *Trafalgar Square: Emblem of Empire*. London: Lawrence and Wishart, 1976.

Mack, William P., and Royal W. Connell. *Naval Ceremonies, Customs, and Traditions*. 5th ed. Annapolis, MD: Naval Institute Press, 1980.

Malinowski, Bronislaw. *Magic, Science, and Religion, and Other Essays*. Boston: Beacon Press, 1948.

Mangin, Edward. "Some Account of the Writer's Situation as Chaplain in the British Navy." In *Five Naval Journals 1789–1817*, edited by H. G. Thursfield, 4–39. London: Navy Records Society, 1951.

Marine Accident Investigation Branch. *Analysis of UK Fishing Vessel Safety 1992 to 2006*. Southampton, UK, 2008.

Mayo, James M. *War Memorials as Political Landscape*. New York: Praeger, 1988.

McCarl, Robert S. "'You've Come a Long Way—and Now This Is Your Retirement': An Analysis of Performance in Fire Fighting Culture." *Journal of American Folklore* 97, no. 386 (1984): 393–422.

———. *The District of Columbia Fire Fighters' Project: A Case Study in Occupational Folklife*. Smithsonian Folklife Studies No. 4. Washington, D.C.: Smithsonian Institution Press, 1985.

———. "Occupational Folklore." In *Folk Groups and Folklore Genres: An Introduction*, edited by Elliott Oring, 71–89. Logan, UT: Utah State University Press, 1986.

McCullough, David. *John Adams*. New York: Simon & Schuster, 2001.

McGuire, Randall H. "Dialogues with the Dead: Ideology and the Cemetery." In *The Recovery of Meaning: Historical Archaeology in the Eastern United States*, edited by Mark P Leone and Parker B Potter Jr, 435–80. Washington: Smithsonian Institution Press, 1988.

———. "Building Power in the Cultural Landscape of Broome County, New York 1880 to 1940." In *The Archaeology of Inequality*, edited by Randall H. McGuire and Robert Paynter, 102–24. Oxford: B. Blackwell, 1991.

McLoughlin, William G. *Revivals, Awakenings, and Reform: An Essay on Religion and Social Change in America, 1607–1977*. Chicago: University of Chicago Press, 1978.

McKee, Christopher. *A Gentlemanly and Honorable Profession: The Creation of the US Naval Officer Corps, 1794–1815*. Annapolis, MD: Naval Institute Press, 1991.

Melville, Herman. *White-Jacket or the World in a Man-of-War*. Boston: L. C. Page & Company, 1950.

———. *Moby Dick*. Oxford and New York: Oxford University Press, 1988.

Merwin, George B., Mrs. *Three Years in Chili*. New York: Follett, Foster, and Company, 1863.

Meyer, Richard. "Image and Identity in Oregon's Pioneer Cemeteries." In *Sense of Place: American Regional Cultures*, edited by Barbara Allen and Thomas J. Schlereth, 88–102. Lexington: University Press of Kentucky, 1990.

———. "Images of Logging on Contemporary Pacific Northwest Gravemarkers." In *Cemeteries and Gravemarkers: Voices of American Culture*, edited by Richard E. Meyer, 61–85. Logan, UT: Utah State University Press, 1992.

———. "And Who Have Seen the Wilderness: The End of the Trail on Early Oregon Gravemarkers." *Markers* 11 (1994): 186–219.

Meyer, Richard E., ed. *Cemeteries and Gravemarkers: Voices of American Culture*. Logan, UT: Utah State University Press, 1992.

———. *Ethnicity and the American Cemetery*. Bowling Green: Bowling Green State University Popular Press, 1993.

Mitchell, Roger. "Occupational Folklore—the Outdoor Industries." In *Handbook of American Folklore*, edited by Richard M. Dorson, 128–35. Bloomington: Indiana University Press, 1986.

Morrell, Benjamin. *A Narrative of Four Voyages to the South Sea, North and South Pacific Ocean, Chinese Sea, Ethiopic and Southern Atlantic Ocean, Indian and Antarctic Ocean: From the Year 1822 to 1831*. New York: J & J Harper, 1832.

Morrow, Patrick. "Those Sick Challenger Jokes." *Journal of Popular Culture* 20 (1987): 175–84.

Muckelroy, Keith. *Maritime Archaeology*. London: Cambridge University Press, 1978.

Mullen, Patrick B. *I Heard the Old Fishermen Say: Folklore of the Texas Gulf Coast.* Austin: University of Texas Press, 1978.

———. "Belief and the American Folk." *Journal of American Folklore* 113, no. 448 (2000): 119–43.

Murray, William M., and Photios M. Petsas. "Octavian's Campsite Memorial for the Actian War." *Transactions of the American Philosophical Society* 79, no. 4 (1989): 1–172.

Myers, Ned. *Ned Myers; or, a Life before the Mast.* Edited by James Fenimore Cooper. Annapolis, MD: Naval Institute Press, 1989.

Mytum, Harold. "Mariners at St. Dogmael's, Pembrokeshire: The Evidence from Gravestones." *Maritime Wales* 13 (1990): 18–32.

———. "The Dating of Graveyard Memorials: Evidence from the Stones." *Post-Medieval Archaeology* 36 (2002): 1–38.

———. "Death and Remembrance in the Colonial Context." In *Archaeologies of the British: Explorations of Identity in Great Britain and its Colonies 1600–1945*, edited by Susan Lawrence, 156–73. London: Routledge, 2003.

———. *Mortuary Monuments and Burial Grounds of the Historic Period.* Manuals in Archaeological Method, Theory, and Technique. New York: Kluwer Academic/Plenum Publishers, 2004.

Nelson, H. M. "The Naval Battle of Medinet Habu." *Journal of Near Eastern Studies* 2 (1943): 40–45.

Newhall, Charles L. *The Adventures of Jack: Or, a Life on the Wave.* Fairfield, WA: Ye Galleon Press, 1981.

Nicol, John. *The Life and Adventures of John Nicol, Mariner.* Edited by Tim Flannery. New York: Atlantic Monthly Press, 1997.

Noble, Sam. *Sam Noble, Able Seaman: 'Tween Decks in the 'Seventies.* New York: Frederick A. Stokes Company, 1925.

Noll, Mark A. *The Rise of Evangelicalism: The Age of Edwards, Whitefield, and the Wesleys.* Downers Grove, Illinois: InterVarsity Press, 2003.

Nordhoff, Charles. *Whaling and Fishing.* Cincinnati: Moore Wilstach Keys, 1856.

Northan, Irene. "Man of Unity: William Henry Allen." *New England Galaxy* 17, no. 3 (1976): 24–31.

Novak, Maximillian E. *Realism, Myth, and History in Defoe's Fiction.* Lincoln: University of Nebraska Press, 1983.

Noyes, Dorothy. "Group." *Journal of American Folklore* 108, no. 430 (1995): 449–78.

Olmsted, Francis Allyn. *Incidents of a Whaling Voyage, to Which Are Added Observations on the Scenery, Manners and Customs, and Missionary Stations of the Sandwich and Society Islands.* Rutland, VT: C. E. Tuttle Co., 1969.

Oman, Carola. *Nelson.* Garden City, New York,: Doubleday, 1946.

O'Riain, Micheal. "Nelson's Pillar: A Controversy That Ran and Ran." *History Ireland*, no. Winter (1998): 21–25.

Oring, Elliott. "Dyadic Traditions." *Journal of Folklore Research* 21 (1984): 19–28.

———. *Folk Groups and Folklore Genres: An Introduction.* Logan, UT: Utah State University Press, 1986.

Orser, Charles E. *A Historical Archaeology of the Modern World. Contributions to Global Historical Archaeology*. New York: Plenum Press, 1996.

Palmer, Roy, ed. *The Oxford Book of Sea Songs*. Oxford and New York: Oxford University Press, 1986.

Parker, A. J. "A Maritime Cultural Landscape: The Port of Bristol in the Middle Ages." *IJNA* 28, no. 4 (1999): 323–42.

Parker Pearson, Michael, ed. *The Archaeology of Death and Burial*. College Station: Texas A&M University Press, 2000.

Parkes, Colin Murray, and Robert S. Weiss. *Recovery from Bereavement*. New York: Basic Books, 1983.

Perry, Frederick. *Fair Winds & Foul: A Narrative of Daily Life Aboard an American Clipper Ship*. 2nd ed. Boston: C. E. Lauriat, 1927.

Phillips, Lawrence. "British and American Naval Tombs on the China Coast." *Mariner's Mirror* 67 (1981): 370–71.

Phillips, Tim. "Seascapes and Landscapes in Orkney and Northern Scotland." *World Archaeology* 35 (2003): 371–84.

Pocock, Tom. *Horatio Nelson*. Pimlico ed, with new preface. London: Pimlico, 1994.

Poggie Jr., John J., Richard B. Pollnac, and Carl Gersuny. "Risk as a Basis for Taboos among Fishermen in Southern New England." *Journal for the Scientific Study of Religion* 15, no. 3 (1976): 257–62.

Poggie Jr., John J., and Carl Gersuny. "Risk and Ritual: An Interpretation of Fishermen's Folklore in a New England Community." *Journal of American Folklore* 85 (1972): 66–72.

Pope, Dudley. *Life in Nelson's Navy*. Annapolis, MD: Naval Institute Press, 1981.

Procter Brothers. *The Fishermen's Own Book*. Gloucester, MA: Procter Brothers, 1882.

Procter, George H. *The Fishermen's Memorial and Record Book*. Gloucester, MA: Procter Brothers, 1873.

Raban, Avner. "The Medinet Habu Ships: Another Interpretation." *IJNA* 18 (1989): 163–71.

Rando, Therese A. *Grieving: How to Go on Living When Someone You Love Dies*. Lexington, MA: Lexington Books, 1988.

Rediker, Marcus. *Between the Devil and the Deep Blue Sea: Merchant Seamen, Pirates, and the Anglo-American Maritime World, 1700–1750*. Cambridge and New York: Cambridge University Press, 1987.

Renner, Louis L. "The Memory of a Brave Man: The Grave of Lieut. John J. Barnard at Nulato." *Alaska Journal* 15, no. 2 (1985): 16–21.

Richardson, Ruth. "Death's Door: Thresholds and Boundaries in British Funeral Customs." In *Boundaries and Thresholds. Papers from a Colloquium of the Katharine Briggs Club*, edited by Hilda Ellis Davidson, 91–101. Woodchester, United Kingdom: Thimble Press, 1993.

———. *Death, Dissection, and the Destitute*. Chicago: University of Chicago Press, 2000.

Ricks, Christopher, editor. *Tennyson: A Selected Edition*. Berkeley and Los Angeles: University of California Press, 1989.

Roberts, Stephen. "Occupational Mortality among British Merchant Seafarers (1986–1995)." *Maritime Policy & Management* 27, no. 3 (2000): 253–65.

———. "Hazardous Occupations in Great Britain." *The Lancet* 360 (2002): 543–44.
———. "Fatal Work-Related Accidents in UK Merchant Shipping from 1919 to 2005." *Occupational Medicine* 58, no. 2 (2008): 129–37.
Robinson, William. *Jack Nastyface: Memoirs of a Seaman*. Introduction by Oliver Warner. London: Wayland, 1973.
Rodger, N.A.M. *The Wooden World: An Anatomy of the Georgian Navy*. New York: W. W. Norton & Company, 1996.
———. *The Safeguard of the Sea: A Naval History of Britain, 660–1649*. New York: W. W. Norton, 1998.
Ross, Miceal. "Anchors in a Three-Decker World." *Folklore* 109 (1998): 63–75.
Rowlands, Michael. "The Role of Memory in the Transmission of Culture." *World Archaeology* 25, no. 2 (1993): 141–51.
Royal Commission on Loss of Life at Sea. *Final Report of the Royal Commission on Loss of Life at Sea, with Minutes of Evidence, Appendix, and Digest of the Evidence*. London: Printed for Her Majesty's Stationary Office, by Eyre and Spottiswoode, Printers to the Queen's Most Excellent Majesty, 1887.
Rule, John. "A Risky Business: Death, Injury and Religion in Cornish Mining c. 1780–1870." In *Social Approaches to an Industrial Past*, edited by A. Bernard Knapp, Vincent C. Pigott, and Eugenia W. Herbert, 155–74. New York: Routledge, 1998.
Samuels, Samuel. *From the Forecastle to the Cabin*. New York: Harper, 1887.
Santino, Jack. "'Flew the Ocean in a Plane': An Investigation of Airline Occupational Narrative." *Journal of the Folklore Institute* 15, no. 3 (1978): 189–208.
———. "Characteristics of Occupational Narratives." *Western Folklore* 37, no. 3 (1978): 199–212.
———. "The Outlaw Emotions: Narrative Expressions on the Rules and Roles of Occupational Identity." *American Behavioral Scientist* 33, no. 3 (1990): 318–29.
Saunders, David. *Britain's Maritime Memorials and Mementoes*. Sparkford, Somerset, U.K.: Patrick Stephens Limited, 1996.
Scrutton, Thomas. "Preventible Loss of Life at Sea." *Journal of the Statistical Society of London* 49, no. 1 (1886): 1–27.
Shipwrecked Mariners' Society. "Memorial of H.M.S. 'Eurydice.'" *The Shipwrecked Mariner. A Quarterly Maritime Magazine* 28 (1881): 280.
Smith, John. *A Sea Grammar*. London: Printed by John Haviland, 1627.
Snyder, Ellen Marie. "Innocents in a Worldly World: Victorian Children's Gravemarkers." In *Cemeteries and Gravemarkers: Voices of American Culture*, edited by Richard E. Meyer, 11–29. Logan, UT: Utah State University Press, 1992.
Sobel, Dava. *Longitude: The True Story of a Lone Genius Who Solved the Greatest Scientific Problem of His Time*. New York: Walker, 1995.
Spavens, William. *The Narrative of William Spavens, a Chatham Pensioner, by Himself*. Introduction by N. A. M. Rodger. London: Chatham Publishing, 1998.
Spinney, J. D. "Some Naval Memorials in the County of Dorset." *Mariners' Mirror* 73 (1987): 191–96.
Stannard, David E. *The Puritan Way of Death: A Study in Religion, Culture, and Social Change*. New York: Oxford University Press, 1977.

Stewart, David J. "'Rocks and Storms I'll Fear No More': Anglo-American Maritime Memorialization, 1700–1940." Unpublished PhD Dissertation, Texas A&M University, 2004.

———. "Burial at Sea: Separating and Placing the Dead During the Age of Sail." *Mortality* 10 (2005): 276–85.

———. "Gravestones and Monuments in the Maritime Cultural Landscape: Research Potential and Preliminary Interpretations." *IJNA* 36, no. 1 (2007): 112–24.

———. "Burial at Sea." In *Encyclopedia of Death and the Human Experience*, edited by Clifton Bryant and Dennis Peck. Thousand Oaks, CA: Sage Publications, 2009.

———. "Naval Monuments and Memorials: Symbols in a Contested Landscape." In *The Historical Archaeology of Military Sites: Method and Topic*, edited by Clarence Geier, Larry Babits, Douglas Scott, and David Orr, 197-207. College Station, TX: Texas A&M University Press, 2010.

Stone, Lawrence. *The Family, Sex and Marriage in England 1500–1800*. New York: Harper & Row, 1977.

Stroebe, Margaret, and Henk Schut. "The Dual Process Model of Coping with Bereavement: Rationale and Description." *Death Studies* 23 (1999): 197–224.

Summerson, J. "The Monuments in the Church of St. Nicholas, Deptford." *Mariner's Mirror* 27 (1941): 277–89.

Tappan, Eva March, editor. *The World's Story: A History of the World in Story, Song, and Art*. Boston: Houghton Mifflin, 1914.

Tarlow, Sarah. "Romancing the Stones: The Graveyard Boom of the Later 18th Century." In *Grave Concerns: Death and Burial in England 1700–1850*, edited by M. Cox, 33–43. York, England: Council for British Archaeology, 1998.

———. *Bereavement and Commemoration: An Archaeology of Mortality*. Oxford: Blackwell Publishers, 1999.

Tarpley, Fred A. "Southern Cemeteries: Neglected Archives for the Folklorist." *Southern Folklore Quarterly* 27, no. 4 (1963): 323–32.

Tashjian, Dickran, and Ann Tashjian. *Memorials for Children of Change: The Art of Early New England Stonecarving*. Middletown, CT: Wesleyan University Press, 1974.

Taylor, E. G. R. *The Haven Finding Art: A History of Navigation from Odysseus to Captain Cook*. London: Hollis & Carter, 1956.

Taylor, Richard P. *Death and the Afterlife: A Cultural Encyclopedia*. Santa Barbara, CA: ABC-Clio, 2000.

Thursfield, H. G., ed. *Five Naval Journals 1789–1817. Publications of the Navy Records Society*. London: Navy Records Society, 1951.

Toelken, Barre. *The Dynamics of Folklore*. Rev. and expanded ed. Logan, UT: Utah State University Press, 1996.

Tomlinson, Barbara. "Battle Reliefs on English Church Monuments." *Mariner's Mirror* 81 (1995): 333–38.

Turner, Victor Witter. *The Ritual Process: Structure and Anti-Structure. Symbol, Myth, and Ritual Series*. Ithaca, NY: Cornell University Press, 1977.

Van Gennep, Arnold. *The Rites of Passage*. Chicago: University of Chicago Press, 1960.

Vincent, E. *Nelson: Love and Fame*. New Haven, CT: Yale University Press, 2003.

Wachsmann, Shelley. "The Ships of the Sea Peoples." *IJNA* 10 (1981): 187–200.
———. "The Ships of the Sea Peoples: Additional Notes." *IJNA* 11 (1982): 297–304.
———. *Seagoing Ships and Seamanship in the Bronze Age Levant*. College Station, TX: Texas A&M University Press, 1998.
Ward, W. R. *The Protestant Evangelical Awakening*. Cambridge: Cambridge University Press, 1992.
Watters, David H. *"With Bodilie Eyes": Eschatological Themes in Puritan Literature and Gravestone Art*. Ann Arbor: UMI Research Press, 1981.
Westerdahl, Christer. "The Maritime Cultural Landscape." *IJNA* 21, no. 1 (1992): 5–14.
———. "Maritime Cultures and Ship Types: Brief Comments on the Significance of Maritime Archaeology." *IJNA* 23, no. 4 (1994): 265–70.
Williams, J. E. D. *From Sails to Satellites: The Origin and Development of Navigational Science*. New York: Oxford University Press, 1992.
Worden, J. William. *Grief Counseling and Grief Therapy*. Third ed. New York: Springer Publishing Company, 2002.
Wurst, LouAnn. "'Employees Must Be of Moral and Temperate Habits': Rural and Urban Elite Ideologies." In *The Archaeology of Inequality*, edited by Randall H. McGuire and Robert Paynter, 125–49. Oxford: B. Blackwell, 1991.
Wyman, Mark. *Hard Rock Epic: Western Miners and the Industrial Revolution, 1860–1910*. Berkeley and Los Angeles: University of California Press, 1979.

Index

Page numbers in italics refer to illustrations.

Abraham H. Howland, 218
Agency, 185, 217–18
Aigburth, 51
Aitken, Michael, memorial for, 206
Akin, Fredric, memorial for, 83
Alexander, 44, 145, 175
Allen, William Henry, memorial for, 76–77, *77*
Allin, Thomas, 105
All Saints Church, Wyke Regis, Dorset, 44, 80, 145, 175
Ames, Nathaniel, 183
Anchor: religious symbolism of, 172, 175–80, *177*, *178*, *179*, *180*, 186, 209; symbolizing life cut short, 54–55, *55*
Andacollo, 1–3
Anderson, Mary Désirée, 21
Andrea Gale, 205
Andrews, William, memorial for, 48
Anglo-American Maritime Memorials Survey, 31–32
Anxiety-ritual theory, 66–68
Aquatic, 83
Arbuthnot, Marriott, memorial for, 175
Archer, HMS, crew memorial for, 65
Argus, 76
Ariadne, HMS, crew memorial for, 82
Atlantic, 25, 145–46
Atwill, Thomas, memorial for, 67, 80, 193

Baker's Island, MA, 37
Barker, Joseph, memorial for, 143

Barlow, Edward: attitude toward seafaring, 211; description of burials, 107–108; witnesses a fire aboard ship, 74
Barron, William, burial at sea of, 118
Barry, John, memorial for, 94
Bassett, Fletcher S.: description of recovering a drowned body, 152; on superstition regarding corpses aboard ship, 108
Battle of Actium, memorial for, 84–85, *85*
Bean, William, memorial for, 49
Béchervaise, John, 42, 60, 102, 160
Beck, Horace, 108, 170, 217
Beck, William, memorial for, 187
Bennett, Thomas Arthur, memorial for, 80, *81*
Benson, Charles, 212
Bereavement and Commemoration: An Archaeology of Mortality (Tarlow), 22–23
Bermuda Lost at Sea Memorial, 202–3, *204*
Bethel movement, 182–83, *184*, 208
Birkenhead, sinking of, 99–100
Bismarck, 214
Boadicea, HMS, crew memorial for, 65, 78
Boatmen's Shelter, 206
Bolitho, William Edward, memorial for, 187
Bolton, William, memorial for, 76
Bombay, HMS, 49, 72–74, *74*, 75
Bonhomme Richard, 88
Boston, USS, 118
Bourchier, Edward, memorial for, 46
Bower, John, memorial for, 167, 195
Bowling, Tom, 93, 229n46

Bridgeo family gravestone, 140
Briggs, Ted, 215
Briseis, 188
Bristol Cathedral, 191
Britain's Maritime Memorials and Mementoes (Saunders), 23
Broad Street Cemetery, Salem, MA, 62
Brooklyn, USS, 88
Brunswick, HMS, 64
Bullen, John, memorial for, 47–48, 93–94, 110
Buller, William, memorial for, 50
Byard, Thomas, memorial for, 109, 174–75

Callao, Peru, 1–2, 161, 221n5
Cambria, 193
Campbell, Colin, memorial for, 49, 72–74, *74*, *75*
Cape Horn, 157
Castaway stories, 161–63, 234n74
Cautionary tales, 95–97
Cedar Grove Cemetery, New London, CT, 70, 164
Cemeteries and Gravemarkers: Voices of American Culture (Meyer), 22
Cenotaph, definition of, 140, 233n14
Census of Fatal Occupational Injuries, 221n8
Chaplains, aboard ship, 232n75
Cheviot, 49
Churchill, Winston, 34–35, 60, 200
Clemens, Samuel, 153
Cobb family cenotaph, *143*, 143–44, 157
Cockbilling yards, 122
Cole, USS: memorial service for, 89; online memorial, 217
Collective memory, 156
Common Burying Ground, Newport, RI, 161
Constantine, HMS, 49
Constitution, USS, 75, 86, 163
Continental (bulk carrier), 215
Continental (clipper ship), 105–6, 120
Copp's Hill Burying Ground, Boston, MA, 136, 138, 172
Cox, John, memorial for, 171
Coxere, Edward, 73, 160, 176, 211
Crane, HMS, 48, 93–94, 110
Cremer, Jack, 73
Crews, Henry, memorial for, 209
Cromwell, Peter, memorial for, 157

Crosby family gravestone, 140
"Crossing the Bar," 197
Crowell, William, memorial for, 109
Crusoe, Robinson, 162
Cumberland, USS, 50

Dana, Richard Henry, Jr.: attitude toward burial at sea, 129; description of a fall from aloft, 46–47; description of life in forecastle, 91; fatalistic worldview of, 56; member of maritime folk group, 18
Danae, HMS, 80
Darling, Grace, 45–46
Darlywyne, 208
Davidson, Charles, memorial for, 197–98
Davis, Thomas, memorial for, 110
Davy Jones, 56, 114, 126
"Deadliest Catch," 206
Deane family monument, 144
Death at sea, causes of: accidents, 206; disease, 62–66; drowning, 46; falls, 46–49; fire, 49; hostile action, 49–52. *See also* Shipwreck, causes of
"Death Car, The," 115
Decatur, Stephen, 86
Deetz, James, 20, 21, 223n52
Defoe, Daniel, 162
Delphey, Richard, memorial for, 76
Demerara, 155
Denison monument, 40, *41*, 144
Dennis, John, memorial for, 136–37, 161
Desolation Island, 155
Despatch, 36
Dethlefsen, Edwin, 20, 21, 223n52
Doliber, Frances, memorial for, 172
"Don't Go Down the Mine," 97
Doterel, HMS, 49
Downey, John, memorial for, 188, *189*, *190*, *191*
Drake, HMS, 88
Drowning victims, recovery of, 152–53
"Dying Truckdrive, The" 97

Eagles, Edgar, memorial for, 46
Eastern Cemetery, Portland, ME, 171
Ebenezer, 49
"Egg Shells," 113–14
Elephant, HMS, 63
Esdaile, Katherine Ada McDowall, 21

Ethnicity and the American Cemetery (Meyer), 22
Eurydice, HMS, 34–35, *35*, 60, 200
Evangelical revival, 181–82
Evergreen Cemetery, Portland, ME, 58
Ewen, Benjamin, memorial for, 47, 198–99
Ewen, John, memorial for, 195–96
Ewer, Walter, memorial for, 133–34, *135*, 187

Falmouth Cemetery, Cornwall, 179, 197
Fatality rates, sailors: comparison to other occupations 9–10, 207; historical, 7–9; in modern United Kingdom, 5–7; in modern United States, 4–5, 221n8
Fengar, Alvan, memorial for, 194
Fiddler's Green, 126
Firefighter lore, 14, 222n38
First Great Awakening, 181
Fitch, Joseph, memorial for, 49
Fittock, Henry, memorial for, 51
Flatman, Joe, 213
Flying Dutchman, 111, 112, 113
Folk group: concept of, 13–17, 222n35; sailors as, 17–20
Forbes, Harriet, 20–21
Fordham, Charles, memorial for, 109
Forest Hills Cemetery, Boston, MA, 177
Forster, William, 139
Foudroyant, HMS, 109
France, John, memorial for, 195
Frazer, J. G., 158
Freer, Bowyer Hamilton Guy, memorial for, 54–55, *55*

Ganges, HMS, 94, *95*, 229n50
Gardner, James Anthony: description of his captain's death, 121–22; description of yellow fever, 63–64; ghost stories, 111, 113, 114
Garrick, Richard, 194
Gebel el-Arak knife, 226n54
General Lyon, 83
"Ghostly Fishermen, The," 112
Ghosts, 110–15, 126–29
Gilberry, Wilfred, memorial for, 1–4, 161
Gilbert, Richard, memorial for, 198
Gloucester, MA: fishermen fatalities, 8, 222n21; Fishermen's Memorial, 24, *71*, 214; Fishermen's Rest (cemetery), 28

Golding, Robert, memorial for, 46
Goldsmith, Tom, 56
"Good death" vs. "bad death," 68–69, 227n109
Graham, James, memorial for, 200
Granary Burying Ground, Boston, MA, 36–37
Grant, Harry, memorial for, 212
Graves, William, 82
Gravestones. *See* Memorials
Gravestones of Early New England, and the Men Who Made Them, 1653–1800 (Forbes), 20
Gray, William, memorial for, 36
Green, Alfred, 45
Grieving process, 158–63
Griffin, John, memorial for, 94
Governor, vessel, 1

Hales, James, monument for, 106, 118–19
Hall, Basil: description of burial at sea customs, 119, 124; memorial for, 195; superstition regarding corpses aboard ship, 108
Hall, Edward T., 15–16
Halsey, Elisha, memorial for, 76
Hamilton, 39
Hammocks, use of as burial shroud, 117–18
Hammond, James Dennis, memorial for, 75
Hand, Wayland, 52, 97–98, 226n64
Haswell, John, memorial for, 75
"Haven of His Love, The," 209, *210*
Havens, Jacob, memorial for, 212
Hawk, Edward, memorial for, 46, 57–58
Heath, Josiah, memorial for, 194
Henry, John, memorial for, 80
Highland Road Cemetery, Portsmouth, 73, *178*
Hill, William, memorial for, 198
Hind, HMS, 113, 114
Holmes, Franses, memorial for, 53
Holy Trinity Church, Hull, 62, 173, 188
Hood, HMS, 214–15
Hopper, William, memorial for, 194
Howard, Henry Bailyss, memorial for, 129, *130*, 212
Humans vs. nature: moment of loss, 57–58, 60–61, 203, 205; on modern maritime memorials, 205; triumph of humanity over nature, 61–62
Humphrey, Daniel, memorial for, 194
Humphreys, John, memorial for, 49
Hurricanes, 38

Impregnable, HMS, 50
Indiana Soldiers and Sailors Monument, 86
Individualism, 147–52

Jackal, HMS, 82
Jack Nastyface. *See* Robinson, William
Java, HMS, 75
Jaws, 206
Jeffery, James, memorial for, 36, 187–88
Jeffery, Samuel Henry, memorial for, 157
Johnson, Tom, memorial for, 215
Jonah (maritime superstition), 112
Jones, John Paul, memorialization of, 88–89
Jordan, Terry, 22
Jurassic Park, 237n6

Kanackas, 79
Kellehear, Allan, 158
Kelly, Samuel, 92, 160–61, 211, 214
King George, 75
Kingston Road Cemetery, Portsmouth, 82, 165
Kroomen, 78
Kübler-Ross, Elisabeth, 158
Kursk, 215

Lady Mary, 208
Langley family monument, 139
Lawrence, Elias, memorial for, 76
Lee, Charles, memorial for, 37
Lee, Richard, memorial for, 194
Leetham family memorial, 188–90
Leggett, William, 124
Lewis, Ida, memorial for, 46
Lewis, William, memorial for, 49
Lightfoot, Gordon, 205
Liminality, 112, 116, 127, 161, 165, 208
Lindsay, Joseph, memorial for, 75
Liverpool, England, 1
"Loss of the *Amphitrite*, The," 45
Lost World: Jurassic Park, The, 237n6
Low, Gilman, memorial for, 177
Lowry, William John, memorial for, 197

M1 (submarine), 211
Macedonian Monument, 86
Mackay, John, 37
Maine, USS, 87
Malinowski, Bronislaw, 66

Manacle Rocks, Cornwall, 36
Mangin, Edward, 170
Mant, George, memorial for, 200
Marblehead Charitable Seamen's Society monument, *146*, 146–47
Marine Accident Investigation Branch, 5
Maritime cultural landscape, 12
Maritime culture: concept of, 11–13 (*see also* Folk group); impact of danger on, 52–56; view of religion, 168–71
Maritime enclaves, 222n32
Maritime values: bravery and duty, 70–76; comparison to state-sponsored memorials, 90–91; failure of, 98–103; self-sacrifice, 82–83; taking care of group, 76–81, 126. *See also* State-sponsored memorials
Mather, Cotton, 168
Maunder, Henry, memorial for, 194
Melville, Herman, 29, 60, 93; attitude toward nasal stitch, 119; description of burial at sea, 116; on the problem of bodies lost at sea, 156–57
Memorials: as a form of social protest, 163–65, 213–14, 217; dating, 224n66; limitations of, 29–31; locations of, 27–28 (*see also* Place, importance of); religious functions of, 187–200; study of, 20–24, 223n53; teaching function of, 91–98; types of, 24–27
Mertola, 45
Meyer, Richard, 22, 52
Miner folklore, 52, 96, 226n64
Ming, Bill, 203
Moby Dick, 29, 60, 79, 93, 156, 205
Monitor, USS, 51
Monmouth, 105
Moore, John, memorial for, 194
Moss Glenn, 46
Muckelroy, Keith, 12
Myers, Ned, 39, 56
Mytum, Harold, 52, 224n66

Nancy, 40
Nasal stitch, 119–20
Naval memorials, 84–91
Neighbour, Herbert, memorial for, 211
Nelson's Column, 85–86
Nelson, Horatio: abhorrence of burial at sea, 111; death of, 50; memorialization of,

87–88; return of body to England, 109, 230n20
Newhall, Charles, 99
Newlands family monument, 72, 144
Newman family monument, 138, 172
Nicholls, Alfred, memorial for, 46
Nicol, John, 62, 99, 100–101
Noble, Sam: attitude toward burial at sea, 129; comparing death to sleep, 117–18; description of burial service, 108
Nordhoff, Charles, 93
Norman, John, memorial for, 109
North Star, 114
Nuestra Senhora de Begona, 1

Octavian, 84–85
Oddy, Thomas, memorial for, 49
Old Burial Hill, Marblehead, MA, 75, 146, 172
Old Burying Point, Salem, MA, 62, 173
Old North Church, Boston, MA, 92
Olive Branch, 60, *61*, 187
Olmsted, Francis, 56
On Death and Dying (Kübler-Ross), 158

Palmer, William, memorial for, 57, *58*, *59*, 137
Pamlico Sound, NC, 153
Peirce, John, memorial for, 50–51, *51*, 200
Pendleton, Isaac, memorial for, 52
Pequod, 60, 93
Perfect Storm, The, 205
Perry, Frederick, 105–6, 116, 117, 120
Pigmy, 49
Pinkham, Seth, memorial for, 109
Pitman family memorial, 53
Place, importance of, 155–56
Plympton St. Mary's, Plymouth, England, 53, *54*
Plymouth Lifeboat Guild, 206
Portland, Dorset, 167
Portland St. George, *28*, 167, 193, 195, 198
Portsea St. Mary's, Portsmouth, England, 145, 179, 184, 195
Poseidon Adventure, The, 206
Powell, John J., memorial for, 62, 173–74
Power relations, 163–65, 213–14, 217
Powers, Thomas Barratt, memorial for, 77, *78*
Prowse family gravestone, 142
Pungo River, NC, 153
Purdie, Joseph, memorial for, 46

Queen, 42–43, *43*, 44, 57, 60, 92, 102, 160

Racer, HMS, crew memorial for, 65
Ramesses III, 84
Ramillies, HMS, 45
Ranger, HMS, 64
Read, John, memorial for, 212
Read family gravestone, *28*, 193
Rediker, Marcus, 56, 169
Redoubtable, 50
Religious symbolism, nineteenth century, 185–86
Richards family gravestone, 136, 139
Richardson, Addison, memorial for, 62, 172–73
Rites of passage, 115
Rixon, Victor, memorial for, 209
Robinson, Thomas, memorial for, 40–41
Robinson, William, 212
Roby, Henry, memorial for, 172
Romantic movement, impact on maritime memorials, 43–44, 147–52
Rosser family monument, 51
Royal Commission on Loss of Life at Sea, 7
Royal Edward, 51
Royal George, 145
Royal Navy Cemetery, Haslar, UK, *28*, 35, 80, 82, 165
Rural Cemetery, New Bedford, MA, 83, 133
Russell, Edward, memorial for, 62, 173

"Safe Within the Vail," 196
"Sailors for My Money," 45
Sailors' Homes, 183
Sailors' Rests, 183
Salem, MA, 37
Samuels, Samuel, 124, 214
Sanderson, John, memorial for, 191–92
Sanford, John, memorial for, 65
Saunders, David, 23
Sayres, N. F., memorial for, 40
Scourge, 39–40, 56
Scriven, Benjamin, memorial for, 49
Scriven, John, memorial for, 198, *199*
Sculcoates Lane Cemetery, Hull, 192
Scurvy, 62–63
Seamen's Bethel, New Bedford, MA, 27, *29*, 79, 93, 145, 154, 184, 205, 218
Seamen's Friend societies, 183

Seaman's Grammar, 63, 107
Searle, Gary, memorial for, 209
Sea Venture, 202
Second Great Awakening, 180–82
Selkirk, Alexander, 162
Serapis, HMS, 88
Serpent, HMS, 37–38
Severn, HMS, crew memorial for, 179
Sheffield, Amos, memorial for, 140
Shipwreck, causes of: running aground, 36–37; storms, 38–41. *See also* Death at sea, causes of
Shovell, Cloudesley, memorial for, 92, 214
Skinner, B. F., memorial for, 82
Skinner, James, memorial for, 98
Smith, Ernest, memorial for, 209, *210*
Smith, John, 63, 107
Smith, Robert (American sailor), memorial for, 98
Smith, Robert (British sailor), memorial for, 53, 192–93, *193*
Smith, Sylvanus, memorial for, 157
Soldiers and Sailors Memorial Arch, Brooklyn, NY, 86
Spavens, William, 101
Speedy, 183
Spielberg, Steven, 206
Spontaneous shrines, 215–17
Stanley, Billy, memorial for, 209
State-sponsored memorials, 84–91. *See also* Maritime values
Stephenson, James, memorial for, 60, 187
Stewart, Charles, memorial for, 49
St. Budeaux Church, Devonport, 76, 92, 109, 157
St. James' Cemetery, Liverpool, 2, 76, 109, 142
St. Michael, 74
St. Mylor Church, Cornwall, 42, 75, 92, 110, 145, 154, 161, 188, 207–8
Stonehouse, Mary, memorial for, 157–58
Stonington, CT: Evergreen Cemetery, 40
"Storm Stories," 206
Straits of Gibraltar, 176
Sturges, Robert, ghost of, 111–12
Superb, HMS, 77
Superior, 49

"Tale of the Shipwrecked Sailor," 162
Tarlow, Sarah, 22–23, 149
Tarpley, Fred, 21
Téméraire, HMS, 76
Tennyson, Alfred, 197
Texas Graveyards: A Cultural Legacy (Jordan), 22
Thames, 51
Theban, 193
"Three Score and Ten," 60
Ticonderoga, 75
Titanic, 205
Toelken, Barre, 14–15, 222n35
"Tombstone Every Mile," 97
Torbay, HMS, 49
Trafalgar Square: as a protest site, 213–14; commemorations of Nelson, 87
Tucker, Samuel, memorial for, 58, *59*
Tucker memorial, 53, *54*, 82
Twain, Mark, 153
Twister, 237n6
Two Years Before the Mast (Dana), 18
Typhus, 63

Vail, Charles, memorial for, 187
Van Gennep, Arnold, 115, 158
"Vanishing Hitchhiker, The," 114–15
Vannarp, Adam, memorial for, 70–72
Varrall, John, memorial for, 27, 48–49
Vasa, 72
Venereal disease, 64
Victory, HMS, 86–87
Vietnam Veterans Memorial, 90, 215
Viking memorials, 134
Virginia, CSS, 51
Virtual memorials, 217
Votive models, 92, 228n43

Wallace, Robert, memorial for, 194
Ward, Luke, 107
Warren, John, memorial for, 64
Weather lore, 40
Weazle, HMS, 36
Webbe, Charles, memorial for, 161
Weeks family gravestone, 142–43
Welburn, Chris, memorial for, 206

Westerdahl, Christer, 12, 23
Western Cemetery, Portland, ME, 144
Williams, George, 164, *164*
"Wreck of the *Edmund Fitzgerald*, The," 205
"Wreck of the *Rambler*, The," 45
Wright, Stephen, burial at sea of, 105

Yellow fever, 63–64
Yescombe, Edward Bayntum, memorial for, 75, 174
Young, Robert, 124

Zoroaster, 133

David J. Stewart is associate professor of maritime archaeology at East Carolina University. A graduate of the nautical archaeology program at Texas A&M University, he teaches courses in the history and theory of nautical archaeology, ship documentation and reconstruction, and maritime culture.

New Perspectives on Maritime History and Nautical Archaeology
EDITED BY JAMES C. BRADFORD AND GENE ALLEN SMITH

The Maritime Heritage of the Cayman Islands, by Roger C. Smith (2000; first paperback edition, 2001)

The Three German Navies: Dissolution, Transition, and New Beginnings, 1945–1960, by Douglas C. Peifer (2002)

The Rescue of the Gale Runner: *Death, Heroism, and the U.S. Coast Guard*, by Dennis L. Noble (2002; first paperback edition, 2008)

Brown Water Warfare: The U.S. Navy in Riverine Warfare and the Emergence of a Tactical Doctrine, 1775–1970, by R. Blake Dunnavent (2003)

Sea Power in the Medieval Mediterranean: The Catalan-Aragonese Fleet in the War of the Sicilian Vespers, by Lawrence V. Mott (2003)

An Admiral for America: Sir Peter Warren, Vice Admiral of the Red, 1703–1752, by Julian Gwyn (2004)

Maritime History as World History, edited by Daniel Finamore (2004)

Counterpoint to Trafalgar: The Anglo-Russian Invasion of Naples, 1805–1806, by William Henry Flayhart III (paperback edition, 2004)

Life and Death on the Greenland Patrol, 1942, by Thaddeus D. Novak, edited by P.J. Capelotti (2005; first paperback edition, 2014)

X Marks the Spot: The Archaeology of Piracy, edited by Russell K. Skowronek and Charles R. Ewen (2006; first paperback edition, 2007)

Industrializing American Shipbuilding: The Transformation of Ship Design and Costruction, 1820–1920, by William H. Thiesen (2006)

Admiral Lord Keith and the Naval War Against Napoleon, by Kevin D. McCranie (2006)

Commodore John Rodgers: Paragon of the Early American Navy, by John H. Schroeder (2006)

Borderland Smuggling: Patriots, Loyalists, and Illicit Trade in the Northeast, 1783–1820, by Joshua M. Smith (2006; first paperback edition, 2019)

Brutality on Trial: "Hellfire" Pedersen, "Fighting" Hansen, and the Seamen's Act of 1915, by E. Kay Gibson (2006)

Uriah Levy: Reformer of the Antebellum Navy, by Ira Dye (2006)

Crisis at Sea: The United States Navy in European Waters in World War I, by William N. Still Jr. (2006)

Chinese Junks on the Pacific: Views from a Different Deck, by Hans K. Van Tilburg (2007; first paperback edition, 2013)

Eight Thousand Years of Maltese Maritime History: Trade, Piracy, and Naval Warfare in the Central Mediterranean, by Ayse Devrim Atauz (2008)

Merchant Mariners at War: An Oral History of World War II, by George J. Billy and Christine M. Billy (2008)

The Steamboat Montana *and the Opening of the West: History, Excavation, and Architecture*, by Annalies Corbin and Bradley A. Rodgers (2008)

Attack Transport: USS Charles Carroll *in World War II*, by Kenneth H. Goldman (2008)

Diplomats in Blue: U.S. Naval Officers in China, 1922–1933, by William Reynolds Braisted (2009)

Sir Samuel Hood and the Battle of the Chesapeake, by Colin Pengelly (2009)

Voyages, the Age of Sail: Documents in Maritime History, Volume I, 1492–1865, edited by Joshua M. Smith and the National Maritime Historical Society (2009)

Voyages, the Age of Engines: Documents in American Maritime History, Volume II, 1865–Present, edited by Joshua M. Smith and the National Maritime Historical Society (2009)

HMS Fowey *Lost and Found: Being the Discovery, Excavation, and Identification of a British Man-of-War Lost off the Cape of Florida in 1748*, by Russell K. Skowronek and George R. Fischer (2009)

American Coastal Rescue Craft: A Design History of Coastal Rescue Craft Used by the United States Life-Saving Service and the United States Coast Guard, by William D. Wilkinson and Commander Timothy R. Dring, USNR (Retired) (2009)

The Spanish Convoy of 1750: Heaven's Hammer and International Diplomacy, by James A. Lewis (2009)

The Development of Mobile Logistic Support in Anglo-American Naval Policy, 1900–1953, by Peter V. Nash (2009)

Captain "Hell Roaring" Mike Healy: From American Slave to Arctic Hero, by Dennis L. Noble and Truman R. Strobridge (2009; first paperback edition, 2017)

Sovereignty at Sea: U.S. Merchant Ships and American Entry into World War I, by Rodney Carlisle (2009; first paperback edition, 2011)

Commodore Abraham Whipple of the Continental Navy: Privateer, Patriot, Pioneer, by Sheldon S. Cohen (2010; first paperback edition, 2011)

Lucky 73: USS Pampanito's *Unlikely Rescue of Allied POWs in WWII*, by Aldona Sendzikas (2010)

Cruise of the Dashing Wave: *Rounding Cape Horn in 1860*, by Philip Hichborn, edited by William H. Thiesen (2010)

Seated by the Sea: The Maritime History of Portland, Maine, and Its Irish Longshoremen, by Michael C. Connolly (2010; first paperback edition, 2011)

The Whaling Expedition of the Ulysses, *1937–1938*, by Lt. (jg) Quentin R. Walsh, U.S. Coast Guard, edited and with an introduction by P.J. Capelotti (2010)

Stalking the U-Boat: U.S. Naval Aviation in Europe during World War I, by Geoffrey L. Rossano (2010)

In Katrina's Wake: The U.S. Coast Guard and the Gulf Coast Hurricanes of 2005, by Donald L. Canney (2010)

A Civil War Gunboat in Pacific Waters: Life on Board USS Saginaw, by Hans K. Van Tilburg (2010)

The U.S. Coast Guard's War on Human Smuggling, by Dennis L. Noble (2011)

The Sea Their Graves: An Archaeology of Death and Remembrance in Maritime Culture, by David J. Stewart (2011; first paperback edition, 2019)

www.ingramcontent.com/pod-product-compliance
Lightning Source LLC
Chambersburg PA
CBHW031432160426
43195CB00010BB/700